Early Professional
Baseball and the
Sporting Press

Early Professional Baseball and the Sporting Press
Shaping the Image of the Game

R. Terry Furst

McFarland & Company, Inc., Publishers
Jefferson, North Carolina

LIBRARY OF CONGRESS CATALOGUING-IN-PUBLICATION DATA

Furst, R. Terry.
  Early professional baseball and the sporting press : shaping the image of the game / R. Terry Furst.
      p.   cm.
  Includes bibliographical references and index.

  ISBN 978-0-7864-6985-7 (softcover : acid free paper) ∞
  ISBN 978-1-4766-0625-5 (ebook)

  1. Baseball—United States—History—19th century.
  2. Baseball—United States—Public opinion. 3. Baseball—United States—Social aspects. 4. Sports—Public relations—United States. 5. Mass media and sports—United States.
  I. Title.
  GV863.A1F87 2014
  796.357'64—dc23   2013047169

BRITISH LIBRARY CATALOGUING DATA ARE AVAILABLE

© 2014 R. Terry Furst. All rights reserved

No part of this book may be reproduced or transmitted in any form or by any means, electronic or mechanical, including photocopying or recording, or by any information storage and retrieval system, without permission in writing from the publisher.

Cover art: Homer Davenport, *When Gambling Controlled*, pen and ink cartoon, 16½" × 21"

Manufactured in the United States of America

McFarland & Company, Inc., Publishers
  Box 611, Jefferson, North Carolina 28640
  www.mcfarlandpub.com

To Angela DiBello, an irrepressible aesthete and inspiration to all who know her.

Acknowledgments

   This book greatly benefited from the contributions of the following people: Maria Reveron-Harrison, Avi Bornstein, Deeadra Brown, Laila Alsabahi, Diane Glynn, Dick Perez, John Thorn, and to the baseball and sport historians, past and present, whose work guided my path. The help of the librarians at the Rare Manuscript Division of the New York Public Library and the annex of the New York Public Library made my research effort an easier task than it might have been. Their help is greatly appreciated.
   I deeply appreciate the help and encouragement of Edward Sagarin and Bernard Rosenberg of City College of New York—their patient confidence in my work will be remembered. The book is dedicated to their memory.

Table of Contents

Introduction	1
I. **Changing Views Toward Man, Recreation, Leisure and Health**	9
Muscular Christianity and the Y.M.C.A.	15
Periodicals, Sport Magazines, Newspapers and the Dissemination of Ideas About Physical Fitness	17
II. **The Amateur Ideal in Baseball**	23
The Rise of Sportsmanship in England	23
Social Class, Status and Amateurism in England	26
The Amateur Rower in England	27
The Amateur Rower in America	28
The Influence of the English on American Sport	30
III. **The Origin of Baseball and the Early Years of the Knickerbocker Base Ball Club**	34
The Abner Doubleday Myth	41
The North American Indian and the Origin of Baseball	42
The Origin and Structure of the Knickerbocker Base Ball Club	43
Baseball Clubs Before and After the Knickerbockers	53
The First Convention and the First Association of Baseball Players	56
IV. **Positive Press**	60
Well-Publicized Events in the Early History of Baseball	62
Recognition and Acclaim of the Skill of Baseball Players and Adoption of the Fly Rule	66
V. **The Baseball Public and the Spectacle of Baseball**	74
The Public	75

Table of Contents

The Baseball Consumer	76
Composition of the Baseball Public	77
The Baseball Public and the Press	80
The Baseball Spectacle and Rule Changes	82
Baseball Strategies	84
The Appeal of Baseball	85
The Rowdy Behavior of the Baseball Audience	87
Club Rivalries	89

VI. The Disreputable Image of Baseball — 93
    Professional Athletics of the Early Nineteenth Century — 93
    Substitution and Revolving: Disreputable Practices
        in the Transformation of Baseball — 97
    Gambling and Corruption in Baseball — 99
    The Championship of Baseball: The Quest for Supremacy — 106
    The Impact of the Championship on Baseball — 110
    The Moral Image of Baseball — 110
    African Americans in Baseball: The Early Years — 111

VII. Compensation and Image in Professional Baseball — 115
    Precursor of Direct Payment to Players: The "Benefit Match" — 115
    Admission Charges and Sharing of Gate Receipts — 119
    Sinecures: An Indirect Form of Player Compensation — 121
    The Adoption of the Rule Prohibiting
        Compensation to Players — 122
    Some Issues Surrounding Salaries — 123
    Player Compensation, Socio-Occupational Background
        and the Professionalization of Baseball — 126
    The Cincinnati Red Stocking Team of 1869–70 — 129
    Player Compensation and the Image of Professional Baseball — 132
    The 1870s: A Time for Decisions in Organized Baseball — 134
    Attempts by the Press to Define the Terms
        Amateur and Professional — 136
    The Image of Professional Baseball — 139

Chapter Notes — 145
Bibliography — 161
Index — 167

Introduction

This book describes and analyzes the process by which the collective image of professional baseball was formed. It traces both the negation and the affirmation of ideas in the sport press that would impede or promote the growth of baseball from a recreational pastime to a spectator sport spectacle in mid-nineteenth-century America. The image grew as a result of a complex of factors. This complex included sports reportage and reading by the baseball public of matters in the sport press, discussion of baseball within social and occupational networks, game attendance and changing evaluations of work and play. These variables did not operate in a simple cause-and-effect relationship, with one variable determining the outcome of another. They combined in complex ways; changing values toward work and play both preserved and undermined sentiments toward baseball. Much of this interactive complex was influenced by the English sports ideal and newly formed attitudes toward recreational pursuits and sport in America.

The sport press was a necessary condition for the collective construction of knowledge about baseball. Therefore, this study traces sports reports of significant events in baseball (e.g., the Cincinnati Red Stockings tour of 1869) and describes the collective processes that helped engender the image of professional baseball.[1] Editorial commentaries, evaluative descriptions, and letters to the editor are analyzed from the standpoint of sentiments toward the older and the emerging orientations toward playing baseball.

In its infancy, baseball adopted an attenuated English sports ideal, which is suggested by the playing rules, by-laws, and the social-recreational approach to playing baseball by clubs like the New York Knickerbockers and the Brooklyn Excelsiors. However, as a more competitive style of play grew in organized baseball, the domains of work and play grew closer together on the ball field, and they coalesced in the minds of the baseball public. Writing about the image of professional baseball in the 1960s, Roger Angell observes:

> Baseball itself has the most enviable *corporate image* in the world. Its evocations and loyalties firmly planted in the mind of every American male during childhood

and nurtured thereafter by millions of words of free newspaper publicity appear to be unassailable. It is the national pastime. It is youth, springtime, a trip to the country, part of our past.[2]

Approximately a hundred years earlier the image of professional baseball was not "firmly planted in the mind of every American male."[3] Instead, there existed a composite of ideas about the game. Disparate notions of what the game of baseball was and should be awkwardly jostled each other and at times came into sharp conflict. The imprint of an older, social-recreational approach to playing baseball was coming into conflict with a newer, more competitive style of play.

Much written about baseball in the sport press reflected this conflict. In 1875 a sportswriter declared, "As a general thing, any professional baseball club will 'throw' a game if there is money in it. A horse race is a pretty safe thing to speculate on in comparison with an average baseball match."[4] This stinging rebuke conveys an image of baseball that was markedly different from the following description of baseball expressed fifteen years earlier: "Here we have ... what we may now term our national game of ball, an amusement at once invigorating and beneficial to health and free from every objectionable feature that in one respect or another characterizes every other outdoor amusement."[5] These strikingly dissimilar sentiments span a period of time in which the image of professional baseball was being formed. By the early 1870s, the attributes associated with the professional game had been set forth by the sport press as a loose configuration of characteristics that included skillful play, payment of salaries, disreputability of players, the recognition of the names of leading players, and an awareness of the clubs they represented.

But what is an image? Kenneth E. Boulding perceives an image as a "loose structure, something like a molecule."[6] In this conception, certain messages have little effect upon the image, but other messages add to it or modify it.[7] When the latter occurs, "the image is built up as a result of all past experience of the possessor of the image. Part of the image is the history of the image itself."[8] Boulding also comments on the significance of an image for social behavior. He notes: "The basic bond of any society, culture, subculture, or organization is a 'public image,' that is, an image the essential characteristics of which are shared by the individuals participating in the group."[9] He goes on to observe, "A public image almost invariably produces a 'transcript'; that is, a record in more or less permanent form which can be handed down from generation to generation."[10] It is this "transcript," in the form of sport news, that provides a starting point for analysis of what I will assume in this book: "We can study the formation of images ... without committing ourselves to any tests of ultimate validity."[11]

From this standpoint, baseball press reportage is assumed to be primarily responsible for shaping ideas about the image of professional baseball. However, the task is not without epistemological difficulties. One underlying problem can be put in the form of a question: Are the image of baseball and the socio-historical reality of baseball one and the same? No, they are not the same. Boulding takes up this thorny problem in a chapter titled "The Image and Truth: Some Philosophical Implications."[12] He points out that he has "considered the dynamics of behavior in terms of what is essentially an abstraction: the image."[13] He has "not considered the question, whether the image is 'true,' or how, if it is true, we know that it is true," because Boulding has been dealing with a "scientific abstraction" and not a "philosophy."[14] Furthermore, he asserts that the subject of knowledge has been regarded as part of philosophy, but he would like "to make a science out of knowledge by the deft substitution of something that is not what the philosopher means by knowledge, namely the image, for the real thing."[15] I will assume baseball is "ontologically irreducible" to an ultimate reality.[16] Newsprint stories provided a basis for people to imaginatively reconstruct events in baseball. These reconstructions were not necessarily isomorphic with the world of baseball — they *were* the world of baseball.

Helping to illuminate this world, writers used a lively prose style that helped to translate descriptions of the event into a new language that facilitated the imaginative or vicarious reconstruction of the reported event. Dramatic adjectives, scintillating verbs and colorful hyperbole enlivened baseball descriptions. Fly balls were "hauled in," batters "wielded the ash," teams that failed to score were "skunked" or "calcimined."[17] Baseball writing was a focal point for the organization of ideas about baseball. However, attendance at games, discussions of baseball matters and the omnipresence of changing attitudes toward work and play all helped to shape our knowledge of baseball.

To analyze ideas about baseball, I rely heavily on the press reports of baseball as historical data. I also treat these reports as representations of a sociological process and apply concepts such as status, deviance, class, and conspicuous leisure, among others, to analyze the process. This approach incorporates the distinctions noted by Cahnman and Boskoff, who point out the differences in the contrasting studies of revolutions by Crane Brinton and Lyford Edwards.[18] They indicate that Brinton, in *Anatomy of Revolution*, uses sociological categories to analyze historical events, while Edwards, in *The Natural History of Revolution*, uses the "data of history" as an illustration of a sociological process.[19] In this book, I emphasize baseball reporting as the data of history. Nevertheless, I also use sociological concepts as analytical tools to gain a better understanding of the transformation of organized baseball from a social-recreational pursuit to a commercial spectator-team sport. One of the difficulties of applying sociological concepts to a historical problem is the tendency to simplify complex social processes by overstating the significance of sociological concepts as explanatory tools. Realizing that an extended narrative can often capture the uniqueness and rich texture of events, in this book the narrative form is sacrificed for the utility of the generalizing capacity of sociological concepts. This approach provides a more flexible framework to apprehend the intricacies between changing values toward work, play, and sport. For these were necessary conditions for the emergence of organized baseball. With an emphasis on sportswriting as a sociological process, a variety of societal events and key changes in American society are omitted from this study in order to give more attention to the process that fashioned the image of professional baseball. For example, the Civil War did have an effect on organized baseball: the number of games played and the number of players diminished slightly during the conflict. However, this had little impact on the sociological process which was underway before the advent of the war. The process continued during the war, although it may have been impeded by the conflict between the North and South. Nevertheless, the war, despite its enormous importance, did not alter the formation of ideas that contributed to the construction of the image of professional baseball. Thus, in this context, the Civil War and other major societal occurrences are scarcely relevant. However, I do touch on the significance of changing values toward work and play, and changing views toward recreation and health, as antecedents for the rise of sport.[20]

Paralleling the question of whether or not the image of professional baseball accurately reflects the socio-historical reality of baseball is the question of whether or not a terminological distinction should be made when referring to either the baseball player or organized baseball. These are separate conceptual entities—the latter denotes the various elements that constitute the organization of baseball, such as the structure of the National Association of Base Ball Players, the format of championships, and the stability of clubs within the association.

The idea of the baseball player suggests a conceptual level where individuals are involved in voluntaristic action and are described as being skillful or having other characteristics. But from a collective standpoint, the notions of baseball and the baseball player combine into one conceptual entity: organized baseball. Therefore, for this book, organized baseball subsumes the idea of the player. Although it is assumed that the sport press was fundamental to the construction of ideas about baseball, the collective impact of rumor, gossip, and discussion within socio-occupational networks cannot be discounted as an important process by which ideas about baseball were shaped, independent of the sport press.[21] Since few data exist which would shed light on how the aforementioned collective processes specifically influenced ideas about baseball, it will be assumed that members of the baseball public would often talk about stories, reportage of games, reports of changes in the rules and so forth as a starting point for discussion about baseball matters.

The theoretical framework outlined above relies heavily on press reportage of events in baseball. This reliance raises the possibility of taking these reports as accurate descriptions of these events. However, I am aware that sportswriters may have unintentionally distorted reportage of events. Misperceptions by them seem to have occurred when inept play on the part of fielders was mistaken for deliberate attempts to "fix" games. Allegations were made in the press, although there was little basis for the accusations.[22] Biases in the reportage of baseball were also present due to the influence of the English sport press on American sportswriters. However, an analysis of the conditions under which distortions took place in the reportage of baseball matters is not the subject of this book, nor is there an attempt to reconcile differences between reportage and what really happened. This is usually the sort of inquiry that historians of the press take up.

For the most part, the analysis of baseball reporting emanates from the cities of New York and Brooklyn. These cities were the centers of early baseball activity and were also the leading centers for news and book publishing. In publications like the *Spirit of the Times*, the *Brooklyn Eagle*, and the *New York Clipper*, sentiments toward the older and newer orientations toward baseball are sought in the form of editorials, commentaries, evaluative descriptions, and letters to the editor. Lengthy passages from sport periodicals and the general press are freely quoted. This does not mean that socio-historical analysis is subordinate to the inclusion of lengthy quotations, or that quotations are a substitute for reasoning. The quotations are merely an adjunct to analysis. Nevertheless, my hope is to be able to communicate the richness and variability of commentaries on baseball. By using this method, I hope to share with the reader, as much as possible, the data from which many of the conclusions of this study have been drawn.

Scholarly histories and serious attempts to reconstruct the beginnings of baseball are sparse.[23] However, there are studies that are comprehensive in their scope and coverage of the early days of baseball. The most noteworthy of these are *Baseball: The Early Years* by Harold Seymour and Dorothy Seymour Mills, "Cash and Glory" by David Quentin Voigt,[24] "The Development of Modern Athletics" by Melvin Adelman,[25] *Ball, Bat and Bishop* by Robert Henderson,[26] *The Book of American Pastimes* by Charles Peverelly,[27] *America's National Game* by A.G. Spalding,[28] "Baseball: The Origins and Development of the Game to 1903" by Jeffrey Laurence Haven,[29] *Sphere and Ash* by Jacob Morse,[30] *Base Ball* by Seymour Church,[31] *Baseball: Diamond in the Rough* by Irving A. Leitner,[32] "A Theoretical Consideration of the Internal Dynamics of Sport" by Martha M. Seban,[33] *Baseball in the Garden of Eden*, by John Thorn,[34] and *Baseball Before We Knew It*, by David Block.[35]

With a few exceptions, many of these works are descriptive, relying mainly on a narrative approach to limn out the complexities of the early history of baseball. A more rigorous approach is found in the works of Adelman, Seymour, Voigt and Seban, Thorn, and Block. In their works, both analytical and descriptive methods are used to trace the infancy of baseball. Although these researchers deal with the professionalization of baseball, none of them specifically analyzes the relationship between the baseball public and the image of professional baseball. Spalding, Henderson, Voigt, Seban, Seymour, Block and Thorn view the professionalization of baseball as the result of the internal machinations of people in baseball.[36] In their works, attention is focused primarily upon factors that facilitate the commercialization of the game. Admission charges, surreptitious payments to players, competitive bidding for players, rule changes, and gambling are some of the factors considered. There is little detailed analysis directed toward external factors. The point of departure for research and analysis is usually occurrences that are intrinsic to baseball. In the works of Thorn and Block, new primary source information about the origins of the game is presented.

Although this study relies on the sport press as a starting point for analysis, the overall emphasis is upon the interplay between the baseball public and events in baseball, leading to collective ideas about baseball. In order to identify and discuss the circumstances which helped shape views about baseball, an overview of the early history of recreation is important. With this in mind, Chapter I touches upon Puritan values, popular sentiments and intellectual ideas toward leisure, recreation, health, and sport in the first half of the nineteenth century in America. Chapter II describes the origin of the rise of the "amateur" ideal and the influence of the English on American sport. A comparison between the origins and uses of the term amateur rower in England and America is undertaken to gain a better understanding of the process involved in the making of the image of professional baseball.

The ideological relationship between amateur and professional athletics is explored in relation to changing values toward work and recreation in America. Chapter III presents an overview of baseball beginnings in New York. The influence of the Knickerbocker Base Ball Club and other clubs preceding them are described. The influence of the English sport ideal and working class sentiments toward baseball are also addressed. In addition, descriptions of prominent clubs, the first association of baseball players, and some of the early issues in baseball are sketched in. In order for baseball to establish itself, it was important that it receive acclaim by the sport press and the support of the burgeoning baseball public. Chapter IV focuses on the various representations in the press of the praiseworthy aspects of the game.

Chapter V describes the earliest features of the relationship between the baseball public and the baseball spectacle. The emphasis is on the manner in which the baseball public was formed and the significance of the transformation of baseball into a spectacle. With this as a theoretical background, it is suggested that the rise of the baseball public was dependent on the reportage in the sport press of a wide variety of matters pertaining to baseball. It is also suggested that the baseball spectacle grew out of the following factors: rule changes, playing innovations, heroism, rowdy behavior, gambling, partisan rooting, and club rivalries. In contrast to the praiseworthy representations of baseball in the sport press, Chapter VI explores negative representations of the game. In this chapter, an analysis is undertaken of gambling, corruption, substitution, and the revolving of players to other clubs. The structure of the championship as reported in the sport press and how they were related to the image of professional baseball is also analyzed. Different representations of compensation to players reported in the sport press are described and analyzed in Chapter VII. The focus here is on delineating the issues related to compensation of players and how the issues affected the image of professional baseball.

I

Changing Views Toward Man, Recreation, Leisure and Health

The image of professional baseball was formed at a time when American society was undergoing social dislocations arising from a complex array of factors. Some of the more important ones were the growth of a more secular society, the spread of the factory system, economic upheavals, urbanization, and increased press circulation. Within this sociocultural compass, a shift occurred in the work-related values of self-discipline, diligence, and fortitude, as the centrality of work in the lives of people diminished. This shift in values could be detected by the changing views of educators, physicians, moralists and others who advocated the benefits of engaging in recreation and outdoor amusements. These changes, both social and cultural, made it possible for middle- and upper-middle class people to expand their play horizons. When this occurred, the time was ripe for a unique experiment in ball playing by a group of merchants, clerks, workingmen and professionals who started playing different versions of children's bat and ball games. Some of these games were Stoolball, Old Cat games, and Rounders. They were played in Europe and the United States in the seventeen hundreds and earlier.

The following questions are raised to help explore the historical background out of which sentiments toward outdoor pastimes were altered, thereby contributing to the social background out of which *organized baseball emerged:* (1) What are the meanings of the terms sport, recreation, and leisure? (2) What kinds of recreation and sport activities existed in the early part of nineteenth century America? (3) How did a lessening of Puritan ideals affect the growth of sport? (4) How did a growing interest in health matters and physical exercise by Americans, and "Muscular Christianity," influence the growth of sport? (5) What were the key intellectual ideas that supported this growing interest in health and exercise?

Sport is an ambiguous term with different meanings for many people. Notwithstanding differences in the meaning of sport and the difficulty of defining it, sport will mean vigorous physical activity which requires trained physical skills, in the context of a game or a contest that requires physical exertion.[1] In addition, sport often, but not always, embodies notions of fair play, has a tradition, recognized rules or procedures, and usually has an organizing body with regulatory power.

During the first three decades of the nineteenth century, the following sports were popular: horse racing, yacht racing, fox hunting, pedestrianism (foot racing), pugilism, blood sports (cockfighting, bear and rat baiting), rowing races, wrestling contests and cricket matches.[2] Closely related to the concept of sport, and equally difficult to define, are the terms "leisure," "recreation" and "amusements." When the aforementioned terms are currently used they generally connote similar meanings, but when applied to nineteenth-century life, they take on different meanings. At mid-nineteenth century, leisure denoted the antithesis of work. Leisure was both a respite from work and a preparation for the all-consuming workweek of sixty hours or more. The idea of leisure being a state of repose and a release from work is suggested by Charles Francis Adams, who wrote in his diary in 1843: "I idled away the morning on Mr. Daniel Greenleaf's wharf. Perhaps this consumption of time is scarcely justifiable; but why not take some of life for simple enjoyments, provided that they interfere with no known duty?"[3] Recreation differed from leisure in that it implied a goal. It was also thought to restore psychic and bodily energies as a preparation for a resumption of work.

Recreational pastimes from colonial times until the latter part of the nineteenth century varied according to the geographical region in which they were practiced. There appears to be no one prevailing practice common to all geographic areas. Leisure and recreational practices varied by social class and according to rural or urban location. Prevalent ideas about recreational activities in the New England states were utilitarian-oriented. Social and legal sanctions were more punitive there than in the Middle Atlantic states or in the South. Recreation generally took the form of barn raisings, quilting parties, house raisings, ship launchings, and other productive, non-sensual activities. Attitudes toward recreation were more liberal in the South than in New England. Hunting, horse riding, country dancing, target shooting, and fishing were popular recreational pastimes, enjoyed by land-owning gentry in the South, who also set the standards for these activities. Conventional ideas about recreational pursuits in the Mid–Atlantic region were more closely aligned with the South, with the exception of Pennsylvania, where Quaker influence mitigated against frivolous pastime. Amusements such as fairs, carnivals, and traveling theater groups were popular, though condemned by the Protestant church. As the cities grew, urban forms of amusement, like Bar-

I. Changing Views Toward Man, Leisure and Health

num's American Museum in New York, became popular. Public lectures and the theater also were part of the amusement scene in the larger cities.[4]

The rise of sport in nineteenth-century America is closely related to the influence of Puritan ideals on leisure, recreation, and sport. Historians are in general agreement that Puritan ideals had an adverse effect on the growth of these activities. Often their analysis is illuminating. But occasionally it is diluted because the terms leisure, recreation, amusement and sport are used imprecisely. One historian uses the terms leisure and sport in the same breath, implying that they are the same phenomenon. Writing about sport and physical education during colonial times, he notes: "Puritans did not condemn *sport* generally, but rather emphasized that any *leisure* activity pursued had to be justified according to the ultimate purpose of life."[5] Other sport historians, discussing Puritanism, are vague in their use of terms. They suggest:

> There were a few *games*, there were memories of games played in England, and there were stories of holidays and festivals told by parents and grandparents.... But work and piety were the watch-words in New England and early attempts at *sport* were immediately suppressed....[6]

Another view of the influence of Puritan ideas on sport is offered by a sport historian who equates leisure with sport. He states:

> Despite the negative influence of the Puritan ethic on the *sporting pastimes* of America's colonial forefathers and young Republic citizens, the semblance of a *leisure* portrait began to come into focus; it reflected sport and recreation taking place in both cooperative and competitive circumstance....[7]

Despite the lack of terminological specificity, the above authors are in agreement that Puritan ideals retarded the advancement of sport.

A more carefully reasoned analysis of the effect of Puritanism on leisure, recreation and sport is accomplished by the sport historians Lucas and Smith.[8] They point out that the "old-fashioned Puritanism," although weakened by the 1820s, still regarded amusements and sports as anathema. This was particularly true in New England.[9] In other sections of the country and in the cities, amusements and sport steadily gained ground. Even in these areas, the legacy of Calvinistic theology was ever-present, and when given the opportunity, ministers railed against encroachments of the Sabbath and licentious amusements. However, their injunctions did not stifle the impulse to play; they only impeded the emergence of recreational pastimes, and limited the pursuit of leisure or sport.[10] Although there were regional differences in the way people viewed recreation, amusements, and sport, many adult Americans in the 1840s regarded them as a waste of time.[11]

It was not that the Puritans or other Protestant sects objected to a playful diversion, or a simple recreational pastime, "provided it was truly refreshing, was not a waste of time, was not done in excess, and was not immoral or sensual."[12] What was objected to was activity that would stimulate the senses rather than relax the spirit; hence, sport and amusements were repressed, because they were thought to be too sensually exciting. Puritans believed that sports would engender sensual appetites leading to excessive behavior, thus enslaving man through pleasure. Excess would misdirect the service of man to God. Participation in nonutilitarian recreation and popular sports was thought to be conducive to excessive behavior and therefore was to be avoided.[13]

Perhaps gambling was the most distasteful activity to the Puritan mind, because it "tempted God's providence for frivolous ends."[14] Since gambling on sport was widely practiced, sport was equated with immorality. This distaste was also embedded in the images evoked by the press where associations were made between sports and the pioneer sponsors of sport, saloons, and poolrooms.[15]

Americans' lack of enthusiasm for organizing sports and partaking in them was not simply due to religious prohibitions. Their apathy can also be traced to a general feeling that sport detracted from time spent at work. This view of Americans and the importance of work was advanced in the writings of British travelers to America.[16] These travelers noted, and so did their American contemporaries, that "Americans were preoccupied with the pursuit of wealth.... The ability to become rich was central to the American dream and accounted for the widely accepted belief in progress."[17] One traveler, William Baxter, a Whig member of Parliament in 1855, said that he rarely heard "field sports referred to even by young men" and "athletic games" were not very popular in America.[18] Baxter also pointed out that "to roll balls in a ten-pin alley by gaslight, or to drive a fast trotting horse in a light wagon along very bad and very dusty roads seemed the Alpha and Omega of sport in the United States."[19] In brief, British travelers saw that "sport was essentially a sporadic phenomenon that was capable of soliciting a great deal of enthusiasm on particular occasions, but in the grand scheme of things was generally not yet part of the mind set of most citizens."[20]

Yet despite Puritan-based moral prohibitions against sport and a general apathy toward athletic games, there was a shift in the views of a variety of influential thinkers, who began to look more favorably at sport and started to appreciate the benefits derived from athletics. This changing viewpoint helped support the beginnings of an athletic movement, which in turn affected the growth of sport. Lucas and Smith remark: "The rise of sport in America, beginning just before the Civil War and emerging full-blown in the 1870s and 1880s, could never have occurred without the revolution of religious and intellectual diversification so prominent at the beginning of the century."[21]

One element of this diversification was a burgeoning liberalism that buffeted the old Puritan-based provincialism, prompting a new awareness of health and the use of leisure time. This intellectual renaissance was most notable in New England, but not unknown in other parts of the country. European intellectual ideas, which included doctrines of German idealism and French utopianism and a nascent American literary romanticism, rivaled views of man molded by Calvinist theology. But ideas alien to Calvinism did not only originate from secular sources. Within Protestant theology, a new model emerged in the form of Unitarianism, which conceived of man as loving and perfectible. Amidst a profusion of new philosophical views of man and a declining Calvinistic ethic, Unitarianism emerged under the leadership of William Ellery Channing.[22] Unitarianism incorporated, although disguised, some of the ideas of Jacques Rousseau. Theologically, Unitarianism was a much softer kind of Calvinism, but with major differences. Channing's liberal theological doctrine was based on the potential for excellence in man. He espoused the right to strive against the material world and to seek leisure and physical exercise after work.[23] Positive attitudes toward recreation and leisure did not stem directly from the social gospel of Channing's Unitarianism, but his attack on the excesses of work and his belief in man's perfectibility helped generate an ambiance in ministerial circles which was conducive to a reinterpretation of leisure and recreation.

Closely related to the doctrine of the "open mind," which was at the heart of Unitarianism, was the "transcendental movement."[24] This intellectual mode of apprehending man and his worldly activity indirectly influenced sport by promoting physical education and instilling an awareness of the importance of developing a harmony among mind, spirit, and body. The thinkers who constituted the transcendental movement were well educated, middle class, lived in the northeast part of America, and were Unitarian in their religious beliefs.[25] They did not hold a single, unified doctrine or philosophy, but they shared two fundamental beliefs: a rejection of the overemphasis on materialism and a conviction of the "power and sanctity of the human spirit."[26] The adherents of transcendentalism were primarily interested in man's spiritual nature, but they were also concerned with the physical body as a home for the spiritual body. The leading figures in this intellectual movement were Ralph Waldo Emerson, William Ellery Channing, Henry David Thoreau, and Margaret Fuller. The most influential of these thinkers were Emerson and Thoreau. Emerson advocated gymnastics, cricket, archery, fishing, and other activities as educative tools for the young, because they were "self-revealing."[27] He also believed that swimming, skating, fencing, and riding taught participants "lessons in the art of power."[28] The views of the transcendentalists were helpful in providing an "ideological background which was favorable to the establishment of organized physical education theory."[29] Their ideas were part of a realization by many writers, journalists, physicians, educators, and the like, of the importance of physical fitness, proper nutrition, diet and exercise. These ideas were conducive to a reinterpretation of leisure, recreation, and eventually sport. But despite the increasing acceptance of leisure and recreation, remnants of Puritanism thwarted the emancipation of amusements and sport.[30]

Changes in Henry Ward Beecher's views toward work, leisure, and recreation reflect the assimilation of new liberal currents of thought with sectarian Protestantism.[31] This intellectual amalgamation of orthodox Calvinism with new, liberal views of man made for an uneasy union. In the early 1840s, Beecher, in his *Seven Lectures to Young Men*, was quick to describe the awful consequences of idleness and the virtue inherent in diligence. He advocated ethical and moral conduct, and also derided amusements. Beecher conceived of God as "overflowing with grace" and not the wrathful God of "Calvin's pre-destinarianism."[32] Men should undertake the working out with God of their own salvation. However, his position on leisure and work changed. His views "shifted away from an unqualified celebration of labor toward a growing appreciation of the arts of repose."[33] Preaching at the Plymouth Church in Brooklyn, starting in 1847, he began to urge members of his congregation to take vacations. In the winter he extolled the importance of "rest and recreation" as compared to "overwork."[34] From his pulpit in the 1850s Beecher attacked the excesses of work and stressed the importance of rest and recreation.

Beecher's espousal of leisure and his condemnation of the excesses of work parallel his attack on Calvinistic orthodoxy. What was unique about Beecher was not the radical change in his view of man, but his blending of religious, moral, and economic ideas. This blending took the form of a pattern that would "tack back and forth between the strenuous and the passive ideals, contradictions awkwardly jostling each other."[35] He at once hailed the development of character of those steeped in poverty and at the same time supported luxury as an indispensable basis for culture. He railed against those who, because of laziness, were not able to raise themselves from the lower stratum of society, but was critical of relentless ambition and the harm done to youthful intellect by excessive industriousness.[36] In *The Meaning of Henry Ward Beecher*, William McLaughlin points out that Beecher made a distinction between "work and drudgery."[37] This difference enabled him to differentiate leisure from idleness, which led in turn to the idea that "leisure was a means for self-cultivation."[38] Furthermore, as McLaughlin notes, this movement, away from a more traditional posture on leisure, had Beecher, as usual, treading on thin ground with many of his evangelical audience. It all seemed somehow too easy, too contrary to the Protestant ethic. There was nothing here about saving the souls of sinners, nothing about men's duty to help the poor with charity and almsgiving. Beecher had to address himself more directly to the problem of stewardship if he wished to overcome the suspicions of those who thought he was advocating not only naturalism, but also materialism and self-indulgence. Nevertheless, Beecher was as inconsistent here as everywhere else. At the same time that he was praising modern technology for increasing leisure, he was praising those who kept their noses to the grindstone.[39] By the 1870s Beecher moved further toward the espousal of recreation by advocating "bowling and billiards, when rescued from the sordid surroundings of the commercial establishment."[40] The inconsistency of Beecher's sentiments toward leisure corresponded to the uneasiness that middle-class Northerners felt about combining traditional values of diligence and hard work with new ideas that espoused repose and recreational exercise.[41]

Muscular Christianity and the Y.M.C.A.

The reinterpretation of leisure and recreation by ministers, clergymen and others was substantially aided by an ethical concept known as "Muscular Christianity." This ethic stressed the importance of sportsmanship, honesty, individual effort, and initiative in the playing of athletic games, such as cricket, football, riding, and hiking.[42] The roots of Muscular Christianity can be traced to the English public schools under the leadership of Thomas Arnold (1828–1842).[43] The ideas on which Muscular Christianity were founded were introduced to American readers in the 1850s by Thomas Hughes, in *Tom Brown's School Days*. It depicted life at Rugby School, emphasizing the role of athletics as a means of inculcating moral, intellectual, and physical attributes in young men. The book not only influenced moralists and educators, but also "strongly influenced Americans of the period ... large numbers of so-called average people."[44]

Charles Kingsley, an English clergyman and author, helped promote the Christian athlete by glorifying the "Church's new social mission through the medium of the perfectly heroic man — the noble embodiment of moral, intellectual, and physical attributes."[45] This message could be found in Kingsley's 1850 book *Alton Locke*. These two books and others helped promote the idea of robust athletics as a means to develop Christian virtues and good health. The message was well received in America, and "very quickly there arose a kind of mysticism about vigorous competitive athletics, a peculiar proneness to emotionalism and a fondness for romantic hero figures."[46]

From their pulpits, Thomas Wentworth Higginson, Henry Ward Beecher, and Henry C. Wright argued that physical prowess and sanctity were compatible. The merging of Christian principles and athletic endeavors was promoted by the work of the Young Men's Christian Association. The Y.M.C.A. was founded in England by George Williams in 1841 and was introduced to the United States in the early 1850s. At this time, the Y.M.C.A. was organized for the study of the Bible and evangelical work. However, the notion of using athletics as a vehicle for Christian virtues became part of their mission. In 1856, the Brooklyn Association Board of Managers considered the building of gymnasiums, but due to financial difficulties and the Civil War, the gymnasium was not erected. Nevertheless, in 1864, at the annual convention of the Y.M.C.A., a resolution to commit the organization to physical education was formally expressed. Five years later two gymnasiums were built: one in New York, the other in San Francisco.[47]

Nurtured by calls for care of the soul through greater care of the body and athletic involvement, the Muscular Christianity "movement" was underway in America at mid-century.[48] Aiding this movement was a constant stream of criticism directed toward excessive toil and pleas to partake in recreational activities. These criticisms came from physicians, intellectuals, educators, editors, and other spokespersons who advocated vigorous outdoor exercise as a panacea for a variety of ills. Rodgers observes that "for a nervous, over materialistic, over constricted nation, which had taken toil to excess, to let go in play, acknowledge the buried call of instinct, had become a more vital duty than work itself."[49]

The athletic movement helped to promote an "expansion of free-time and free-time activities."[50] A variety of spokespeople broadcast what they believed to be the debilitating effects of city life and excessive toil on the health of the urban dweller and the nation as a whole. Foreign visitors such as Charles Dickens, Frederick Bremer, Herbert Spencer, and Sir Charles Lyell all commented on the excessive toil and poor health of city residents.[51] From the medical profession the word "neurasthenia" was coined in the 1860s. It became synonymous with an assortment of neurological complaints. Sleeplessness, back pains, depression, headaches, were all thought to be manifestations of general exhaustion. S. Weir Mitchell, a Philadelphia neurologist, gave some credibility to the threat of an epidemic of neurasthenia when he published *Wear and Tear or Hints for the Overworked*.[52]

In the 1850s, George W. Curtis, editor of *Harper's*, reminded his readers of the ill effect of the rapid tempo of their daily lives. He urged people to take up outdoor exercise as a way to ameliorate the rigors of their daily life. In the same period of time Frank Queen, editor of the *New York Clipper*, called for construction of gymnasiums to foster good health for young boys. *Godey's Lady's Book* gave constant attention to the health needs of its feminine readers. Advertisements began to appear in the *New York Tribune* in the 1850s, calling for the family to take "gymnastic lessons." Books like Dr. R.T. Tail's *The Illustrated Family Gymnasium* underscored the importance of physical exercise for maintaining good health.[53] The recreation movement and the "cult of strenuosity grew together, minimizing the distinction between usefulness and sport, toil and recreation, the work ethic and the spirit of play."[54]

The rise of baseball was related to the change in values toward work and leisure. The values that supported the pursuit of work-oriented goals and the insistent busyness of Americans were challenged by a "growing praise of play and recreation" which chastised Americans for their excesses of work.[55] "Thrift, diligence, and self-discipline," the values that had been the cornerstone of the nineteenth-century work ethic, were being eroded by a combination of plentitude of factory-produced goods, "carrying new amenities" to the middle class, and the debilitating effect that factories were having on "creativity and independence in work."[56] From the 1850s onward, positive sentiments toward baseball parallel a trend that began attacking "the excesses of work and a growing praise of play and recreation as anecdotes to the violent all-consuming busyness of the Americans."[57]

Periodicals, Sport Magazines, Newspapers and the Dissemination of Ideas About Physical Fitness

In the first half of the nineteenth century, educational publications and periodicals helped to popularize ideas related to physical well-being. One idea that surfaced and gained currency at this time was that deliberate exercise would enhance the functioning of the body. Publications such as the *American Journal of Education*, the *Annals of Education and Instruction*, and *Godey's Lady's Book* sensitized the growing reading public to the need for a proper diet, dress, and exercise as a means to good health.[58] The idea that physical exercise and recreation might be beneficial to man was not new. Franklin had advocated frequent exercise in running, leaping, wrestling, and swimming in the mid-eighteenth century, as a means to maintain good health and strengthen the body. Jefferson's dictum, "Strong body makes the mind strong," certainly carried credence in light of his avid horsemanship, nearly until the end of his life.[59]

Adding to the growing idea of the benefits to be gained from physical exercise was the state of Americans' health. Historian Arthur Cole notes:

> The health of the American people in the middle of the nineteenth century reflected the survival of pioneer optimism and neglect. Although the traditional ague and fever prevailed only on the frontier and in rural backwaters, careless and uncleanly conditions in the more thickly settled towns and cities bred diseases which quickly assumed an epidemic character.[60]

In New York's working-class sections in lower Manhattan, inadequate sewage and excrement from animals and humans provided a breeding ground for disease. These conditions contributed to New York's having the "highest death rate of all American cities."[61] A writer of the time, H.W. Bellows, said: "Want of proper sewerage and ventilation, absence of forethought in providing open spaces for the recreation of the people, allowance of intramural burials and of fetid nuisances, such as slaughter houses, and manufactories of offensive stuffs, have converted cities into pestilential inclosures."[62] These deplorable conditions were undoubtedly responsible for the outbreaks of cholera in 1854, and smallpox in 1861, in New York. The 1854 epidemic killed close to two thousand five hundred people.[63]

The reality of the poor health and the susceptibility of Americans to diseases was commented on by the editor of *Harper's Monthly*. He states that young Americans were "a pale pasty-faced, narrow-chested, spindle-shanked, dwarfed race — a mere walking manikin to advertise the last cut of the fashionable tailor."[64] The editor of *Harper's* was not alone in his concern for "the ill health of Americans; authors, statesmen and others who had access to the public spoke out on what they believed to be the "sorest need of the people ... [for] some recreation that would offer relaxation from business cares and sedentary employments."[65] Helping to champion recreation and sport as a panacea to the general ills of the populace were men like Oliver Wendell Holmes, the statesman Edward Everett, and author Thomas Wentworth Higginson. Everett urged "noble athletic sports, manly outdoor exercises, which strengthened the mind by strengthening the body and bring man into a generous and exhilarating communion with nature."[66] Higginson advocated ice-skating as one form of recreation in a series of articles in the *Atlantic Monthly*.[67] Holmes was an admirer of boxing and engaged in walking and rowing. He also advocated international horse racing as a fillip to imbue patriotism. He suggested that if pugilism were introduced into the clergy "we should have better sermons and infinitely less quarrelsome church militant."[68]

The theme that physical exercise was important for maintaining health was also adopted by physicians and educators who spread a recreational gospel in their books and articles.[69] Their efforts did much to soften middle-class views toward sport. A sport such as baseball could be viewed within a context of its being a healthful physical exercise rather than a frivolous pastime or child's play. The burgeoning interest in health matters, recreation, and sport was greatly aided by sport magazines, newspapers, and baseball guides. They did much to disseminate the rules and changes in the rules, publicize rivalries, and report on the weekly outcome of matches. Consequently, information about matters of health, recreation, sport, and particularly baseball, gained a wider audience.

One of the early advocates to take up the theme of physical exercise and sport as being beneficial to health was John Stuart Skinner, the founder of the *American Farmer* (1819). Almost as soon as the publication began, it expanded coverage to include articles which expressed Skinner's views that exercise, recreation, and sport were necessary for the "well-rounded American." Articles were devoted to "fox hunting, horse racing, and dogs."[70] Skinner's knowledge of sports, particularly English sports, was helpful in providing

I. Changing Views Toward Man, Leisure and Health 19

a wide variety of articles on the subject. His interest in sport culminated in a regular section in 1825 called "Sporting Olio." The *American Farmer* was one of the earliest magazines to report on sport on a regular basis.[71] However, "sport literature" in the early nineteenth century was often viewed as being vulgar and rather disreputable by a substantial portion of the general American reading public. "Sporting magazines suffered from an association with tavern-life, gambling, and general smoking-room stories, just as drama suffered because of its early relationship with prostitution."[72]

Despite negative sentiments toward sport, the *American Farmer* prospered. Skinner's success did not go unrecognized by other aspiring publishers, who, like Skinner, saw the economic potential in writing about sport. Between 1826 and 1835, seven new sporting magazines were started, although only two lasted for more than three years. In 1829 Skinner's "Sporting Olio" was expanded into a new monthly magazine called *American Turf Register and Sporting Magazine*. In 1830, there appeared the *Cabinet of Natural History* and *American Rural Sports*. The following year William T. Porter's *Spirit of the Times and Life in New York* was started. The *Spirit of the Times* was the only sport magazine of the period, other than the *Turf Register*, to last longer than three years.[73] The influence of these publications was considerable. Sport historians indicate that the *Spirit of the Times* "must be considered a contributing factor in popular attitude changes in the pre–Civil War."[74]

Porter's *Spirit of the Times* and the *American Turf Register*, which Porter purchased in 1839, were the leading sport publications of the day. However, Porter suffered financial losses and "allied himself" with George Wilkes.[75] The magazine retained the name of *Porter's Spirit of the Times* until 1859, when it was renamed *Wilkes' Spirit of the Times*.[76] With Wilkes as the owner and Porter as the editor, the *Spirit of the Times* achieved a national reputation and was relied upon for accounts of sport events by newspapers.[77]

The third decade of the century saw a rapid increase in the publishing of a wide variety of printed material.[78] At this time the founding of both newspapers and magazines increased in America. The number of newspapers increased from 802 in 1828 to an estimated 1,218 by 1834.[79] in New York "the number of newspapers and monthly magazines, without including periodical publications issued at longer intervals," was 65. In the state of New York, the number was 263.[80] New York was fast becoming the publishing center of the nation, a position which it attained in the 1850s. The impact of this outpouring of printed words onto the people evoked comments by a writer for the *American Almanac and Repository of Useful Knowledge for the Year 1834*. He states:

> The periodical press, comprising newspapers, magazines, reviews, & c[*sic*], devoted to religious, politics, literature, arts, science ... is one of the momentous consequences of the invention of printing. Periodical publications especially newspapers disseminate knowledge throughout all classes of society and exert an amaz-

ing influence in forming and giving effect to public opinion in all civilized countries.[81]

Print media stories about baseball, which emanated from sporting periodicals, daily and Sunday newspapers and sporting guides, were significant in shaping ideas about baseball.[82] Newspapers had been occasionally reporting on sports in the 1830s. Foot racing, rowing matches, cricket, prizefighting and cockfighting were all commented on at different times in the *New York Transcript*, the *New York Sun*, and the *New York Herald*. These "one-cent dailies," started in the 1830s, were "loud," seeking to pander to the tastes of the "new urban masses." "Police court reporting," "illicit sex relations," prizefights and horse racing were regularly reported.[83] At times the *Sun* would excoriate the prize ring as being debasing and an inhumane practice, but nevertheless, it carried news of matches that stirred public interest. Later the *New York Times* (1851) and the *Tribune* (1841) also railed against prizefights and baseball; however, they still covered some of the more notable matches, apparently to please the wide public interest generated by these contests.

The *New York Clipper* was established in 1853 by Frank Queen. It became one of the most important sport periodicals of the day, and according to one sport historian, the "prime popularizer" of baseball in the 1860s.[84] *New York Weekly Mercury*, in the 1840s, and the *Brooklyn Eagle*, in the 1850s were two regular contributors to reporting on baseball before the Civil War. In the 1860s, Bennett's *New York Herald* gave "considerable space to baseball, prize fighting, and horse racing."[85] But the commercial potential of baseball was realized earlier by the press. Seymour points out that "the interaction between the game and the sporting page was apparent by the 1850s. Baseball news sold newspapers and newspapers sold baseball."[86]

As more baseball games were played, it became increasingly difficult for editors and writers to cover many of the more notable contests. Therefore, editors enlisted the aid of local correspondents, club secretaries, and fans to supply them with accounts of contests.[87] In the mid–1850s, accounts of games were brief, running usually less than several hundred words, but toward the end of the decade, the length of stories increased to "full-columned descriptions." By the 1860s "inning-by-inning accounts of both match games and intra-squad games could be read."[88] In the 1850s, the dime novel made its appearance. This popular form of literature "reached a much larger audience than any earlier fiction in America."[89] However, before 1885 the subject of sport in the dime novel was only an occasional occurrence. One exception to this trend was the annual edition of *Beadle's Dime Base-Ball Player*, published from 1860 to 1881 by Beadle and Adams.[90]

Perhaps the success of the *Dime Base-Ball Player* was due to its editor, Henry Chadwick, the leading baseball writer of his day. His "prodigious" amount of writing on the game gained for him the sobriquet "Father of Baseball ... Nestor of American Sport."[91] Chadwick started reporting on cricket in the 1850s.[92] The influence of his native England is evident in his writing; he consistently stressed the virtues of gentlemanly deportment in the playing of both cricket and baseball. Baseball historian Voigt describes Chadwick as "fearless." He also remarks:

> His chief targets were crooked players, drunken players, and rowdy players. Nor did he spare clubs from charges of mismanagement. Although his attacks were blistering, he was prudent enough to speak of evildoing in general terms, and rarely named specific villains.[93]

In a personal sketch, although not giving specifics, Chadwick notes that he covered baseball starting in 1851 for every important sport weekly and daily paper in the metropolitan area, although he is usually thought of as a baseball writer for the *Brooklyn Eagle* and the *New York Clipper*.[94]

William Cauldwell, the editor of the weekly *Sunday Mercury*, may also be one of the earliest writers covering baseball.[95] In May 1 of 1853, and in July of the same year, he mentioned a match between the Gothams and the New York Knickerbocker baseball clubs. These were the first press accounts since 1845, when there was a brief mention of a contest between New York and Brooklyn. *Beadle's Dime Base-Ball Player* was the first of a number of baseball guides which appeared in the nineteenth century. Other prominent guides were *DeWitt's Base-Ball Guide* (1868–1885); *Spalding's Official Baseball Guide* (1878–1939); *Reach Baseball Guide* (1883–1939) and *Wright and Ditson's Baseball Guide* (1884–1912).[96] The primary purpose of these guides was the advancement of the playing and the instruction of baseball. The editors emphasized the rules and regulations of the game, the formation of clubs, and the names of the officers and delegates to the annual baseball convention. Voigt points out:

> The guidebooks of the seventies were published by outsiders who willingly paid in order to get their advertisements before a growing baseball-minded public. Thus, subsidized, commercialized baseball managed to keep its public regularly informed on rule changes, league membership changes, seasonal performances and statistics, and informal chatter about players and clubs.[97]

At first, the baseball guide served as a quasi-official "compendium of the game."[98] Later, the baseball guide became the official register of professional baseball, the DeWitt guide of 1872 became the official guide for the National Association of Professional Baseball Players.[99]

The groundswell of interest in recreation, health, and sport before the Civil War is inextricably related to a transformation of religious and intellectual views of man in America. The spirit of intellectual reformation and the romantic evangelical thrust of American religious life engendered a concern for individual and community health, and a growing interest in recreation and sport. Although this burgeoning interest in health, recreation, and sport gained momentum during the fourth and fifth decades of the nineteenth century, there still existed at this time a legacy of Puritan ideals which helped maintain a suspicion of sport. Hence, there was not a unity of conviction among people about either participating in or viewing sport. The changing views, and at times the contradictory opinions of Henry Ward Beecher, suggest an uneven assimilation by Americans of new liberal ideas about recreation and sport. Nevertheless, expressions of the excesses of work and the praise of recreational pastimes could be heard from the pulpit and read in both the popular press and religious periodicals. The resonant voices and lucid prose of thinkers like Emerson, Thoreau, Holmes, Fuller, Channing, Higginson, and others formed a chorus in praise of recreational diversions as a palliative for overwork. Their message was clear: it was not through a slavish devotion to work or in self-discipline that a man's spiritual essence manifested itself, but rather through the free expression of play in the context of outdoor pastimes and athletic pursuits. The publishing of a variety of printed material was the principal means by which people gained knowledge about health matters and the idea that physical exercise would promote better health. The *American Farmer* was one of the early publications to link physical exercise and sport as being beneficial to health. About the same time, newspapers began commenting on sport. It was the sport periodical, however, that focused its attention on sport, and by virtue of that attention became the prevailing pundit on sport matters and the dispenser of sport information. Similarly, but in a narrower sense, baseball guides provided the masses with a similar service.

New meanings about health, recreation, and sport were also popularized by the works of Thomas Hughes and Charles Kingsley. *Tom Brown's School Days* greatly influenced the pursuit by young men for physicality, intellect, valor, and fortitude through athletics. The Y.M.C.A. provided a means by which Christian principles and athletic endeavors could be combined into a recreational gospel extolling virtues to be gained through strenuous exercise and sport. The stage was set, ready for the entrance of the unique experiment in ball playing and ultimately the inception of organized baseball. Before discussing the early years of organized baseball and the sport press, we will turn to the influence of the English on American sport and on the ideals that guided the playing of the game.

II
The Amateur Ideal in Baseball

At the outset, baseball was played mainly as an outlet for athletic exercise and social amusement, rather than an opportunity for a hotly contested game. Underlying this mode of play was a code of conduct emphasizing fair play and sportsmanship. In the late 1850s, this code began to wane and eventually was supplanted in the 1860s by a "win" ethic whereby aggressive competition was to become the *sine qua non* of organized baseball. Co-extensively during this period, there existed an ideational conflict between recreational and professional baseball. The conflict was influential in drawing into sharper focus the essential characteristics of professional baseball. Helping to delineate these characteristics, the press served as a lively forum where ideas about baseball were promulgated, tested, and debated. Before setting forth the ways in which the press described amateur and professional baseball, we need to trace the social background from which the terms amateur and professional sport arose in England and America. By doing so we can identify the social processes contributing to the production of meanings associated with amateur and professional baseball. This will help generate an understanding of the conflict between the two.

Our inquiry will seek answers to the following questions: (1) What is the relationship of sportsmanship to the inception of amateurism in early nineteenth-century England? (2) What part did social class and status play in the social processes that led to the rise of amateurism? (3) What function did the term amateur serve in England and America? (4) What sports in England and America were the first to adopt the term amateur? (5) How did English sport influence American sport?

The Rise of Sportsmanship in England

In the early part of the nineteenth century, the elite of English society began to embrace life in the country more than life in the town. This bucolic lifestyle included an emphasis upon field sports, such as fox hunting, pheasant shooting, angling, riding, and falconry.[1] The tenant farmer, yeoman and freeholder were excluded from these activities by both custom and game laws.[2] Although legal, social and economic circumstances clearly separated the country squire from other rural people, it was the manner in which he pursued field sport that gave him an added distinction to that of sportsman.

A tacit code of conduct surrounded his hunting activities. This code entailed the idea that the prey be given an opportunity to evade the hunter — in other words, a "sporting chance." For the English squire the hunt was not only an opportunity to engage in a contest between man and animal; it also represented moral principles that reflected his social position. The training of hunting dogs and horses for the hunt and the inclusion of obstacles (fences and ponds) ensured a more entertaining and challenging undertaking. The following descriptions of English field sports at the turn of the nineteenth century suggest this approach to hunting:

> The pleasures of good English sporting used to consist in the conscious pride of art — in watching and training the fine instinct of the dog against the finer instinct of the bird — in the power of the man to pursue and in his skill to strike his wild and wary prey — to follow "over hill, over dale, through bush, through briar," with an activity that declared health and vigour, and a perseverance that indicated the keen sense of delight with which the sport was urged. The difficulty constituted all the glory of success.[3]

The lifestyle of the country squire influenced men throughout England and other countries. One historian notes:

> The ideal of gentility made every man want to look like an English country gentleman whose dress was in part determined by his sports and pastimes. The stovepipe hat originally designed to protect the head of the hunting man was worn by fishmongers, policemen, cricketeers, and the Oxford and Cambridge crews even when rowing.[4]

At approximately the same period of time, similar ideas of sportsmanship arose in the English public schools in the context of playing folk football games. Early in the nineteenth century, a traditional form of football was played by the masses and at schools like Eton, Harrow, Winchester, and Charterhouse. The game was rough and often violent. But for a number of complex reasons, documented by Dunning and Sheard in *Barbarians, Gentlemen and Players*, the game was transformed at Rugby School with the introduction of civilizing rules which helped to limit the violence and engender ideas of fair play and sportsmanship.[5]

Under the leadership of Thomas Arnold (1828–1842), the social structure of Rugby School was transformed to incorporate an emphasis on team games, such as football and cricket, as a means to instill character values. Arnold believed in the "character forming properties of team-games."[6] The idea of training young men in character ideals was in accord with the desire of parents who wanted their sons' education to prepare them for participation in a "class which was the principal reservoir from which the country's military leadership was recruited and whose values, correspondingly, stressed virtues such as strength, courage and physical prowess."[7] Parents wanted sons to be trained as gentlemen by means of "'manly' education tempered by 'civilizing' restraints and, therefore, denotative of high social status."[8]

The game that began at Rugby School was "radically different from that played by the lower classes; that is a type of football devoid of socially 'contaminating' lower-class associations and, therefore, appropriate as a game for 'gentlemen.'"[9] What distinguished rugby from the football of the masses was an ideal code of conduct that emphasized a balance between aggression and skill, spontaneity and control, the individual and the group. The same ideas incorporated into the playing of Rugby football also served as an ideology for the playing of other competitive team games throughout the nineteenth century. The components of this ideology are: (1) the pursuit of the activity as an end in itself, producing pleasure with a corresponding "downgrading of the achievement, striving, training and specialization"; (2) "self-restraint" should be displayed by the "masking of enthusiasm" in victory and disappointment in defeat; (3) the idea that fairness in the playing of the game, and an emphasis on "voluntary compliance with the rules and a chivalrous attitude of 'friendly rivalry' towards opponents," should be the norm.[10]

It is difficult to establish with any certainty how the code of conduct of the English country squire and the code of game-playing conduct at English public schools influenced each other. It seems reasonable to assume that members of the English public schools, who were drawn from the land-owning gentry, adopted ideas toward proper deportment in all sports (field, as well as games) from common knowledge held within this social stratum. In brief, these ideals intertwined to produce an approach to sport that was predominant throughout England in the nineteenth century. The coalescing of these ideals helped to form an amateur ethos. But as Dunning and Sheard point out:

> The amateur ethos existed in a relatively inchoate form. It was, that is, an amorphous, loosely articulated set of values regarding the functions of sport and the standards believed necessary for their realization. However, with the threat posed by incipient professionalization in the north, the amateur ethos began to crystallize as a highly specific, elaborate and articulate ideology.[11]

Other than the family, the principal means of nurturing and transmitting the amateur ideal were English private and athletic clubs. As early as the eighteenth century, the English athletic clubs, principally the Marylebone Cricket Club (1788) and the Jockey Club (1750), helped to share the ideal of athletic deportment. In the case of the Jockey Club, proper athletic deportment did not preclude wagering and the offering of prizes to both jockey and owner.

Their spirit of sportsmanship was demonstrated by their being the first to initiate a "set of weight allowances whose theoretical purpose was to equalize the opportunities of horses of different ages."[12] In these clubs, the loose strands of values and attitudes associated with gentlemanly athletic participation began to take shape. Although private clubs had been in existence since the seventeenth century, it was not until the first three decades of the nineteenth century that they began to flourish.[13] The Guards (1813), the Oxford and Cambridge (1830), the Carlton (1832) and the Reform (1837) were some of the numerous private clubs established at this time.[14] By their rules and regulations, the English clubs were able to establish a collective ethos which radiated a standard for sports decorum. Although the code of sport behavior is difficult to define, it embodied a non-serious approach to athletic contests. The emphasis was on deportment: facing defeat or embracing victory should be done gracefully. One should neither complain of a loss nor gloat over a win. Competitive struggle was encouraged, but within bounds recognized by all gentleman athletes.

Athletic contests, especially rowing, were highly visible. They provided English gentlemen with opportunities to demonstrate restraint over their emotions before others. More important, athletic competition facilitated a symbolic demonstration of values deemed essential to gentlemanly conduct. Physical strength, courage, and perseverance were qualities that could be exhibited in varying degrees in sports like rowing, running, cricket and rugby. Moreover, these qualities were to be combined ideally with a certain style, where grace and a flair for giving the opposition an equal opportunity to succeed became the hallmark of the amateur ideal.

Social Class, Status and Amateurism in England

Sport sociologists have effectively argued that in England and in Canada, changing class relations prompted the ruling class to structure sports to conform to their own ideals and meanings—particularly ideas about amateurism.[15] During the first half of the nineteenth century in England, gentleman sportsmen were relatively secure in their social position. The English elite played cricket with paid players who were from working-class backgrounds. "Gentlemen" played alongside their "socially inferior" paid players, and shared the same dressing rooms. On occasion, they would join them in eating and drinking, which usually followed a cricket match.[16] This social intermingling was possible because "gentleman players" could "contemplate defeat" at the hands of "professionals" and accept it with "equanimity."[17] Professional players posed little social risk to gentleman players because the latter were "exceptionally secure" in the "stability of their power and status in society at large."[18] Nevertheless, the class structure that ordered the relationship between gentlemen and professional cricket players was not "immutable." As Dunning and Sheard note:

> Industrialization, urbanization and the related process of *embourgeoisement* began, from the start of the nineteenth century, slowly to erode the foundations on which the basis of their power crumbled, particularly as they became subject to a mounting bourgeois threat, so they began commensurately to experience status insecurity. And as that occurred, professional cricket emerged as a controversial issue and the old pattern of free and easy mixing on the cricket field gave way to a more class-exclusive pattern.[19]

The principal outcome of status insecurity for cricket was the drawing of a sharp distinction between those who participated in sport as a recreational outlet and those who did so as a vocation. Forms of "ritual subordination," such as calling gentlemen players "sir," and "symbolic subordination," such as separate dressing rooms for professionals, were used to underscore the social inferiority of the professional.[20] Another device used to diminish the social threat the professional posed to the gentry was the placing of the professional's initials after his surname on the scorecard, while the gentleman players' initials were placed before their surname. Professionals were also expected to perform "menial duties around the grounds."[21] Gruneau points out that in the 1850s and 1860s in Canada, "amateurism emerged ... as a regulative strategy of social closure by an insecure and somewhat reactionary bourgeoisie surrounded by the expansion of democratic 'rights' and entrepreneurial capitalism."[22] Similar to England, the Canadian "dominant class" struggled to maintain their "superior rank and aristocratic power" through the "dramatic representational value of 'leisure class' games."[23] Amateurism was an important ideological tool used by the economic and political elite to thwart the inroads of the underclass who threatened elite conceptions of sport.

The Amateur Rower in England

Manifestations of status insecurity were not limited to those who played cricket. Fear of the erosion of status position could also be found in competitive rowing in England. Aristocratic young men who participated in competitive rowing as a recreational outlet began to draw a distinction between themselves and those boatmen who rowed for a living by adopting the designation "amateur."

In eighteenth-century Europe, the term amateur was not used to denote *participation* in athletic contests. Instead, it was associated with an "upper class *patron* of and *enthusiast* for sport."[24] It seems that the English expropriated the term from the French, who used it denote "aristocratic collectors and connoisseurs of the fine arts."[25] By the beginning of the nineteenth century in France, it appears that the term amateur had begun to connote athletic participation by elites. In this context, the term was also used interchangeably with the term gentleman.[26] But in the early part of the nineteenth century in England, the term began to take on a different meaning when young upperclassmen at schools and universities took up rowing.[27] Their recreational rowing sharply differed from that of the Thames boatmen who rowed for a living. From the sixteenth century these boatmen had been organized into guilds, and as part of their training, apprentice boatmen would compete in rowing races.[28] Although these races aroused public interest, it is difficult to say if they stimulated interest in rowing among the upper class. Yet a relationship between the Thames watermen and the amateur rower did exist: the watermen were occasionally retained as coaches by schools and universities. However, because of their superior rowing skills, they were excluded from competing in organized competitions.[29] This prohibition was the first "amateur clause" which specifically "excluded anyone who earned his keep with his hands."[30] Although the specification was based on an occupational distinction between the amateur rower and the Thames watermen, the distinction was implicitly grounded in social class differences. Later the social distinction became more apparent. At mid-nineteenth century, the amateur rower was defined as one who was not "by trade or employment a mechanic, artisan or laborer."[31] The definition of an amateur rower was applied in 1871 when the Henley Regatta Committee declined an entry "on the grounds that the crew included people who were or had been mechanics, artisans and laborers."[32] Although professional rowing existed in England early in the nineteenth century, it was amateur rowing that caught the public's attention. Perhaps the reason for this, other than the excitement generated by the races, was the growth of the amateur ideal.

The Amateur Rower in America

It is difficult to pinpoint in America, as was the case in England, the emergence of the idea of amateur athlete.[33] But since America followed the British in their organization of sport, it is likely that the idea emerged in America after the English had nurtured their own notions of the amateur athlete. Similar to the English, competitive rowing in America started with harbormen who rowed for a living and occasionally competed in races for wagers.[34]

From the colonial period, skilled oarsmen earned a living by rowing ship pilots and tradesmen out to meet incoming ships. Rowing contests occurred in the latter half of the eighteenth century "but they attracted little, or no, public attention."[35] However, in the first two decades of the nineteenth century, a number of rowing contests for wagers were reported in the press.[36]

II. The Amateur Ideal in Baseball

The leading contests occurred between a boat named the *Knickerbocker* and another boat named the *Invincible*. From 1807 until the 1820s the two boats were matched against each other. In one race in 1820, the *New York Gazette* reported that they raced for a wager of eight hundred dollars.[37] These races and others were "sponsored by the boat builders themselves to demonstrate, indeed advertise, their skill in building boats."[38] During the 1820s and 1830s recreational boat clubs first appeared.[39] In 1834 a number of these clubs merged to form the Castle Garden Amateur Boat Club Association (CGABCA). The association was composed of young men drawn from "prominent families."[40] The use of the term amateur connoted that the members of the association did not earn a living as watermen, nor did they participate in competitive rowing for money. The latter idea was underscored when the association was invited to compete in a regatta in Poughkeepsie. However, the constitution of the association forbade "any club to row for money, or take part in a regatta or races with any club or clubs independent of those belonging to the association."[41] The primary purpose of a club within the association was to promote rowing as a "social diversion" and not as a competitive activity.[42] However, each year the CGABCA held regattas in June and September in which races were held.[43]

In addition to the Castle Garden Association, there existed another confederation of boat clubs called the Independent Boat Club Association. This association differed from the Castle Garden Association in that its rules were "less stringent."[44] The clubs were more competitive, and although the members were "white collar," they were not drawn from the city's elite as were the members of the CGABCA.[45] By 1842, the Castle Garden Amateur Boat Club Association held its last regatta.[46] The end of the association and the collapse of other rowing clubs indicated the decline of club rowing in New York. However, races of "harbormen and professionals" continued until the late 1850s.[47]

In about 1855, the Empire City Regatta Club (ECRC) was formed. This club differed from previous rowing clubs in that its members did not compete in races or row for recreation. The purpose of the club was to sponsor races for prize money, usually four hundred dollars per regatta.[48] They published "challenges in the leading sports journals for large amounts in contrast to privately arranged contests a decade earlier."[49] One of the leading scullers of the time, William H. Decker, offered to race "anybody for a thousand to five thousand dollars."[50] These challenges and annual regattas sponsored by the ECRC and the newly formed New York Regatta Club (1859) produced rowing races that were a "major attraction for the huge throngs, often estimated at 10,000 people...."[51] From the mid–1850s and into the 1860s, professional rowing was popular. However, after the Civil War, interest declined and amateur rowing ascended in the forms of collegiate and club rowing.[52]

Yet ambiguity still surrounded what constituted an amateur rower. In

1872 twenty-seven rowing clubs met and set forth rules and regulations to govern amateur rowers, thereby establishing the National Association of Amateur Oarsmen (NAAO).[53] In their deliberations, a lively debate ensued over what an amateur rower was. Some representatives wanted to adopt the English definition which excluded all artisans and manual workers from amateur competition. However, the definition agreed upon was that "one who does not enter into an open competition for a prize, or who has never taught, pursued, or assisted in the pursuit of athletic exercise as a means of livelihood, or who has not been employed in or about boats or on the water."[54] Despite this definition, "professionals and semi-professionals remained a part of the rowing scene until the last decade of the nineteenth century."[55]

It appears that the principal reason for the inclusion of the term amateur in the CGABCA was to denote that their rowing activities were social and not occupational. This probably stems from a desire not to be associated with working-class men who rowed for a living and who also raced for prizes and betting wagers. While this is not certain, it is clear that in the case of the NAAO they explicitly stated in their charter the desire to be distinguished from those who raced for money or those who, in some way, were occupationally tied to rowing.

The Influence of the English on American Sport

The influence of the English on American sport in the nineteenth century has been analyzed by sport historian Jennie Holliman. She observes that England had a greater influence on American sport than all other countries combined.[56] She notes:

> Most sports came from Europe. No better advertisement of an amusement could be offered than to say it had been successfully practiced in London. When a man from England went through the country with new pastimes, tricks or plays the American people straightway adopted them, enjoying the belief that they were following the latest fashion of London.[57]

Holliman contends that not only were American ideas about sports influenced by the English, but Americans were also dependent on them for sporting equipment and books on sport. She goes on to point out that much, if not all, sport equipment came from England and Holland. In the first half of the nineteenth century, saddles, rods, reels, tackle, riding habits, and shuttlecocks came from England. Holland provided Americans with sleighs and fishing equipment. Americans looked toward English sport books as guides to their sporting activities. Books such as "John Lawrence's *Philosophical and Practical Treatise on Horses* and Pierce Egan's *Boxiana* ... furnished sporting knowledge to the Americans who either read them or extracts from them published in a few periodicals in the United States."[58] Books of English origin, which were not generally available, were excerpted in the sporting press. Some of these were Johnson's *Shooter's Companion*, Johnson's *Sportsman's Dictionary*, the *English Hunting Directory* and the *Annals of Sporting and Fancy Gazette*.[59] Even when Americans began to initiate their own sporting publications:

> English sport writers and English periodicals and sport books were used as models or guides. Not a book nor a periodical dealing with sports of the United States was published at this time which was not under the direct influence of the English as to contents and as to form.[60]

Publications such as the *American Farmer* (1819) and the *Spirit of the Times* (1831) were influenced by the English. Articles appearing in the *American Farmer* on science and health were of English origin. The *Spirit of the Times* had a London correspondent who authored a column called "From our Liverpool Correspondent." Articles and extracts were taken from *The London Sporting Magazine*. *The New York Sporting Magazine and Annals of the American and English Turf* were modeled on *The English Sporting Magazine*.[61] Very few books on sport were written by Americans during this time,[62] and most were versions or abridged compilations of English sporting books. The author of *The American's Shooter's Manual* (1827) admits to having made a compilation of information from the "best standard books, which of course were English."[63]

Holliman concludes her analysis of the influence of English sport on American sport by noting that "practically every phase of sporting life in America was tinged with the English influence."[64] While the influence of the English on American sport and American life was widespread, there was often an ambivalence by Americans toward things English. Writing about England's heritage in America, historian Barbara Solomon summarizes this ambivalence nicely by pointing out that "forward looking Brahmins appreciated the paradox of their community which, though anti–English in principle, often abased itself before English standards."[65]

Another historian, Stephen Hardy, writing about sport and recreation in Boston, tells us:

> Much of the sporting impulse stemmed from a tendency to mirror English social fashion. As one contemporary analyst noted, "anglomaniacisms" had much to do with the greater acceptance of outdoor sports by men and women alike. While the patriot might cringe at the love of things English, there was some compensation, she concluded; for "anglomaniacism" has made it here in America, because in England, the fashion [sic] to ride, to cycle and to play games.[66]

Perhaps part of the mixed view that Americans held of the English was due to Americans' belief in the view that the English held of them. Larzer Ziff, writing about how American writers broke away from English literary convention, offers this view:

> Americans had always been edgy about the English view of them. They responded

at times with abject humiliation and at other times with defiant aggressiveness to English criticism, revealing in either response a deep prerational attachment. England still stood as parent. What had the youthful nation to show as compensation for the rich cultural inheritance it had forsaken when it cut the family ties?[67]

The acceptance, and at the same time denial of things English, manifested itself in American sport by the intent of sportsmen not merely to emulate the English, but a desire to improve upon the qualities of English sports. This was the case with baseball. The founders of the New York Knickerbocker Base Ball Club retained elements of the English sporting tradition, mainly a code of conduct which deemphasized competition and emphasized the social and the athletic benefits to be gained from playing baseball, and thus laid the groundwork for America's national game.

The emergence of amateurism can be traced to English field sports in the early nineteenth century. Ideas of sportsmanship arose from giving the prey an opportunity to escape, thereby making the hunt more challenging for the hunters. During this time, similar ideas in football pertaining to fairness, self-restraint, friendly rivalry, and the game as an end in itself, gained popularity in English public schools. These ideas were nurtured under the guidance of school masters who believed that playing football in accordance with the above-mentioned principles helped instill character values. English private and athletic clubs also helped to shape and to transmit ideas about this ideal code of game-playing conduct during the nineteenth century.

In England and America, class backgrounds of amateur and professional rowers played a part in their separation and the meanings attached to each other. In England, the underlying reason for separation was a combination of class and status. Unlike cricket, upper-class rowers did not want to associate with occupational rowers. Neither did they want to compete against them, for they were usually outclassed. In America, the reasons for the distinction between amateur and professional rowing appear to be less related to class than to a desire by amateurs to disassociate themselves from the disreputability of the professional athlete, and a desire to maintain a distinction between those who rowed for fun and those who took rowing seriously. In England, changing class relations heightened status insecurity among elites, prompting invidious distinctions between amateur and professional rowers. In America, the desire to maintain rowing as a conspicuous form of leisure and the status of being an amateur engendered a distinction between amateur and professional.

The social process which gave rise to the concepts of amateur and professional rowing in England and America corresponds to the process responsible for the emergence of the concepts of amateur and professional in baseball. The reason for this is the following: in the cases previously cited, play activities were transformed into competitive contests, thereby becoming symbolic vehicles for the transmission of social and moral meanings about the relationship between two sets of interrelated factors—work and sport, and status and class.

As struggles in social relationships continued in England and America, notions of what constituted an amateur or a professional took on more definite meanings. No clear-out distinctions existed between the two during the mid-nineteenth century. However, in both countries, the factors of social class and status were not the only influences in determining why people strove to be deemed an amateur and shunned the label of being a professional. Gambling on sport, "fixed" contests, and the commercialization of sport helped create an aura of moral impropriety which lowered the status of the professional and raised the position of the amateur. Although Americans were ambivalent about things English, the pervasive influence of English sports, equipment, books, magazines, and immigrants placed England in the position of a leader in matters of sport. As we shall see in the next chapter, English children's books of games had an important influence on the emergence of baseball.

III

The Origin of Baseball and the Early Years of the Knickerbocker Base Ball Club

An overview of the origin of baseball in America is the starting point for a discussion of the beginnings of the New York Knickerbocker Base Ball Club and other organized baseball teams in New York. Seeking the origin of baseball in America has been a preoccupation of writers such as the nineteenth century baseball writer Henry Chadwick, baseball historians David Voigt, Robert Henderson, Harold Seymour, David Block and John Thorn, the baseball player Albert G. Spalding, and others. They have endeavored to unravel the multiplicity of bat and ball games that can be traced to baseball's origin. This quest unfortunately has created myths and ambiguity surrounding the progeny of baseball, as we would recognize it today. The search has been stymied by a lack of primary historical data and the complexity of tracing the innate capacity of ball games to morph according to culture, geographic locale, technology, and serendipitous circumstances.

The origin of baseball is often associated with what baseball historians call the Doubleday myth: a belief in the legend that the game of baseball was invented by Abner Doubleday in 1839, at Cooperstown, New York. The tale was popularized by the conclusion of a committee (1907) appointed by Albert G. Spalding, a well-known player, and other prominent men in baseball, and a book written by Spalding (1911).

Before this time, baseball historians had already asserted that baseball was an outgrowth of rounders, a favorite game of English children. If these historians are correct, how and why did baseball come to America? We would also like to know how the influence of the English on American sport affected the organization of the Knickerbocker Base Ball Club. What other baseball clubs arose after the formation of the Knickerbockers? How and why did baseball change from a lighthearted recreational activity to a more competitive contest? What evidence is there to link the American Indian with the origin of baseball? In order to answer how and when baseball came to America, we have to look again at the influence of the English on American sport.

There is a consensus among baseball and sport historians that baseball has multiple antecedents. These beginnings date from ball games in seventeenth-century Europe and more directly from early nineteenth-century America as it evolved into baseball as we would recognize it today.[1] In a quest for an origin of baseball there have been numerous

Knickerbocker Base Ball Club, recognized by baseball historians to be one of the early prominent organized baseball clubs. Circa 1845. Woodcut illustration in Spalding's 1911 book *America's National Game*.

interpretative twists and turns by baseball and sport historians as they seek to document baseball's lineage. One prominent account is noted by baseball historian Harold Seymour, who states: "The unquestionable link between baseball and rounders was proved in 1939 by Robert W. Henderson, a librarian. His examination of early game books for children demonstrated that the rules for rounders and baseball were at first identical."[2]

However, the pioneering work by Henderson on the origin of baseball does not stand the scholarly scrutiny of David Block (2005). He effectively argues that the case for the English game of rounders as a progenitor of baseball is based on erroneous scholarship of Henderson, who asserts that a boy's game of ball called base ball was played in England in the eighteenth and nineteenth centuries. As it evolved in England, the name of the game changed to feeder and rounders, according to the locale where the game was played. In England, the rules for the game appeared in print in 1829, under the name rounders. Similarly, in America the rules for rounders appear in the *The Boy's Own Book* (3rd English edition), also published in 1829. The rules for rounders were reprinted in 1835, and were called base or goal ball. These rules were revised in 1839 and called "base ball." From this transformative sequence, Henderson concluded that older forms of base ball, and more directly rounders, led directly to "base ball." Block persuasively argues that the name rounders was merely a "regional nickname" that arose in the west of England and denotes a game that was not, from the standpoint of rules, the lineal antecedent of baseball.³ Moreover, Block argues that the name rounders cannot be found in the "historical annals of England or the United States before 1828," but the name base ball appears "at least 7 times" in eighteenth-century writings, thus appearing more than thirty years before the term rounders. Baseball and rounders took diverging paths in nineteenth-century America, the former becoming a game that facilitated a more aggressive form of play, while the latter retained its traditional underpinnings.⁴

Nevertheless, to Henderson's credit, he reminds us that the difficulty of establishing the origin of baseball is related to the following factors: (1) the history of ball games; (2) the dissimilarity of names under which similar games of ball were played; (3) the lack of historical data; and (4) propaganda surrounding the origin of baseball. Ball games can be traced back to the ancient Egyptians, who used ball games as religious rituals. Some ancient societies used ball games as part of their religious rites and as a preparation for life. Increasing secularization of society ended the religious significance of ball games. Ball games may have emerged spontaneously in Europe, or may have been imported by travelers, or a combination of the two. An early game that used a bat and ball and required more than two players, was a game called "stoolball." Henderson notes that stoolball was the first game recorded as being played in the American colonies by the Pilgrims in 1621. But before this game made an appearance in America, it was played in England during the sixteenth century. Henderson gives us this description of the game:

> Stoolball was very simple at first, befitting a game in which young men and women played together. A three-legged stool was upended. A batter stood before the stool either bare-handed, or with some form of a bat. A player was "out" if a ball hit the stool, or the ball was caught after being struck, and another player took his place at the stool. The winner was the player who scored the greatest number of hits.⁵

At different times, stoolball, like other simple ball games, underwent variations in how the game was played. Stoolball was also played under different names in the same country; Henderson points out that as the number of bases in the playing of stoolball increased it "became known under other names; one of them was 'baseball.'"⁶

III. The Origin of Baseball

The earliest use of the term baseball "so far located, was made by the Reverend Thomas Wilson, a Puritan devine [sic] at Maidstone, England." In 1700, he wrote disapprovingly of "morris-dancing, cudgel-playing, baseball and cricketts, and many other sports on the Lord's Day."[7] The next usage of the term baseball is found in a book published in 1744 by John Newberry called a *Little Pretty Pocket-Book*, a book of children's games. It consists of thirty pages of alphabetically listed games. After each letter, there appears a woodcut illustrating a game, followed by a rhymed description of it, and afterward a "Moral." One of the games listed was "Base-ball," which was described as follows:

> The Ball once struck off,
> away flies the Boy
> To the next destin'd Post,
> and then Home with Joy.
> moral
> Thus Britons for Lucre
> Fly over the Main;
> But, with Pleasure transported,
> Return back again.[8]

The woodcut shows three young players involved in a hit-the-ball-running type of game. Bases are marked by posts, while a player stands ready to hit the ball, another stands ready to serve the ball, and the third player at one of the posts stands ready to run. In the text of the poem, the game is called "Base-ball." This was a rudimentary form of baseball.

The Little Pretty Pocket-Book passed through eleven editions between the years of 1744 and 1790. It was a popular children's book of the time, and the game of base ball was known and played by English boys.[9] Attesting to the popularity of the game of base ball, Henderson quotes from a letter by Mary Lepell (a.k.a. Lady Hervey) dated November 14, 1748. She mentions the playing of base ball by the family of Frederick, Prince of Wales. She wrote: "All this last summer they played abroad; and now, in the winter, in a large room, they divert themselves at base-ball, a play all who are, or have been school-boys, are well acquainted with."[10] Jane Austen also recorded "base-ball" in her book *Northanger Abbey*, published in 1818, but written in 1789.[11]

After having established the popularity of base ball with English school boys, Henderson returns to the question, how and when did the game come to America? He admits that the question "can never be satisfactorily answered. It may have been brought by English children who crossed the Atlantic with their families. In all probability, it did, but this, so far, cannot be proved. We do know it arrived in book form."[12] In short, English boys' books of games are an important source of knowledge about base ball. During the eighteenth and nineteenth centuries, it was not uncommon for compilers of books of

Boys playing a ball game in 1838. A version of an early ball game. Woodcut courtesy John Thorn.

games to plagiarize games from other books. Hugh Gaine, a well-known New York printer, pirated the first American edition of Newberry's *Little Pretty Pocket-Book*. This first edition was advertised in the *New York Mercury* on August 30, 1762. The book used the term "base-ball" for the first time in America and also included the first illustration of the game printed in America.[13] In 1786, a Philadelphia publisher, W. Spotswood, published the second edition of a *Little Pretty Pocket-Book* and in 1787 the book "was pirated a third time" and published by Isaiah Thomas of Worcester, Massachusetts.[14]

Games of bat and ball were played by young men and children at this time. A rudimentary game of baseball was played by Washington's soldiers at Valley Forge. One of the soldiers, George Ewing, noted in his diary on April 7, 1778, that he "exercised in the afternoon in the intervals playd at base."[15] Yarning Lansing Collins, a student at Princeton in 1786, recorded in his diary that he had had "a fine day, play baste ball in the campus but am beaten for I miss both catching and striking the ball."[16] The eighteenth century could be called the "infancy of base-ball." The game was well known in England and occasionally played in America under different names, and in a "primitive form." Apparently, no definitive rules had been established. In brief, the game was "handed down by word of mouth, or practical demonstrations from generation to generation."[17]

Part of the complexity of tracing the early history of baseball is that similar ball games were known under different names according to country and locale which and where they were played. In England, the name rounders began to supplant other names such as "feeder," which was also used to describe baseball. This was in part due to a compilation of boys' games published in London in 1828 called *The Boy's Own Book: A Complete Encyclopedia of all the Diversions, Athletic, Scientific, and Recreative*. It was published by Vizetelly, Branston and Co., and compiled by William Clarke. It was a success. Three thousand copies were sold without any advertising in less than three months. *The Boy's Own Book* passed through seven editions. In the second and third editions, there were changes in the names of some games, one of which was the game called rounders. Henderson suggests that the name rounders was substituted for baseball because the former name was in "more general use" than the name baseball.[18]

The game of rounders was played in the following manner: sides are picked without a set number on each side; at one time the number of players was limited to eleven; each player of the side at bat stood in turn in a large batter's box while the pitcher served the ball to the batter; at times, and at different locales, the batter could wait until he was served a "good ball"; and, if he struck at the ball and missed three times, he was out.[19] The field for rounders was laid out in a diamond-shaped pattern with stones or posts as bases. The bases were spaced twelve to twenty yards apart. If the batter hit the ball, he ran in a clockwise direction around the bases (just the opposite direction in baseball). An out was registered if the batter missed the ball three times, or was struck with the ball before reaching one of the bases ("soaking"), or if the batted ball was caught. The sides would change when a player was put out (unlike baseball, where three outs constitute the end of an inning). The object of the game was to score the most runs; that is, for the batter to make a complete circuit of the bases.[20] There was no set number of innings in rounders; the duration of the game was open to negotiation between the opposing sides.

In some places, ball games closely resembling rounders were called Town Ball, Round Ball, or the Massachusetts Game. For example, Town Ball differed from baseball or rounders in that the batter's box was placed between two bases, making it a fifth base. The "home" plate was the fourth base. In this version of rounders, the runner did not have to make a complete circuit of the bases.[21] These early forms of baseball were played before 1829. There were no printed rules, nor was there a criterion by which rules could be made uniform. But with the publication in 1829 in Boston and England of *The Boy's Own Book*, the rules of rounders were printed. In this book, the rules for many base-running games were laid down for the first time. *The Boy's Own Book* was a "tremendous contrast" to similar books of games "which emphasized piety, morals and instruction of mind and soul."[22] It gave instead specific instructions and rules for games. Shortly after the publication of *The Boy's Own Book*, the company of Lilly, Wait, Colman, and Holden, of Boston, in 1834 published a book called *The Book of Sports* by Robin Carver. He acknowledged his indebtedness to *The Boy's Own Book* for the copying of games printed in his book. In *The Book of Sports*, the game of rounders was reprinted and the name was changed to "Base or Goal Ball." Carver pointed out that "Base" or "Goal Ball" "is known under a variety of names, it is sometimes called 'round ball' but I believe that 'base' or 'goal ball' are the names generally adopted in our country."[23]

The use of the term baseball in subsequent publications of books of games and pastimes continued. In 1835, the firm of Cory and Daniels, of Providence, Rhode Island, did the same thing that was done by Lilly, Wait, Colman, and Holden in 1834. They published a small book of games for children drawing on *The Boy's Own Book* of 1829 by reprinting the rules for rounders and substituting the heading "Base" or "Goal Ball."[24] In 1839, S. Babcock of New Haven published a book called *The Boy's Book of Sports: A Description of the Exercises and Pastimes of Youth*. The publishers acknowledge that they drew upon *The Boy's Own Book*. In the section of "Games at Ball," the name of "Base Ball" is used to describe the same game that had been described in other boys' books of sports as "rounders" and then "Base" or "Goal Ball." It is here that players are instructed for the first time to run counterclockwise. The illustration of "Base Ball" in *The Boy's Book of Sports* of 1839 was a reprint of the woodcut illustrating "Base" or "Goal Ball" in Robin Carver's *Book of Sports* of 1834.[25] While there is no direct evidence that the New York Knickerbockers and other New York teams before the Knickerbockers relied upon any printed books of rules to formulate their own brand of baseball, the great popularity of Carver's *Book of Sports* and *The Boy's Book of*

III. The Origin of Baseball

Boys playing a ball game depicted in Robin Carver's 1834 *Book of Sports*. Woodcut courtesy John Thorn.

Sports (which totaled several editions and ran into thousands of copies before 1842) "must have resulted in the knowledge of a 'diamond-shaped' field for a base-running game in the minds of hundreds of boys."[26] It is likely that the origin of the Knickerbocker rules and other team rules "came directly or indirectly from these popular books of boy's games."[27]

The Abner Doubleday Myth

The beginning of the Doubleday myth can be traced to the findings of six men who were all prominently associated with baseball. These six men constituted a commission which was instituted in 1905 and funded by A.G. Spalding, one of the major figures of baseball in the nineteenth century. After two years, the commission issued a report. It was based primarily on the recollection and testimony of Abner Graves, a boyhood playmate of Abner Doubleday. On the basis of three letters, the commission concluded that the game was created and named by Doubleday in 1839.

The creation of the commission stemmed from a controversy over the origin of baseball. Henry Chadwick, called the "Father of Baseball" and "Nestor of American Sport," had claimed in the 1860s that baseball was a direct descendant of rounders.²⁸ He repeated this claim in a letter written to the Spalding Commission.²⁹ The same claim can be traced to the American historian C.A. Peverelly in his *Book of American Pastimes*, published in 1866, which flatly declared that the game of baseball came from rounders. But both James Montgomery Ward, a well-known player of the early days of baseball, and A.C. Spalding contended that baseball was entirely an American invention. Perhaps because of nationalistic tendencies in the country at the turn of the century and the chauvinistic fervor of Spalding, the commission heavily relied on one letter written by Abner Graves.

This was an error on the part of the commission, as Henderson argues. He compares Graves's letter to another letter written a number of years later by Graves. This letter appeared in a book titled the *Story of Cooperstown* by Ralph Birdsall, published in 1918. The comparison between these letters reveals some inconsistencies and what appears to be an error on the part of Graves. Henderson points out:

> The date of the invention of baseball by Doubleday is set by Spalding at 1839, on the letter of Graves, which said "either the spring prior or following the Log Cabin and Hard Cider campaign of General Harrison," actually this would have been 1839 or 1840. As a matter of fact, Doubleday was not in Cooperstown in 1839 or 1840. He entered West Point Military Academy on September 1, 1838, and was not in Cooperstown on leave or otherwise in 1839 or 1840. In Graves' letter to Birdsall he gave the date 1838 or 1839.³⁰

Henderson also points out that Graves's "hazy recollection" was imprecise on a number of other relevant points, such as where Doubleday went to school or whether or not Graves was present when Doubleday allegedly outlined with a stick in the dirt a diamond-shaped baseball field.³¹ In short, Graves was recollecting events that took place sixty-eight years earlier.

It is likely that Doubleday, like hundreds of others, was playing a ball game which varied in name and in form in different locations in America. But the game they played was not the same as the one which was initiated by a group of young men in New York in 1842. Prior to 1842 the major differences that existed in the various bat-and-ball games played by Americans was that runners were put out by opposing players who threw the ball at the runner; stakes were used instead of bases; base runners ran clockwise; and the distance between bases was less than 90 feet. But in 1842, these practices were modified to introduce what might be called the modern game of baseball.

The North American Indian and the Origin of Baseball

In relation to the origin of baseball, a brief comment should be made in reference to a possible link between the introduction of baseball to Americans and North American Indian ball games. Early accounts of Indian ball games by George Catlin at mid-nineteenth century and later by Stewart Culin early in the twentieth century emphasized that Indian ball games were serious affairs, often pitting one tribe against another, in struggles that lasted an entire day. Careful preparation for the games was made by rites of fasting or purification by water. The games had religious significance: usually their purpose was to ensure the perpetuation of the tribe by demonstrating strength, courage, and endurance in the playing of ball games. It is likely, although not certain, that these games were known to Americans.

However, the extent of the knowledge and the influence of Indian ball games on American ball games is difficult to assess for this reason: there appears to be no record of any kind that would indicate that Americans were influenced by Indian ball games and used them as a basis for the playing of baseball. Moreover, the press during the early years of baseball never mentions Indians in relation to baseball and no baseball historian has ever suggested a relationship between the two. Nevertheless, it might be argued that the press and other influential people suppressed the connection between baseball and games of North American Indians because they considered Indian adults as "child-savages," and therefore did not want to contaminate the American version of the origin of baseball.[32]

For the sake of further discussion, if we again assume there was widespread knowledge about Indian ball games, how is it that white Americans did not adopt these ball games? The answer simply is that Americans, in matters of sport, followed the English and not the Indians. Furthermore, Stewart Culin points out that in "all ball games" played by American Indians, the ball is never touched by the hand. Touching the ball by the hand was "strictly forbidden." Of course, in the game of baseball the ball is touched by the hands of the players.[33] Ironically, it appears that the American Indians learned the game of baseball from "whites." Culin suggests that the Indians

> absorbed European ideas, many of which have in time become difficult of recognition as foreign in origin. An excellent example of incorporation is found in the Navaho game of baseball. In spite of tribal traditions, it appears that the Navaho learned the game [baseball] from the whites when they were imprisoned at the Basque Redondo after 1863.[34]

The Origin and Structure of the Knickerbocker Base Ball Club

The New York Knickerbocker Base Ball Club, established in 1845, was one of America's pioneers of organized baseball club. The New York and Magnolia base ball clubs preceded the New York Knickerbocker Base Ball Club by two years. Unfortunately, the origin and the early days of the Knickerbocker Club and other base ball clubs are not well understood, because of the lack of data on many of the early players and officers of these clubs, and the lack of club records between 1846 and 1854.[35] Complicating matters, a paucity of data on the circumstances under which ball playing, usually a child's game, was undertaken by adults at this time, makes even a brief analysis a tenuous enterprise. Nevertheless, enough is known, much of it documented, to establish the general characteristics of the Knickerbocker Club and the social-recreational orientations they had toward playing baseball.

Charles Peverelly, a sportswriter of the period, was one of the early writers to describe the origins of the Knickerbockers. He states:

> During the years of 1842 and 43, a number of gentlemen, fond of the game, casually assembled on a plot of ground in Twenty-Seventh Street — the one now occupied by the Harlem Railroad Depot. It was customary for two or three players, occasionally during the season, to go around in the forenoon of a pleasant day and muster up players enough to make a match.[36]

Peverelly goes on to point out: "A party of gentlemen formed an organization, combining together health, recreation, and social enjoyment, which was the nucleus of the now great American game of Base Ball." He also notes that "no person can obtain admission in the club merely for his capacity as a player. He must also have the reputation of a gentleman."[37]

Harold Peterson has shed some light on the early Knickerbockers by obtaining a heretofore unknown journal of Alexander Cartwright. Cartwright was one of the prime organizers of the Knickerbockers and, according to Peterson, the man who "vandalized the simple, childish game then known as town ball or baseball [and] introduced adultness and complexity to a directionless kiddie pastime."[38] In 1845, Cartwright was a man of twenty-two. He was employed as a teller in the Union Bank of New York and was also a member of the volunteer firefighting company known as the Knickerbocker Engine Company. He and other young men, who were drawn from the ranks of clerks, merchants, Wall Street brokers, lawyers, and possibly some artisans and clothiers, would frequent an area in New York called Murray Hill. There, next to "Sunfish Pond" from 1842 to 1845, these relatively prosperous middle- to upper-middle class men would informally meet and play ball.[39] Peterson attributes Cartwright with having introduced "a carefully drafted diagram" which "stationed his friends around a perfect ninety-foot square and placed the batter at the fourth 'home' base instead of a special batter's box several feet toward the first base." He also dictated that there be only three men in the outfield, removed two roving short fielders, put one of them at an entirely new position he called "short stop," and abolished one of the two catchers behind the batter.[40]

Robert Henderson, one of the pioneers of historical research on baseball, attributes the origin of baseball to the popularity of several boys' books of sports which contained rules and diagrams for games of ball which were similar to the ones adopted by the Knickerbockers in 1845. He states that "there need be no mystery about the genesis of the Knickerbocker rules. They came directly or indirectly from these books of boys' games."[41] Henderson attributes the origin of the rules to a Mr. Wadsworth. He points out that one of the club's original players and first president, Duncan F. Curry, had related, "On one afternoon when the group was at play Mr. Wadsworth presented for consideration a diagram of a baseball field laid out substantially as it is today. The plan caused a great deal of talk," said Mr. Curry, "but finally we agreed to try it."[42]

Whether it was Cartwright or Wadsworth who was the first to introduce an explicit set of rules is not crucial to a general understanding of the early history of baseball. What is important is that the modifications that were introduced transformed a game commonly associated with children and adolescents into a lively, absorbing adult pastime, one that captivated the interest of participants and provided entertainment for spectators. One of the more significant innovations was the establishment of the distance of ninety feet between bases. Henderson summarizes the importance of this innovation. He notes: "Five feet less would have given base runners an enormous advantage. Five feet more would have given infielders too much time to scoop up a ground ball and get it to the first baseman. But at ninety feet, plays at first base are decided by a step."[43]

Instead of throwing a ball at a runner ("soaking"), as was the custom in earlier ball games such as rounders, the defensive player could now throw to a man at one of the bases, or could attempt to tag the player on offense, to make an out. No longer were the bases an aggregation of rocks or standing wooden poles; they were now square flat plates. Nine men constituted a side instead of an irregular number of players. These nine players would bat in order as agreed by both sides before the start of the game. The number of outfielders was reduced from five to three with the removal of two free-roving "short fielders." One of these fielders was put at a new position called shortstop. Another important modification was "three hands out, all out." Only three men needed to be retired instead of the whole team (as was the practice in cricket). This change greatly helped to enhance the tempo of the game, to say nothing of the opportunity of getting out of the sun for a while.[44]

In 1845, these rule changes would be codified and serve as a model for the teams that would emerge in the 1850s, after the Knickerbockers. The rules adopted on September 23, 1845, incorporating these changes, were:

> 1st.— Members must strictly observe the time agreed upon for exercise, and be punctual in their attendance.
> 2nd.— When assembled for exercise, the President, or in his absence the Vice-President, shall appoint an Umpire, who shall keep the game in a book provided

for that purpose, and note all violations of the By-Laws and Rules during the time of exercise.

3rd.—The presiding officer shall designate two members as Captains, who shall retire and make the match to be played, observing at the same time that the players put opposite to each other should be as nearly equal as possible; the choice of sides to be then tossed for, and the first in hand to be decided in like manner.

4th.—The bases shall be from "home" to second base, forty-two paces; from first to third base, forty-two paces, equidistant.

5th.—No stump match shall be played on a regular day of exercise.

6th.—If there should not be a sufficient number of members of the Club present at the time agreed upon to commence exercise, gentlemen not members may be chosen in to make up the match, which shall not be broken up to take in members that may afterwards appear; but, in all cases, members shall have the preference, when present, at the making of a match.

7th.—If members appear after the game is commenced they may be chosen in if mutually agreed upon.

8th.—The game to consist of twenty-one counts, or aces; but at the conclusion an equal number of hands must be played.

9th.—The ball must be pitched, and not thrown, for the bat.

10th.—A ball knocked out of the field, or outside the range of the first or third base, is foul.

11th.—Three balls being struck at and missed and the last one caught, is a hand out; if not caught is considered fair, and the striker bound to run.

12th.—If a ball be struck, or tipped, and caught, either flying or on the first bound, it is a hand out.

13th.—A player running the bases shall be out, if the ball is in the hands of an adversary on the base, or the runner is touched with it before he makes his base; it being understood, however, that in no instance is a ball to be thrown at him.

14th.—A player running who shall prevent an adversary from catching or getting the ball before making his base, is a hand out.

15th.—Three hands out, all out.

16th.—Players must take their strike in regular turn.

17th.—All disputes and differences relative to the game, to be decided by the Umpire, from which there is no appeal.

18th.—No ace or base can be made on a foul strike.

19th—A runner cannot be put out in making one base, when a balk is made by the pitcher.

20th—But one base allowed when a ball bounds out of the field when struck.[45]

The founders and early members of the Knickerbockers were influenced by a burgeoning enthusiasm in America for recreational exercise. They were also influenced by the British gentry's ideal of sportsmanship and fair play. Albert Spalding, one of the leading players of the 1860s, observed that the Knickerbockers "had been organized after the pattern of the ancient Marylebone Cricket Club of England, which for centuries more or less, had made every rule for the government of cricket."[46] Supporting Spalding's view, historians have recognized the influence of the English on the formation of men's clubs and cricket clubs in New York, Brooklyn, and Staten Island. Pessen notes that the Union Club of New York was "molded after the clubs of Lon-

III. The Origin of Baseball

An illustration from the *New York Clipper* of the Eagle and Gotham baseball clubs playing a match in 1857 at the Elysian Fields, in Hoboken, New Jersey. Woodcut courtesy John Thorn.

don."[47] The St. George Cricket Club of New York, located on Staten Island (1840), was composed mainly of prosperous English immigrants and "was the most influential club not only in New York but throughout the nation."[48] Other cricket clubs in New York and Brooklyn had similar compositions. Some of the leading baseball players of the 1850s and 1860s, such as George and Harry Wright, were former cricketers.

Another connection between cricket and baseball has been uncovered by Adelman, who attempts to demonstrate when and between whom the first match game of baseball occurred.[49] Contrary to what has been recognized by historians as the first *match game* of baseball between the Knickerbocker Base Ball Club and the New York Club on June 19, 1846, Adelman argues that the first match game was reported in the *Herald* on October 21, 1845.[50] He points out, "The *Herald* reported that a baseball contest would be played between the New York Club and a team known as the Brooklyn Club at Elysian Fields."[51] The results of the contest were not reported by the *Herald*, "but four days later it noted that the New Yorkers defeated the Brooklyn Club in a rematch, 37 to 19."[52] Not much is known about the New York Club, but Henry Chadwick, the preeminent baseball and cricket reporter of his day, claimed that the New York Club was formed prior to the Knickerbockers, but nevertheless he felt that the Knickerbockers deserved the "honor" of being called the "pioneer" club of baseball.[53] It is likely that the New York Club had an informal organization, knew members of the Knickerbockers, and had played cricket.[54] Little is known about the Brooklyn Club, but by comparing the box scores of the Union Star Cricket Club of Brooklyn with the box scores of the Brooklyn Club, it is apparent that "over half the names of the Brooklyn team correspond with those that appeared in the box scores of the Union Star's contests."⁵⁵ Adelman also notes that members of the Star Cricket Club and the Knickerbocker Club were present at the New York Club's anniversary dinner in 1845.⁵⁶

But the connection between the English and the Knickerbockers goes further than the members of the Knickerbockers dining with members of an English cricket club. Both Voigt and Seymour point to the adoption by the Knickerbockers of the English aristocratic orientation toward sport. Seymour observes: "To the Knickerbockers a ball game was a vehicle for genteel amateur recreation and polite social intercourse rather than a hard-fought contest for victory."⁵⁷ Playing a "boy's game introduced a note of exclusiveness" to the club. He goes on to say that Knickerbocker "rules and regulations emphasized proper conduct, and the entire tone of their organization was more akin to the atmosphere surrounding cricket."⁵⁸ Voigt reaches a similar conclusion about the influence of the English on the Knickerbockers. Like Spalding, he suggests that the Knickerbockers modeled themselves after the Marylebone Cricket Club of England.⁵⁹

He also sees upper-middle and upper class men in New York and Philadelphia as attempting to distance themselves from the "rabble" by belonging to the right gentlemen's club.⁶⁰ The emphasis on play, combined with social activities, made these clubs outlets for conspicuous leisure.⁶¹ By doing this they "aped the British styles."⁶² But the Knickerbockers' emulation of the English was not total. They followed the English by incorporating their sport ideal and organizational structure into the principles which guided the formation of the club. However, unlike the English, the Knickerbockers did not follow the competitive style of play found among English cricketers here and abroad.⁶³ The Knickerbockers endorsed a sport ethic which emphasized a lighthearted, self-sacrificing approach to playing baseball. The fraternal pleasures and amusements to be gained from playing baseball were foremost in importance to these men.

The organizational structure of the Knickerbocker Club was a formal one. The use of profanity and disputation of an umpire's decision were prohibited. Offenders were subject to fines of 10 cents and 25 cents respectively for each offense. Fines were also imposed for failure to follow the orders of the team captain. Being absent from practice (Monday and Thursday at 4:00 p.m.) or from monthly meetings was also punishable by fines. In 1860, the rules were still strictly enforced. This is indicated by a letter from A.P. Bynders, a member of the club, to James Wenman, an officer of the club, informing the latter that he, Bynders, had "forfeited" his "membership" because he had been absent, apparently from practice. The letter makes clear that Wenman was aware that Bynders was appearing "at court" and consequently he could not be present at practice. Despite this, Bynders concludes his letter by resigning from the club because of a lack of time to devote to his duties as a club member.[64] The democratic nature of the Knickerbockers stipulated that if the captain left the field without reason, or was derelict in his duties, he too was subject to a fine. It is noted in the Club Books that even "President Davis was fined 50 cents for using improper language."[65]

The administration of the playing rules and bylaws was delegated to the officers of the club, consisting of a president, vice president, secretary, and three directors, all of whom were elected for one-year terms. The officers decided when and with whom the Knickerbockers should play match games, and whom they would admit or not admit as members. The levying of fines and the suspension or expulsion of members was also the responsibility of the officers. Members of the Knickerbockers were expected to buy and launder their uniforms, pay assessed club expenses, and pay club dues ($5.00 per year).[66] The relatively formal organizational structure of the Knickerbocker Club is again indicated by a resolution that was adopted on April 4, 1857, which details rules for the use of lockers and uniforms: (1) Every member to be furnished with closet and key and shall appear to take charge of the same within two weeks from the commencement of playing. (2) Every member must have his apparel marked with his initials in his closet after exercise and keep same locked. (3) Members shall not wear the apparel of a fellow member without his permission. (4) Members shall not attempt to open the closet of a fellow member. (5) For any violation of the preceding rules a fine of fifty cents will be charged. (6) All clothes found out of place in the rooms will be taken care of and the owner must pay fifty cents for the redemption of each article to keeper of the rooms.[67]

The Knickerbockers were gentleman sportsmen, but not in the British aristocratic sense that family and wealth were requisites to class position. They were gentlemen by reason of their occupations and their attainment of a "certain standing in the community."[68] Furthermore, their ability to "devote every Monday and Thursday" afternoon to playing baseball, and the "financial obligations" that membership entailed, signified a degree of exclusiveness.[69] The Knickerbockers constituted a "status group," in that they were accorded a "special social esteem."[70] They were admired and imitated by other baseball clubs of the early 1850s.[71] It is difficult to ascertain to what extent their prestige existed outside of baseball in their formative years, but it is likely that they drew attention to themselves and were the center of attention.[72] They presented the sight of adults playing a game usually associated with children, on weekday afternoons, in accordance with a strict observance of rules and regulations, while dressed in blue woolen pantaloons and white flannel shirts, adorned by straw hats.[73] In all likelihood these adults at play evoked an image of an "abstention from labor and a certain social standing."[74] The effect they might have produced on others was to project an image of "conspicuous leisure.[75] For the English sportsmen, participation in sport was primarily an extension of his class position. Sport and social structure were inseparable for the English sportsman in the first half of the nineteenth century.[76]

One principal difference between the English approach to sports and the emulation of them by the Knickerbockers resides in the American emphasis upon success. At this time, values toward work were being transformed in America. The competitive economic striving of Americans was not lost with the rise of sport for the masses. In the second half of the nineteenth century, the lessons learned in economic competitive striving were applied to baseball and other sports.[77] Winning baseball games became an expression of the deeply-rooted value of success.[78] This does not mean that the English did not enjoy winning in cricket matches and football games, but victory or defeat did not have the same significance it had for Americans. The English sportsman was secure in his status position. A win or a loss did not alter his status. The English sport ideal signified that "striving to win, at all times [was] to be kept subordinate to the production of pleasure."[79] This ideal waned with the change of class relationships in nineteenth-century England, and the rise of professional cricketers and Rugby players.[80]

Baseball historians have correctly emphasized the recreational and social goals of the Knickerbockers, but have neglected to recognize a burgeoning competitive spirit within the club starting in the mid–1850s.[81] The principal expression of a more aggressive-competitive playing of baseball within the Knickerbockers and throughout organized baseball was signified by the advocacy of "substitution," the nine-inning game, and the fly rule. It is not known for certain if a fraction of players, perhaps younger ones within the Knickerbockers, championed a more lively game: a contest wherein the players strove to implement skill and strategy as the principal means to obtain victory. However, it is known that the Knickerbockers enrolled William Fenn Wadsworth into their membership ranks. He was a skilled first baseman for the Gothams. He may have been enticed in 1854 to play for the Knickerbockers for an "emolument," a term used to signify a compensation, in this case for participation as a player.[82] Wadsworth was also active as an advocate at the National Association meetings in 1857 for changes in the game, particularly the length of the game (seven or nine innings), which was usually played to 21 runs. At first, he urged playing seven innings but later supported a nine-inning game, which was resisted by a conservative faction of the club. Players "were desirous of changing the rules of the game, from the easy mode in which they have hitherto played it; and with that view, called a convention of all the clubs to discuss the revisions of the rules."[83] This initiative may have engendered the subsequent revision of the rules in the 1851 and 1858 conventions, which prompted a more lively and entertaining contest.

Many of the issues and controversies of organized baseball in the 1850s

III. The Origin of Baseball 51

stemmed from an increasing focus upon victory. One of the principal manifestations of a burgeoning competitive orientation to playing baseball was the practice of a club substituting, for a game, one or more players of average ability with players from another club who were known for their exceptional ability, to gain a competitive advantage. The initial playing rules of the Knickerbockers provide a remedy for the problem of not having a sufficient number of players (eighteen) to constitute a match. If there were not a "sufficient number of members" present to constitute a match, "gentlemen" could be called upon to join in the game. However, sometime after 1845 and before 1855, a resolution was adopted by the Knickerbockers which restricted this practice.[84] Those who favored substitution reversed the resolution against it at a meeting of the Knickerbockers held on August 22, 1855. It was decided at this time to rescind the resolution that restricted the number of players and forbade the "introduction of strangers or members of other Clubs from being taken into the match, when the specified numbers of members of our own club are on the ground."[85] The minutes of this meeting go on to note:

> This gave rise to a very spirited and entertaining discussion as to the propriety of admitting members of other clubs to play in our matches, the extent to which it should be allowed, and what courtesy was necessary and proper in view of maintaining our respectability and pleasure in the national game of Base Ball.[86]

The vote in favor of substitution was a close one with thirteen members voting in favor of it and eleven members in opposition to it. The reintroduction of the rule permitting substitution and the closeness of the vote suggest that, contrary to previous characterizations of the Knickerbockers by baseball historians, the Knickerbockers were more competitively oriented than previously believed. It is likely that a more competitive game was advocated by younger players and that this clashed with the views of older players. An entry in the Knickerbocker Club Books on December 6, 1856, suggests this: "The minutes of the two last meetings were read by the Secretary and approved with the exception of the report of the last meeting wherein the word *old Fogy* was compared with the name of one of the members which was considered by the meeting as personal and was erased."[87]

Some baseball historians describe the Knickerbockers as a "silk-stocking aggregation,"[88] or "an exclusive, upper-leisure class affair, whose members constituted a sort of exercise-seeking social aristocracy."[89] The Knickerbockers were not members of the upperclass, nor did they attempt to restrict the game to members of their class as a form of elitism.[90] Adelman has shown that the early Knickerbockers were drawn primarily from the upper-middle and middle classes, and their policy of rejecting match games with other clubs was not engendered by a desire to "monopolize" the game, as Seymour has asserted, but rather by a reluctance to publicize the playing of a game that was usually associated with children or young adults.[91] While I agree with Adelman, it also seems likely that the turning down of matches with other clubs by the Knickerbockers was an attempt to maintain their noncompetitive posture against the inroads of competition within and without the club. Adelman also argues that the Knickerbockers could have arranged matches with cricket clubs who, at the time, occasionally played baseball. But possibly, because of their insecurities associated with playing a child's game, they were reluctant to openly announce their organization and arrange matches before 1851.[92] They appear to have limited their baseball playing to intra-squad matches.

Engaging in athletic competitive striving is an ancient practice, epitomized by organized athletic games held during the Golden Age of Greece. Men throughout the ages have intermittently engaged in agonistic forms of athletic competition. Therefore, it is not surprising that competitive striving would arise among the Knickerbockers and other similarly organized baseball clubs in the 1850s. The specific impetus to more competitive matches is not clear. It is likely, but not certain, that the entrance of younger players into senior clubs, and the growth of Junior Base Ball Clubs with their younger members, contributed toward advancing a more lively game. It is plausible that younger players were opposed to the older play ethic in baseball because it limited their potential for real and symbolic rewards in a culture that was espousing the achievement of success though competition.

At mid-nineteenth century, Americans thought "lessons" could be learned from "competitive striving."[93] A prominent theme in "conduct of life books" after the Civil War was that the building of character could be enhanced through competitive striving. In a book titled *The Young Man's Friend*, the author, Daniel Eddy, extolled the virtues of competition by comparing life to a racecourse where all people were attempting to capture the prize.[94] Eddy also told his readers that the qualities needed for success could be gained by comparing man to the workings of a steam engine "with muscle power providing the ironwork, brain the engine power, and steam the force."[95] The theme of physical training as a means to success was elaborated on by others such as Kenneth H. Wayne in *Building the Young Man* and William Mathews in *Getting On in the World*.[96]

A competitive spirit within the early years of organized baseball can also be related to competitive contests between volunteer fire companies in New York and Brooklyn. Before mid-nineteenth century, volunteer fire companies were composed of young men who delighted in competing against other companies to see who would be the first to reach a blaze. The volunteer firehouse was one of the centers of urban sporting culture.[97] Firemen were not paid; the position was honorific and sought after by young men. In each firehouse, groups of young men and boys called "runners" would lead the inevitable race to the fire by helping to clear a path. These informal competitions permitted the firemen to exhibit their gaudy uniforms and colorfully decorated fire engines. In the 1840s firemen "sported red flannel shirts, high black boots, blue-black trousers, shiny leather belts, and blue coats."[98] Winning was important to these men. "Getting passed" in the race to the fire was a "crushing defeat."[99] Firemen were accused of being more interested in the competition than in extinguishing the fire.

The relationship between a more competitive spirit among the Knickerbockers and other clubs in baseball and competition in volunteer fire companies has some support in information uncovered by Harold Peterson in a book about Alexander Cartwright, one of the founders of the Knickerbocker Club.[100] Peterson notes that "many of the Knickerbockers were firemen," including James Whyte Davis, William A. Woodhill and Alonzo Slate, who were firemen in the Oceana Hose Company No. 36.[101] Walter Avery, another Knickerbocker player, belonged to Hose Co. No. 1, while "other Knickerbocker names—Curry, Keeler, Lee, Talman, Taylor, Vredenburgh—occur frequently in the fragmentary surviving records" as members of other volunteer fire companies.[102] Alexander Cartwright belonged to the Knickerbocker Engine Co. No. 12, and Peterson claims that Cartwright "sentimentally named his new baseball club for it," although he does not adduce any data to support this contention.[103] Peterson also points out that the Mutual Hook and Ladder Company was the place where the New York Mutual Base Ball Club was organized.[104] Peterson suggests that "the volunteers were really the first organized teams and their competitions among the first organized team contests. They were so competitive (to the point of fist fights) that the extension of rivalry to the ball field was natural."[105]

Baseball Clubs Before and After the Knickerbockers

Organized baseball clubs existed before and at the time the Knickerbockers were organized. Some of the more prominent clubs were the New York Ball Club, the Brooklyn Base Ball Club, the Eagle Base Ball Club, the Olympic Ball Club of Philadelphia, and the Magnolia Base Ball Club.[106] These clubs played variations of boys' old cat ball games. They appear to have influenced the formation of the playing rules adopted by the New York Knickerbockers, although there is no historic record of a direct lineage between the rules by which these clubs played baseball and the Knickerbockers' rules. Instead of "innovators," the Knickerbockers were "consolidators."[107]

Press notices in the form of descriptions of baseball appeared in the 1820s. In 1823, an announcement of young men playing baseball appeared on April 25 in the *National Advocate*. The unknown writer describes "a company of active young men playing the manly and athletic game of 'base-ball,' and notes that a game will be played the following week."[108] There is no record of the scores of these games or detailed descriptions of how the game was played.

The Washington Club appeared around 1850. In June 1851, they challenged and played the Knickerbockers to a match game which they lost 21 to 11.[109] This was probably the first match game played since the Knickerbockers had played the New York Club in 1846.[110] In a return match played later in June, the Knickerbockers were again victorious, but by a slimmer margin: 22 to 20. The following year the Washington Club reorganized and changed their name to the Gotham Club.[111] In 1854 the Eagle, Empire and Excelsior Clubs were formed. During the next three years, nineteen other clubs arose. The majority of these teams were organized in New York and Brooklyn. Some of the more prominent clubs were the Putnams of Brooklyn (1855), the Eckfords of Brooklyn (1855), the Baltics of New York (1855), and the Mutuals of New York (1857).[112] During this time, "the Knickerbockers dominated baseball in the New York area. Their form of organization was adopted by other clubs, and their playing rules became generally accepted as "the New York game." Many of the new clubs deliberately emulated the Knickerbockers. The demand for their bylaws grew so heavy that they had a hundred copies printed for distribution, and even allowed their secretary to list his address in the *Sunday Mercury*."[113] The Excelsiors, the Eagles, and the Independent Baseball clubs had similar regulations for playing ball and almost identical constitutions.

In addition to emulating the Knickerbockers from an organizational standpoint, these clubs also emphasized the playing of baseball as a recreational form of exercise and the social benefits derived from playing the game. In an article reporting on a win by the Putnams over the Excelsiors, 21 to 15, the writer goes on to describe the social festivities which occurred after the match. He notes:

> The "Putnams" then escorted their late antagonists, and a large number of other invited guests—many of whom were members of other Clubs—to Trenor's Dancing Academy, South 8th Street, Williamsburgh, where the whole party were entertained most hospitably, the members of the Putnam Club constituting themselves a "Vigilant Committee," for the purpose of dispensing the refreshments they had so liberally provided for their guests. The tables having been cleared, the President of the "Putnams," Mr. Samuel Godwin, made a few brief remarks in which, in eloquent terms, he alluded to the advantages they derived from the practice of outdoor games, and the good effects they all experienced, both socially and physically, by the practice of base ball.[114]

With the formation of the Eckford Club in 1855, the occupational composition of organized baseball continued to change. The composition of the Eckford Club signaled the beginning of an occupational change of members of baseball clubs from non-manual and white collar workers, who were mostly clerks, merchants and some professionals, to a greater representation of

III. The Origin of Baseball

A ticket of admission to an 1844 ball held for the Magnolia Ball Club. Possibly the first depiction of men playing baseball. Woodcut courtesy John Thorn.

skilled, semi-skilled, and manual workers, who were mainly skilled craftsmen, mechanics, butchers, proprietors, and shipwrights.[115] The Eckfords (1855), the Atlantics (1855), the Newarks (1855) and the Mutuals were baseball clubs that represented a more aggressive competitive orientation and the changing social class composition of baseball.

A finding by John Thorn in the *New York Herald* of November 2, 1843, announcing presumably an intramural game of baseball, suggests that a baseball club by the name of the Magnolias of New York played at the Elysian Fields in Hoboken, New Jersey, in 1843. The announcement was signed by President John McKibbin, Vice-President Joseph Carlisle, and Secretary Andrew Lester. Thorn assiduously traces the working background and business associations of McKibbin, Carlisle, and Lester. Carlisle was the owner of Magnolia Lunch and Saloon, he served time in Sing Sing Prison for bigamy.

Further research in the flash weekly the *Whip* suggests that the "Magnolia Lunch" may have been a meeting place for "assignations." Thorn goes on to note that would provide the "names, addresses, specialties, and prices of brothels and their residents." Lester was the owner of a billiard parlor. Thorn concludes that the officers of the Magnolia baseball club "had impeccable working-class, sporting, ruffian, and political associations of the sort that historians until now have presumed to emerge only with the unruly Brooklyn clubs of the mid–1850s, notably the Atlantics."[116]

The First Convention and the First Association of Baseball Players

As the formation of baseball clubs spread throughout most of the major cities of the Northeast in the 1850s, it became apparent that an organizing body was needed to regulate and generally oversee the playing of baseball.[117] Spalding notes that, prior to the creation of the National Association and the adoption of uniform rules, "the game had been controlled as to its playing rules largely by local prejudices. It was played under one set of rules in New York and another in New England, and other still widely different regulations were applied to the game elsewhere."[118]

Entries in the New York Knickerbocker Club Books indicate that the Knickerbockers, Gothams, and Eagles met on April 1, 1854, to "arrange a set of rules to govern each club alike in playing the game of Base Ball." They also met on December 15 of the same year for a dinner. Out of these gatherings, a set of rules was adopted to regulate play among clubs.[119] The following year the *New York Herald* reported: "Base Ball Clubs, in order to preserve an organization, have formed a central body composed of delegates from respective clubs." The meeting was presided over by Thomas Van Cott, one of the leaders of the Gothams.[120] After these tentative attempts to codify the rules, the Knickerbockers took the initiative and called a convention. In 1856, it was reported that "at a regular meeting of the Knickerbocker Base Ball Club" a "resolution was adopted" to call a convention of the "various Base Ball Clubs of the City and vicinity" by requesting the "various" clubs to select three members to meet at "number 462 Boomer St. in the city of New York, on Thursday, the 22 day of January 1857." The article goes on to mention that "the object of the convention is to promote additional interest in base ball by the getting up of grand matches on the scale not heretofore attempted."[121] Each of the following clubs was represented by three delegates to the convention: Knickerbocker, Eagle, Gotham, Empire, Baltic, Putnam, Excelsior, Bedford, Nassau, Continental, Union, and Olympic Clubs. All of these clubs came from Manhattan, Brooklyn, or Long Island.[122]

The Knickerbockers "submitted [to the convention] a new code of laws, in which they clearly defend every part of the game; and, with a view to making the game more manly and scientific."[123] One of the rules submitted by the Knickerbockers advocated catching the ball on the fly instead of on the bound. The introduction of the fly rule touched off a controversy that lasted until the early 1860s. The ostensible issue was whether or not a batter would be called out if a ball he hit was caught on one bounce or if it was caught on the fly. The debate had deeper implications. Fueled primarily by the *Spirit of the Times*, the issue of the adoption of the fly rule evoked latent concerns over the skill and manliness involved in playing baseball as compared to cricket. The press argued that the adoption of the fly rule would injure the hands and make the game too much like cricket.[124] Prior to 1864, in most games, a ball caught on one bounce put the batter out. Starting in 1856, editorials in the *Spirit of the Times* urged the adoption of the fly rule. In November of that year a writer for the *Spirit of the Times* commented:

> An important improvement in the fielding of this match, was shown by several fine catches being made on the fly, instead of the child's play from the bound. This reform is not only more manly, but adds very much to the quickness of perception, and nerve and determination, which makes up the necessary qualifications of a complete fieldsman, either at base ball or cricket.[125]

Later that month the *Spirit of the Times* reminded readers that "we threw out a hat last week, namely, that the rule of baseball should be altered, and the striker should not be out unless caught out direct from the bat and not from the bound."[126] Toward the end of the year, the *Spirit* again advocated the implementation of the fly rule. In addition, it was suggested that if the ball was caught on the fly it would constitute two outs instead of one. But if the ball was caught on the first bounce, it would still count as one out. This suggestion was not implemented.[127] The convention of 1857, after discussion in committee, did not adopt the fly rule:

> The advocates of the reform finally acceded to a proposition of their opponents, namely that if a man was caught out before the ball touched the ground, that then the players who were running to the different bases, or home, could neither make an ace nor base, but had to return to their original position.[128]

With this rule a man was still out if the ball was caught on one bound.

The convention also passed a substitution rule. In an effort to regulate the practice of substitution, the convention adopted a rule which prohibited players from playing with a team unless they were a "regular member of the club which they represent, for thirty days prior to the match." It was also resolved that a player could not hold membership "in more than one club at the same time."[129]

The most dramatic rule change implemented at the 1857 convention, in terms of enlivening the game from the viewpoint of both the players and spectators, was the nine-inning game. Until that time the outcome of the game was decided when one team scored 21 runs. Before the initiation of the nine-inning game in 1857, much of the tension of the game was diluted when one team scored 21 runs, the number needed to win. But with the advent of the nine-inning game, the outcome of the game was still uncertain until the last out was made.

The second convention was held in March 1858. At this time, the baseball players created a governing body called the National Association of Base Ball Players. The stated purpose of the association was to "improve, foster, and perpetuate the American game of Base-Ball and the cultivation of kindly feelings among the different members of Base-Ball Clubs."[130] This broad objective included addressing major concerns of clubs. Therefore, it was not surprising that the issue of player substitutes would again be raised.

In an account of the convention of 1858, it is noted that Dr. L.B. Jones, one of the officers of the Excelsior Club, had made a "very strenuous objection to the 'clause' which prohibited a player from playing on another team unless he was a member of the team in question for thirty days." Dr. Jones argued that no substitutions should be permitted under any circumstances. His argument was rejected. The thirty-day rule was retained. The writer of the account agreed with Dr. Jones's position. However, he suggests:

> The party of base-ball or cricketeers [sic] who failed to bring their regular players on the ground should be the losers and no substitutes should be allowed.... Indeed, we should consider it more credible for a club to have played a losing if an up-hill game with the loss of a crack player of their own club, than to win one with the borrowed aid of an outsider.[131]

The National Association of Base Ball Players attempted to stifle the practice of substitution "by extending the probationary period from thirty to sixty days, but without success."[132] The desire for winning was too prevalent; teams who desired to substitute were able either to flout the rule or to devise means of circumventing it. The substitution of players signified the beginning of the end of playing baseball primarily as a social-recreational activity. Moreover, it indicated the onset of the commercialization of the game. Polite, sportsmanlike notions of playing the game as a thing in and of itself began to give way to playing the game as a means to an end.

Another issue of the 1858 convention was a controversy over the admission of junior clubs. These were clubs whose members were not twenty-one years of age. In many cases, these junior clubs were "formed to serve as feeders for senior clubs, and by 1858 there were at least sixty of them in the area metropolitan."[133] The members of the convention turned down the request for admission of junior clubs. The *Spirit of the Times*, in a prophetic editorial, criticized this action:

> We are only afraid of the legislation of those "pseudo" Senior Clubs, which are composed of apologies for men, who with plenty of money, and a proportionate lack of strength of body and energy of spirit who wish to make the game a means of showing off their figures in fancy dress, and their wealth in fancy dinners, who are so lazy that, in a short time, *they will become worse than some cricket clubs who hire professional players to do their work, and they do the blowing*.[134]

In 1860, thirty younger clubs established the National Association of Junior Base Ball Clubs.[135] A growing interest in baseball by young men helped swell the ranks of potential players for the growing number of senior clubs. In writing about the growth of baseball in Brooklyn, Spalding observes:

Junior organizations had been formed in that city during the years in which their seniors were winning laurels, and before 1860 the older clubs were glad enough to find recruits for their ranks from strong players who were being developed in their minor organizations. In 1859 the Stars and Enterprise clubs, both juniors, had been drawn upon by the Excelsiors, who profited greatly in securing several players, among them, from the Stars, James Creighton, afterwards famous as a pitcher.[136]

The geographical representation of clubs had also increased. Before the 1859 convention, clubs were almost exclusively located in New York, Brooklyn, and Long Island. But thereafter, clubs from New Jersey, Pennsylvania, and upstate New York began attending the convention. By the mid–1860s, the game had spread throughout the country.[137]

The origins of baseball, obscured by myth, half-truth, and a paucity of primary historical data, present a challenge to baseball historians who seek to decipher baseball's lineage. Attempts by historians to uncover the origins of baseball lack definitions of what the game is and what it is not. This omission fosters ambiguity in the evolutionary lineage of the game. This is not surprising given the scholarly challenge, the geographic locale, technology, culture, and the serendipitous circumstances that propel children and young boys to reconfigure ball games. Perhaps the only consensus by historians who endeavor to elucidate the origin of the game is that it has multiple progeny. Ball games such as town ball and round ball, preceded by older ball games like one cat and stoolball, are likely progenitors of ball games called baseball in the 1820s. From a different perspective, the inception of baseball as we would recognize it today can be located in the machinations of a small group of middle- to upper-middle class young men who modified old cat ball games and referred to it as "base ball." It is likely that these men had direct or indirect knowledge of ball games played by American children and adolescents.

Eventually, the Knickerbockers' de-emphasis on competition, and other clubs' adoption of this orientation to playing baseball, succumbed as the dominant mode of play in baseball, and were superseded by a more competitive victory orientation to playing baseball. However, the lighthearted approach to the game espoused by the Knickerbockers and other clubs stood in opposition to an encroaching commercial ethos, and gambling on games provided grist for the sport press.

IV
Positive Press

Central to the formation of the image of professional baseball in the press was the negation and the affirmation of notions about the game. In order for baseball to prosper it was also vital that it disassociate itself from the image that cricket had established in the press as the pre-eminent bat-and-ball game in America. It was argued in the press that cricket required greater physical courage and more playing skill than baseball. As baseball matured, the press also sought to negate the idea that baseball was a child's game. It sought to establish baseball as a "manly game," as cricket was considered to be. To accomplish this the press began to urge the reformulation of baseball rules. For the most part, the press wanted a more lively and a more physical game. The press began to focus on the skill of baseball players as a means to affirm its superiority over cricket and to represent baseball as the "National Game."

In this chapter, a variety of representations in the press, depicting the praiseworthy aspects of the game, will be explored. In this context, we would like to answer the following questions: How did baseball overcome its early image as a child's game? What events in baseball contributed to its early acclaim? What was the relationship between playing skill and positive evaluations of baseball?

The work of Gusfield provides an analytical lead in the exploration of the meanings that were collectively formed and associated with organized baseball.[1] In his study of the prohibition of alcohol, he relies on the utilization of an idea that makes a distinction between symbolic meaning "which is not given in its immediate and manifest significance but what the action connotes for the audience that views it." Thus, an act acquires "a meaning which is added to its immediate intrinsic significance."[2] It was critical for baseball to disassociate itself from a number of immediate symbolic connotations, especially the idea that it was a boys' game, and later on that players were disreputable. New meanings emerged in baseball that overlaid its "immediate intrinsic significance."[3]

IV. Positive Press

In the 1850s, the press reported the benefits to be derived from participating in baseball. The early positive sentiments expressed in print media toward organized baseball parallel sentiments expressed toward cricket and physical exercise. Baseball and cricket were associated with "manly" attributes.[4] Both were seen as beneficial to health and the development of character. Furthermore, these were "manly games" in the sense of being contests "that seemed to test, and therefore dramatize and inculcate" masculine qualities as positive character traits.[5] The terms "manly" and "healthful," used to describe baseball, are similar to the terms and phrases used to depict cricket in the press. A writer for the *New York Tribune* uses the phrase "healthy and invigorating exercise" to describe the playing of cricket.[6] A writer for the *New York Herald* also observes that cricket is "extending itself to all parts of the country as a healthful and exciting exercise."[7] An invidious comparison between cricket and baseball can be found in an editorial in the *Spirit of the Times*. The editor writes: "Baseball is the favorite game, as it is more simple in its rules and a knowledge of it more easily acquired. Cricket is the most scientific of the two and requires more skill and judgment in the use of the bat especially, than baseball."[8]

Henry Chadwick was a staunch advocate of the lessons to be learned from playing baseball and cricket. He observes that cricket "teaches a love of order, discipline, and fair play."[9] One of the early references recommending ball playing as a healthful and manly exercise appeared in 1846 in the *New York Tribune*, under the heading of "City Items." There is an account of a man who has been accidentally struck by the "bat of a boy" who was playing ball with some other boys in the "park." The writer goes on to urge that the "park be set apart exclusively for ball-players" and that by taking this action, "accidents may thus be prevented, and a healthful exercise for dyspeptic youngsters secured."[10]

During the 1850s the press consistently described baseball as a manly and healthful exercise. In reporting a contest between the Eagle and Gotham baseball clubs, a writer for the *New York Herald* suggests: "The game of baseball is fair soon to be as popular as the favorite game of cricket and right glad we are to see these healthful and manly exercises so frequently indulged in."[11] The *Spirit of the Times*, in a brief account of a Knickerbocker meeting, notes that baseball is "an excellent game for exercising every muscle of the body, therefore good for persons of a sedentary habit."[12] Similar advice is given two years later when the *Brooklyn Eagle* recommends "ball-playing [as] a fine healthy, enlivening, manly sport."[13] In a letter to the editor of *Harper's Weekly*, the writer describes the popularity of the game "in nearly all the villages and among the rural districts in New York." The writer goes on to say that "it is by no means difficult to find enough who are desirous of engaging in so healthful and agreeable an exercise of a pleasant summer evening."[14]

Health benefits, manliness, and character values were not the only appeals used to promote baseball. Nationalism was also associated with playing baseball, and baseball was suggested as a deterrent to the evils of the barrooms. A writer for the *Spirit of the Times* comments: "The fine American game seems to be progressing in all parts of the United States with new spirit, while in New York and its neighborhoods, its revival seems to have been taken up almost as a matter of national pride."[15] The same sport periodical, reporting on the National Convention of Base Ball Players in 1857, calls baseball the "National Pastime," and exhorts each young man to "take up baseball and quit his barrooms and other night amusements and seek the open air."[16]

In an article describing a match between the Excelsiors and the Knickerbockers in 1859, the *Brooklyn Eagle* calls baseball "our National game." The writer notes:

> Yesterday afternoon, fully six thousand people were collected together on the grounds of the Excelsior Club ... a more orderly or respected concourse we have never seen, and it was truly gratifying to see so many persons of both sexes — for the test provided for the ladies was crowded to its utmost extent — participating in the enjoyment afforded by the manly and noble exercise and exciting and exhilarating game. Here we have in this club, what we may now term our National game of ball. An amusement at once invigorating and beneficial to health, and free from every objectionable feature that in one respect or another characterizes every other outdoor amusement.[17]

Rhetoric in the press, throughout the 1850s and into the 1860s, stressed the playing of baseball as a means to instill civic and national pride, to gain better health, and to develop positive character traits. Enhancing this viewpoint were a number of well publicized events in baseball.

Well-Publicized Events in the Early History of Baseball[18]

The positive image of baseball was aided by the attention and acclaim given to events in baseball, including the Fashion Race Course series in 1858, the Silver Ball Match of 1861, and several playing tours conducted by leading teams in the 1860s.[19] These events brightened the image of the game.

In 1858, baseball's first all-star game was played at the Fashion Race Course near Jamaica, Long Island. Players were selected from the leading teams in Brooklyn and Manhattan. Players for the New York team were selected from the Knickerbockers, Gothams, Empire, and Union Base Ball Clubs. Brooklyn players were selected from the Putnam, Excelsior, Atlantic, and Eckford Base Ball Clubs. However, for the last game, the Brooklyn team loaded their line-up with players from the redoubtable Atlantic and Eckford teams in an effort to secure the series.[20] This series set the stage for one of the early rivalries between Brooklyn and Manhattan and provided a showcase for the skill of the leading players of the day.[21]

IV. Positive Press 63

The first all-star games pitting the best players from New York and Brooklyn in a best-of-three series held at the Fashion Race Course on Long Island in 1858. The New York teams prevailed. Woodcut courtesy John Thorn.

The Fashion Race Course series was the first time admission was charged, but the fifty cents charged gave the spectators the opportunity to see which city had the best players. The series was determined by the best of three games. In mid–July the New York team scored the first victory, with a 22 to 18 win over Brooklyn. The second game was played a month later in August. It was a relatively easy victory for Brooklyn. They beat the New York team 29 to 8. A short time later New York went on to capture the series by winning the third game 29 to 18.[22] Seymour observes that "the important point about the Fashion Course series at the time, was the interest it stirred and the thousands of new converts it made for the game."[23] Part of the attraction of the series was the rivalry generated between New York and Brooklyn, the quality of play, and an atmosphere of excitement and glamour in anticipation of a unique entertainment event. A writer for the *New York Times* describes the multitude of people gathered for the first game of the series. He observes:

> Of every style and variety were the vehicles which conveyed the thousands to the ground — whose numbers certainly could not have been short of eight thousand according to some computations. The grand stand was densely crowded with spectators. Some four or five hundred being ladies, numerous other ladies being in carriages. There was a variety of vehicles densely packed along the entire home stretch, and entirely around the arena allotted to the players, and inside of this line of carriages was a dense mass of human beings, the front ranks of whom were compelled to sit or lie on the grass to allow others in the rear to view the players.[24]

Brooklyn avenged the loss of the unofficial championship of the cities in 1861 in a match arranged by the founder and editor of the *New York Clipper*, Frank Queen. The game was similar to the Fashion Course series, in that leading players were selected from the top teams in New York and Brooklyn, thereby constituting another all-star confrontation between these cities. Queen awarded a Silver Ball to the team whose players scored the greatest number of runs. The Silver Ball Match took place on October 21, 1861, in Hoboken, before a crowd estimated to be "about 10,000."[25] The Brooklyn all-stars won the game, beating the New York all-stars 18 to 6. The significance of the game was similar to the effect that the Fashion Race Course series had: it provided a means for organized baseball to display the talents of its best players. Writing about the Silver Ball Match, a writer at the turn of the century said: "The enthusiasm shown by the spectators and players at this game had never before been paralleled in that the contest did more toward placing base ball upon a substantial footing before the general public than everything which had preceded it."[26]

Memorial to Jim Creighton, famed pitcher and noted batsman for the Excelsior club. He died in 1862, at the age of 21, of an injury sustained while batting in a game on October 14 against the Unions of Morrisania. It is believed he ruptured his bladder after taking a "mighty" swing and succumbed to the injury after four days. Photograph courtesy John Thorn.

The dominant theme in reporting the Fashion Race Course series and the Silver Ball match was the high quality of skill employed by the players. A writer for the *New York Times* comments on the quality of play: "The play on both sides was of the very highest order. It would be almost invidious to particularize... [but] Wright in the field gave some extraordinary displays of good judgment and fine play."[27] A similar observation of skillful play in the Silver Ball match was made by a writer for the *Brooklyn Eagle*. He observed: "The game throughout was well contested, both sides acquitting themselves admirably both in fielding and batting.... The effective pitching of Creighton, and good play of Pearce as catcher, elicited much admiration from the spectators."[28]

Equally important to the establishment of a positive image of baseball were several tours conducted by leading teams of the day. These tours, like the Fashion Course series and the Silver Ball Match, helped spread interest in the game and provided a showcase for the talents of the players. Although New York and Brooklyn were the centers of baseball in the 1850s and mid–1860s, the game of baseball was spreading throughout the East and into the Midwest. By 1860 the game had been started in San Francisco.[29] This interest in the game helped make it possible for the Excelsiors of Brooklyn to go on tour in 1860. The *Brooklyn Eagle*, in 1860, announced the forthcoming tour. It noted, "The Excelsior Club, of South Brooklyn, has in contemplation a grand excursion during the ensuing summer, which, if consummated, will be one of the most interesting features of the season."[30] The writer mentions the scheduled matches which included cities in New York State, Massachusetts, Rhode Island, Connecticut, Maryland, Washington, and Pennsylvania. The writer also points out that the "excursion ... would add greatly to the advancement of the popularity of the game of base ball in every locality visited."[31] The Excelsiors toured western New York, winning all of their six games. Before starting their tour they played the powerful Atlantics. They won, by the score of 23 to 4. They then extended their tour and their string of victories by beating all-star teams from the cities of Baltimore and Philadelphia. Although the Excelsiors planned to play teams in Washington, Rhode Island, Boston and Connecticut, they never did. After their trip to the South, they again played the Atlantics. However, this time the redoubtable Atlantics won by the score of 15 to 14, thus ending the Excelsiors' unbeaten string of victories. Commenting on the tour of the Excelsiors, Albert Spalding, one of the early stars of the game, said that the "record of consecutive victories, the tidings of which were flashed over the State, created a profound sensation, and bred a strong desire on the part of lovers of the game in every city having a team to see the invincible Excelsiors."[32]

The second major tour of the 1860s was undertaken by the National Base Ball Club of Washington, D.C. During the season of 1867 the Washington club set out and played ten games in a number of different Western cities. They included Columbus, Louisville, Cincinnati, Indianapolis, Chicago, St. Louis, and Rockford, Illinois. After vanquishing teams in these cities by scores of 90 to 10 (Columbus), 53 to 10 (Cincinnati), 88 to 12 (Buckeyes), 82 to 21 (Louisville), 106 to 21 (Western Club of Indianapolis), 113 to 26 (St. Louis), and 53 to 26 (Empire Club of St. Louis), the Nationals went onto Rockville, Illinois, to play the Forest City Club.[33] They "suffered their first and only defeat; [they were] utterly crushed and humiliated by the unexpected drubbing by the school boys." They lost 29 to 23. The day after they went on to play and defeat the Chicago Excelsiors by the score of 49 to 4.³⁴ Despite the charges in the Chicago press that the Nationals threw the game to the Forest City team, the tour permitted people to see the excellent play of the Washington team.³⁵

Recognition and Acclaim of the Skill of Baseball Players and the Adoption of the Fly Rule

The growth of playing skill in baseball coincided with the recognition and reporting of this skill in the press. Articles extolling the virtues of playing baseball and descriptions of playing skill helped to combat the earlier image of baseball as a child's game.³⁶ Early acknowledgments of the skill needed to be a first-class player can be found in the reporting of the controversy surrounding the adoption of the fly rule. In the 1850s, the practice of catching the ball on the bound, combined with the traditional identification of baseball as a child's game, limited the recognition of baseball as a skillful undertaking, especially when it was compared to cricket. The game of cricket was generally thought to be more manly and skillful, because of the practice of catching the ball on the fly and the reputed complexity of the game. A writer for the *Spirit of the Times* compares baseball to cricket in terms of skill and complexity. He points out that "every school in the city should have a cricket or baseball club attached to it."³⁷

Catching the ball on the fly. Circa 1860. Woodcut illustration in Spalding's 1911 book *America's National Game.*

Cincinnati Red Stockings, the first openly professional baseball club. In 1869 the club recorded 89 consecutive victories, the only professional baseball club to do so. Photograph courtesy John Thorn.

Since cricket was considered more skillful than baseball in the 1850s, it was often suggested that baseball players take up cricket to improve their skills in playing baseball.[38] This reasoning is employed in an article in the *Brooklyn Eagle*, where it is noted that "playing cricket benefits base ball players.... In the former case a base ball player improves his batting by learning to defend his wicket in cricket, thereby greatly improving his sight in judging a ball...."[39]

This view, although a predominant one, was not shared by all. In a letter to the editor of the *Spirit of the Times*, a reader bitterly complains that cricket is dull compared to baseball. He states:

I have heard a great deal about the manly sports of "merry England," and have always had a great respect for experts in the athletic game of the Britishers. Cricket has been specified as a game requiring the greatest quickness of eye, and activity of limb, and I have heretofore looked upon it as glorious sport, full of intense though innocuous excitement. In my lamb-like innocence I have always, until yesterday, supposed cricket to be a diversion, an amusement, a pastime, a holiday recreation, and nothing but ocular demonstration could ever have convinced me of my great mistake.... Cricket is not a game, it is a popular fallacy to suppose it is, but it is a solemn ceremony periodically performed with a great seriousness by deluded Englishmen who think they're having fun. Fun! A cricketeer has no more appreciation of genuine fun than a dead jackass has of a fancy horn pipe. Grim are the cricketeers, and desponding; smileless, dejected, forlorn, and bilious. The pilgrim fathers, holding an out-door evening prayer meeting on a side hill in four feet of snow in the middle of February, were a gay set of jolly dogs compared to these rueful cricketing Englishmen out for a days [sic] pleasure.[40]

Nationalism was also occasionally interjected into comparisons between baseball and cricket. A writer for the *Spirit of the Times*, reporting on the "final meeting" of the baseball convention of 1857, comments on the attempt by delegates to have the fly rule adopted. He states:

They, accordingly, submitted a new code of laws, in which they clearly defined every point in the game; and with a view of making the game more manly and scientific, they proposed, that no player should be out on a fair struck ball, if it was only taken by the fielder according to the old rule, after it had touched the ground once and was then caught on the bound; but that the ball must be caught in the air before it touched the ground or the player was not out. This rule, Section 16, was discussed in committee, some objecting to it as being too much like cricket, some thought that it would hurt the hands more than taking the ball on the bound....[41]

After reporting on other proposed changes in rules, the writer goes on to argue for the adoption of the fly rule. He points out: "Above all, let not Americans reject a manly point in the game merely because it is English, and hurts the hands (which it does not, if played in a scientific manner); for surely, what an Englishman can do, an American is capable of improving upon."[42]

The call to patriotism as a basis for the support of the adoption of the fly rule is understandable, since the press had heretofore described baseball as the national game. The Knickerbocker Club helped to sustain the publicity surrounding the fly rule by deciding to play the season of 1859 with the fly rule. It was reported in the *Spirit of the Times* that a match between the Knickerbockers and the Excelsiors was

arranged solely for the purpose of testing the respective merits of the catch on the fly and that on the first bound ... and the result was such to satisfy any unprejudiced mind of the superiority in every respect of the former method. In fact, this is the only material difference in the fielding seen in a first-class cricket match and a similar match at base-ball, that in any way gives the former any claim to superiority; indeed, even now, as a general rule, far better fielding is seen in a majority of our base-ball matches, than what the cricket clubs display; and but for the catch on the bound, which so often gives rise to a display in the field unworthy the efforts of the merest tyro, we should certainly claim for base-ball the merit of affording more frequent opportunities for brilliant fielding in one match, than can be had in a dozen cricket matches.[43]

The consistent efforts of the press culminated in the adoption of the fly rule before the season of 1864. A *New York Herald* editorial in 1869 recognizes that baseball could no longer be considered unskillful or child's play. It states: "The game now has been reduced to a science, and the objection which was formerly made to it, on the ground that, compared to cricket, it was child's play, can no longer be raised."[44]

In the press reports of games in the late 1850s, a shift can be discerned from earlier reports that emphasize the benefits to be derived from playing the game, to reports

Henry Chadwick, one of the pioneer baseball writers. His reporting for the *New York Clipper* and summaries in *Beadle's Dime Base-Ball Player* were influential on the development of the game. *Henry Chadwick, the Father of Baseball*, painting by Dick Perez, oil on gesso panel from a black and white photograph, 2008.

that emphasize the skill of play. The shift in emphasis also implies a recognition by writers that, at a particular level of play, baseball was becoming more of an entertainment vehicle for people, instead of a vehicle for the development of their health and character. Accounts of games and articles on baseball in the late 1850s and onward are less likely to contain praiseworthy statements extolling the virtues of baseball and the benefits to be derived from playing the game. Writers are more likely to focus on the quality of play, tacitly recognizing the entertainment interests of fans, rather than attempting to proselytize readers into playing baseball.

Press accounts of baseball are brief in the early 1850s, as compared to later accounts. The outcome of the match, a crude box score, accompanied by some praiseworthy comments about the effect of the game upon physical fitness and character, were the usual fare. But by the end of the decade, the quality of play and the names of players are being singled out. An example of an early report on baseball can be found in a description of a game played in 1854 between the Gotham and Eagle Base Ball Clubs:

> The game of base-ball is fair soon to be as popular as the favorite game of cricket and right glad we are to see these healthful and manly exercises frequently indulged in. Many base-ball clubs have recently been organized and below we give the scores of two games which were played during the past week.[45]

The report ends by citing the score of the games. But there is no description of the offense and defensive plays in the games, nor is there a singling out of players for the quality of their play. As the decade wore on, the reports of games began to mention the quality of play. In an account of a game between the Stars and Niagara teams in 1859, the quality of play is the focus of the story: "On the part of the Stars, we especially noticed the excellent play of Manley at first base; his catching was beautiful. S. Patchen, at short-field, played admirably, and Tracey caught behind very effectively."[46]

The trend toward an emphasis on performance continued into the 1860s, as newspapers and sporting journals expanded their descriptions of the quality of play exhibited in games. A writer for the *Brooklyn Eagle* comments on a match between the Excelsiors and the Putnams in 1860:

> Of the play of the respective parties on Saturday, we have little else to do than to award to all, more or less, the highest praise, not only for individual instances of skill in the several departments of the game, but collectively for the gentlemanly conduct that characterized the proceedings throughout. We observe that every position was apparently so well attended to by each occupant, that no change was rendered necessary on either side, a circumstance that we do not remember witnessing on any previous occasion this season.[47]

Earlier that year a writer commented on the "skill" and "beauty" of play in a game between the Olympics and the Marion Baseball Clubs. He states:

> Cartwright, Wyant and Humphreys, of the Marion, played with much skill — Wyant especially, as short-stop, being very effective. The batting of the Olympics was excellent and their entire play good. Rockwell, as catcher, and Condit as third base, made some beautiful play in catching, while Rushmore, H.J. Murray [sic], and L.J. Murray handled the bat with telling effect.[48]

In a report of a game in 1863 between the Stars and Empire baseball clubs, the story emphasizes the high level of performance:

> The play of the Stars in this match was excellent throughout. True, they committed errors now and then, but their skillful fielding, in a majority of instances, and their truly splendid batting, fully compensated for the few mistakes that were made.
>
> Of those worthy of special mention for excellence of fielding we would name Norton, at left field, Waddel, at first base, and Herbert, a worthy young player at second base. But all marked their play with good fielding in a majority of the innings, the skill displayed in this department being worthy of the high reputation of the club.[49]

Starting in the early 1860s, a description of every inning began to appear in reports of the more prominent games. In a game between the Union and Excelsior clubs in 1863, the writer uses an inning-by-inning format to describe the game. Having described the first three innings, he goes on to say:

The fourth and fifth innings yielded the Excelsiors but two runs, one in each inning, their batting, as a general thing, not being up to their standard, for though the Unions fielded well in many respects, it was not such fielding as we saw them display in their last match with the Eckfords.

...In these same innings the Unions added four runs to their score, two more catches by the Excelsiors giving them half the number. The score at the close of the 5th inning stood 11 to 6 in favor of the Unions.... The four last innings yielded but 3 runs to the Excelsiors, the fielding of the Unions being very good indeed, especially the play of the catcher, who put out 6 players in 3 innings, one catch he made being "a beauty."[50]

The trend toward more descriptive reports of games continued into the 1870s and beyond. Writers reporting on baseball games in the 1870s were prone to a colorful but exaggerated style of prose. Reports of games would start with a brief description of the crowd, playing conditions and the names of leading players. A short summary would follow, then an inning-by-inning description of the game would commence. The report of the game would conclude with another summary and a boxed score. Typical of this kind of reporting is a lengthy description of a game between the Boston club and the Mutuals of New York. The writer notes in part:

> In the next three innings the Bostons layed duckeggs, owing to their inability to punish Matthews pitching, Hatfield capturing four of them on high flies to left field, one catch being a beauty.... In the meantime the Mutuals showed Harry Wright pretty plainly that they could knock a hard ball about as well as the next nine, and rather better than most nines....[51]

Henry Chadwick, disturbed by the overblown style of prose, reproaches the hyperbole of a fellow writer:

> The way some base ball reporters "pile on the agony" in the description of matches throws the blood-and-thunder dramatists and yellow-covered novel writers into the shade. Listen to a Cincinnati genius. Hats off now and hold your breath: "Every base was full. George Wright stepped to the bat amidst a stillness as of death when the 'boldest held his breath for a time' to make the run ... to tie the game, and save the club from their first defeat on their own grounds."[52]

The recognition and acclaim of the playing skill of the baseball player in the press became more evident as the decade of the sixties came to a close. Writing about the transformation of sport in the second half of the century, a sports analyst observes:

> With modernization in business and industry, new psychological transformations suitable to the emerging work styles occurred. Sports, featuring the self-assured independent athlete-performer in a context in which the "inner-directed," achievement-oriented businessman was hailed as the epitome of success, enjoyed wide-spread popularity. The multi-talented baseball player was a model of the successful craftsman.[53]

Ellul notes that sport is "tied to industry because it represents a reaction against industrial life" and that it is "linked with the technical world because sport itself is a technique."[54]

While the above analogy comparing the baseball player to the successful craftsman has merit, it should also be noted that playing skill was not simply a calculated demonstration of craftsmanship, but rather a spontaneous act occurring within the emotionally charged atmosphere of organized baseball. Here playing skill was embodied in daring, one-handed catches, overpowering hits driven beyond the outstretched hands of fielders, reckless base running, and the implementation of imaginative strategies. These acts and others had the ability to "shock," thus enhance the dramatic appeal of the players and "to make the moment of performing all important."[55] Baseball had become a vehicle for transmitting "familiar experience into new forms, giving the bleak and meaningless a sudden luminosity."[56] The increasing level of playing skill and growing club rivalries signified a "dramatic commentary" on the values of striving and success.[57]

However, the spirit of play was not easily suppressed in organized baseball. Belief in the recreational and social benefits of playing baseball kept reemerging as the seriousness of the game moved steadily forward. An editorial in the first half of the decade of the sixties called for a return to "muffin matches" instead of the "serious affairs" which denoted baseball. In referring to muffin matches, the editorial states:

The 1868 cover of the first edition of *DeWitt's Base-Ball Guide*, offering information and statistics about the game. Henry Chadwick was the editor starting in 1869. Woodcut courtesy John Thorn.

> These fun provoking games, we are glad to see, are again coming into vogue, among our ball players, and we think it is about time they should, for real recreation has not been enjoyed in a large majority of the games played this season. In fact ball matches of late years got to be quite serious affairs and some have inti-

mated that ball playing has become quite a money making business, many finding it to pay well to play ball.[58]

The editor goes on to urge a reinstitution of muffin matches between the least proficient players of prominent teams. The use of the term "muffin," in addition to denoting a substantial difference in skill, also connoted a less serious, more recreational approach to playing baseball.[59]

Positive ideas about organized baseball were formed in the press, primarily through the association of baseball with notions of health, recreation, manliness, and nationalism. This image was enhanced by the increasing skills of players who were able to display their talents in the Fashion Race Course series of 1858, the Silver Ball Match, and the Excelsior tour of 1860. Skillful play, spirited competition, club rivalries, and partisan rooting all contributed to baseball's disassociating itself from the idea that it was a child's game. The social-recreational orientation to playing baseball fitted nicely into the ongoing health and exercise movement in America. Furthermore, the identification of baseball by the press as a builder of reputable character helped raise the esteem in which baseball was held. The conjuncture of the above elements was responsible for establishing an ideological superstructure that was to stand in opposition to nascent commercial practices.

The aforementioned matches heightened feelings of nationalism and collective sentiments that baseball indeed was the national pastime. With an upsurge of laudatory comments in the press about baseball, there is a corresponding decline in the press of invidious comparisons between baseball and cricket. This development not only marks the emancipation of baseball from the imprimatur of cricket, but also presages the decline of England as a reference group for American sports. Nonetheless, the influence of the English still held sway until the turn of the century.

V

The Baseball Public and the Spectacle of Baseball

The formation of the baseball public was essential to the image of professional baseball in the press. It stemmed from reports on a wide variety of baseball matters and the exchange of baseball information by way of social and occupational communication networks. Part of the impetus to the growth of the baseball public was the transformation of the game from a recreational-leisure pursuit into an entertainment spectacle. Baseball as a spectacle grew out of the following factors: rule changes, playing innovations, club rivalries, and rowdy behavior and partisan rooting of members of the baseball audience. In analyzing these factors it will be helpful to know how the social class composition of the baseball public is related to the rise of the baseball spectacle. How did members of the baseball public identify with the playing of baseball? What part did the press play in the growth of baseball?

Before delving into the factors that were responsible for the rise of baseball as a spectacle, the concepts of public and baseball public need to be explicated, and distinctions need to be made between the crowd and the audience. By doing this, some light will be cast on the collective structures and underlying processes responsible for the construction of meanings about baseball. Can baseball historians help in clarifying the distinction between a public and the baseball public? Unfortunately, they have not attempted to make such a distinction. Nevertheless, their work is helpful, but limited, in dealing with the problem at hand. Voigt and Adelman simply use the term public, instead of baseball public, when collectively referring to baseball. Seymour uses the terms "baseball devotees," "sporting crowd," and "people" when he collectively refers to baseball.[1] His use of these terms, at times, obscures whether or not he is referring to what Turner and Killian have dubbed "distinct publics."[2] Or is Seymour simply referring to a general public? It is not clear what kind of public he is referring to. Despite the lack of guidance from baseball historians, distinctions will be made between the baseball public, the crowd, and the audience. But before doing this, it will be helpful to first touch on some aspects of the idea of a public.

The Public

The concept of a public and its study have been of major interest to sociologists and other social analysts.[3] Blumer suggests: "We refer to the public as an elementary and spontaneous collective grouping because it comes into existence not as a result of design, but as a natural response to a certain kind of situation."[4] For Blumer the emergence of a public is an outcome of an "issue," which requires a "collective decision arrived at through a process of discussion."[5]

Park, in his analysis of the crowd and the public, arrived at a conception of the public by contrasting it with the idea of the crowd. The public contains individual differences, whereas the crowd is "controlled by one common drive."[6] Furthermore, although the public consists of opposing views, it is also governed by "abstract norms.... Once accepted, the abstract norms function as a new force in collective life...."[7] Similar to Blumer, Turner and Killian explain the emergence of a public in terms of an "issue." They state:

> A public is a dispersed group of people interested in and divided about an issue, engaged in a discussion of the issue, with a view to registering a collective opinion which is expected to affect the course of action of some group or individual.[8]

Benson points out that a public consists of "inhabitants of a specified public entity, having the right *or claiming the right*, explicitly, or implicitly, to influence government actions, directly or indirectly."[9] In this sense, public opinion means to take a "position" or "stand" which is "favorable, unfavorable, undecided, and variations thereof — held by individuals (or groups)...."[10]

The difficulty in the treatment of the emergence of a public by Blumer, Turner, and Killian, and to some extent by Park, is their emphasis on the idea of an issue or opposition as a starting point for an explanation of the emergence of a public. In the sense used above, an issue suggests differences of opinions and the beginnings of conflict. While these possibilities may develop as a public emerges, they are not necessary conditions for the existence of the baseball public. If crucial issues and strong opposition existed in baseball before the mid–1850s, they were not reported in the print media, nor have they been written about by scholars.[11] It was not until the late 1850s that issues and opposition arose and began to appear in print media. But before this, people attended baseball games, read about baseball, and talked about the game. Thus, a baseball public did exist in an inchoate form, but nevertheless it was a public, despite the apparent absence of conflict.

The term public opinion is used by writers and researchers in a variety of ways. Often when the term is used, there is an underlying assumption that an independent, causal relationship exists between public opinion and the public policy taken by a group. However, there is little hard evidence that exists to justify this assumption.[12] The research reported in this book does not attempt to demonstrate a causal relationship between baseball public opinion and actions in baseball. Nor is there an attempt to reconstruct baseball public opinion. What is attempted is an analysis of the formation of the image of professional baseball.

A lead in the understanding of the baseball public stems from Tarde's analysis: "The transformation of any and all groups into publics can be explained by an increasing need for sociability, which necessitates the regular communication of the associates by a continual current of common information and enthusiasm."[13] In addition to the need for sociability, Tarde notes that publics emerge in response to "new interests."[14] Lasswell's work is also helpful in leading to a formulation of the idea of the baseball public. He states: "It should be pointed out that everyone is not a member of the world public, even though he belongs, to some extent, to the world attention aggregate. To belong to an attention aggregate it is only necessary to have common symbols of reference."[15] Following the leads of Tarde and Lasswell, the phrase baseball public will mean a collection of individuals who consumed baseball, both directly and indirectly, through a common informational background which included attendance at games, the playing of baseball, knowledge of baseball matters through reading newspapers, sporting journals, baseball guides, and discussion with others, resulting in generalized ideas about baseball.

As indicated earlier, baseball historians who have written about the infancy of baseball have not always been specific or consistent when referring to the consumers of organized baseball.[16] Terms such as crowds, fans, spectators, and public are often used interchangeably, accompanied by brief descriptions which treat baseball spectators (the direct consumers) and the public (the indirect consumers) as one. Although the two overlap to an extent, they are not identical nor are they mutually reducible to each other. Distinctions can be made empirically and conceptually between the two.

The Baseball Consumer

Contemporary research on sport consumption has found that "most consumption tends to be indirect."[17] Although an estimate of the percentage of indirect consumption is difficult to calculate, today people experience sport indirectly, mainly through television, radio, electronic media, reading, and talking about sport. This, of course, does not replicate the conditions in the nineteenth century, but it does sensitize us to the possibility that not all members of the baseball public attended baseball matches; they may have, to a certain extent, consumed baseball indirectly, vis-a-vis the press and social networks. From a conceptual standpoint, the baseball audience and the baseball public are not identical. The baseball audience is directly influenced by the spectacle of baseball, which intensifies emotions, producing a variety of responses. For the most part, the audience reacts predictably, responding to plays on the field which signify team loyalties and feats of skill, etc. The audience is also unpredictable. At times it will paradoxically unite, transcending individual differences and allegiances. The baseball audience is a complex of different expectations which contribute to both its predictable and unpredictable nature.

In contrast, the baseball public, depending on its stage of growth, is a diffuse collectivity, which acknowledges the right of others to have different viewpoints about matters pertaining to baseball. It is a reflective entity, whereas the audience is a spontaneous assemblage.[18] Audiences also differ from baseball crowds. Audiences can be distinguished from crowds in that they have a predetermined specific purpose known to all its members. The crowd does not have a specific purpose; it is more likely that a purpose will arise through its assemblage. Audiences meet at predetermined times in innumerable places with fixed boundaries. Audiences have a patterned form of interaction and polarization. Crowds have modes of interaction between the masses and their focus, but, comparatively, they lack regularity of stimulus and response.[19] However, as theoreticians have shown, both the crowd and the audience have common features. Therefore, the phrase baseball audience is used throughout this dissertation instead of the phrase baseball crowd.[20]

Composition of the Baseball Public

Although baseball historians have not explicitly taken up the idea of a baseball public, nor have they made distinctions between an audience and a crowd, can their work be of help in identifying the composition of the baseball public? I believe that their work can be helpful if we assume that the baseball public and the baseball audience, if not identical, were certainly similar in their make-up.

Seymour writes:

> It seems likely that middle-class and professional people and the sporting crowd formed the bulk of weekday attendance. It is hardly likely that ordinary workingmen could get away on weekdays, except for bricklayers, longshoremen, carpenters, and various part-time workers who might have some days off between jobs.[21]

Adelman comments on the middle-class composition of the baseball audience. He remarks: "Far from attracting fans from all social ranks, New York's spectator sports prior to the Civil War came from no further down the social scale than more prosperous members of the middle class."[22] He goes on to point out that after the Civil War:

Depiction of an early baseball grandstand, circa 1870. *The Grand Old Game*, digital painting from a black and white photograph, painting by Dick Perez, 2008.

> Attendance at baseball games was more broadly based than other spectator sports ...[although] the lower class neither played nor attended baseball games. In essence, those groups that did not participate in organized baseball did not watch the contests of New York and Brooklyn teams.[23]

Additional insight into the composition of the baseball public can be derived from descriptions in the press of baseball audiences. An account from the *St. Louis Post-Dispatch* depicts the character of the baseball audience. The account states:

> A glance at the audience on any fine day at the ball park will reveal the presence of representatives of all respectable classes. Telegraph operators, printers who work at night, traveling men who go out on the road at nightfall, men of leisure ... men of capital, bank clerks who get away at 3 P.M., real estate men who can steal the declining hours of the afternoon, barkeepers with night watches before them, hotel

V. The Baseball Public and the Spectacle of Baseball

clerks, actors and employees of the theaters, policemen and firemen on their day off, strangers in the city killing time, clerks and salesmen temporarily out of work, steamboat captains, clerks and mates, merchants in a position to leave their stores with a notice to the bookkeeper that they will not be back to-day, call board operators who need recreation after the experience of the noon hour, baseball players, semiprofessional and amateur; workingmen with the lame hand; butchers, bakers, candlestick makers, mechanics out on strike; lawyers in droves, an occasional judge, city officials ... the Mayor's private secretary, and last, but not least, doctors....[24]

In an issue of *Western Monthly*, a colorful description of an audience at Dexter Park in Chicago is given:

The immense audience disposed, for the most part, on the seats of the "grand stand," a favored hundred or two in the cool piazzas and balconies of the Club House; an adventurous Gideon's band, mostly made up of sports, amateur and professional, congregating in front of the Club House, a score of reporters thrown out, like a company of skirmishers, well into the field, and the remainder of the throng scattered promiscuously about the skirts of the field, in carriages or otherwise,—the game commences. If it happens to run pretty evenly, or even if the score is kept down to a low figure, the interest of the crowd is intense. Every good play of any member on either side is hailed with huzzas, partly from amateurs who admire the feat, but chiefly from bettors who have put money on the players' side. At the end of each inning the ears of those in the vicinity of the Club House are saluted with all sorts of propositions for wagers. A stolid-looking fellow with a big neck wants to "go another fifty" on the Ultramarines. A small individual with a sharp nose, a quid of tobacco, and a pocket-handkerchief tied about his neck, desires to hazard a hundred dollars that the Pea Greens don't make three more runs. A terribly excited young man, who has evidently had some training at grain-gambling but little at field sports, announces, in a voice quivering with excitement, his willingness to hazard ten to fifteen on the Pea Greens. Anon somebody makes a proposition, which is received with a general hoot and a suggestion to "soak your head." The same demonstrations occur, in a less degree, in other parts of the Park. In fact, two-thirds of the persons in the vast throng have money or hats—which, unfortunately, cost money—hazarded on the game, and every heart is beating high for the deciding event. It seems as if each of those ten thousand hearts had received the pulsation and momentum of all the others. At length the game is over. Those who went purely to see the sport have enjoyed without distraction a fair exhibition of manly skill and strength, and just a healthy degree of excitement. Those who foolishly put their means at hazard have had too much anxiety for enjoyment, and come away glowing or gloomy, according to their luck.[25]

The likelihood that the majority of the baseball audience and the baseball public were middle class is given further support when we consider that baseball parks in the 1860s and early 1870s were some distance from the centers of population. The Union Grounds and the Capitoline Grounds were located approximately four miles from the center of Brooklyn. This made it especially difficult and expensive for a fan from New York to witness a game. The cost of the ferry and the expense of a trolley, plus the cost of admission and the possible loss of at least a half-day's wages, often made it prohibitive for lower-class working men to go to baseball games. In 1876 it was estimated that the cost for a local mechanic to take his family to a Ladies Day Game in Brooklyn was $2.47. This included the cost of transportation and the $1.25 lost in wages by taking off a half-day.[26] The idea of spending a day's wages on a baseball game must have deterred many of those who might have wanted to attend.

The baseball public and the baseball audience, in their infancy, more than likely comprised middle to upper-middle class men in their twenties and thirties, who were mostly brokers, merchants, proprietors, shop owners, artisans and professionals. In the late 1850s the composition of the two changed to encompass a broader socio-economic segment of the population, which included skilled craftsmen and low white-collar workers. Women also began showing a greater interest in baseball by attending matches. The first Ladies Day was established by the Knickerbockers in 1867. Members were "requested to invite their wives, daughters, and girlfriends, and [they] appointed a committee to see that 'suitable seats or settees' were available for them."[27] Seymour hints that the increase in rooting and rowdy behavior by spectators was due to changes in the social class composition of the fans.[28] Although the composition of the baseball audience changed from upper-middle-class to mostly middle-class, it does not appear that this change affected the deportment of spectators. The shift in the composition of the baseball audience was not great enough to account for the growth of rowdy behavior at baseball games. Baseball spectators, whether upper-middle class or middle class, generally shared similar attitudes toward decorum in public places. Although the baseball audience and the baseball public overlap, the distinction between the two permits the following speculation: as the baseball audience became known for its boisterous behavior, upper-middle-class men, presumably not wanting to tarnish their professional and semi-professional occupational reputations, attended fewer baseball matches. This does not mean that these men did not retain their interest in playing, reading or talking about baseball, but as members of the baseball public, their consumption of baseball may have become more indirect.

The Baseball Public and the Press

The origin of the baseball public and the beginnings of the professionalization of baseball did not occur in a cultural vacuum; a number of social, economic, and cultural factors helped provide a social matrix out of which the baseball public emerged. The mid-nineteenth century was a time when the effects of industrialization and immigration, the growth of transportation, and the rise of urban centers all acted to help promote the growth of entertainment.[29] From this tangled web of influences, the baseball public emerged, but it could not appear unless there were extended chains of interacting groups which formed a complex communication network.[30] People who

V. The Baseball Public and the Spectacle of Baseball

played or enjoyed watching the game of baseball belonged to assorted groups, such as occupational groups, political and social clubs, volunteer firefighting companies, and recreational clubs. It was through the circulation of attitudes, rumors, speculation and sports news that the baseball public was formed and ideas about baseball nurtured.[31] But most important, it was the press that carried baseball news which helped shape ideas about baseball in the baseball public's mind. This assumes that an aggregate of upper-middle-class and middle-class men in the 1850s were relatively open to the influence of newsprint stories about baseball.[32] Theoretical writings and empirical research on the effects of mass media provide a basis for the idea that people under given conditions are susceptible to the influence of mass media. Davison et al. note: "In some cases the influence of communications may be traced to the fact that *very little information of any sort* on a given topic is available."[33]

In addition, the writers note that mass media exert a "powerful influence" on directing the "degree of attention" people will give a subject they are interested in.[34] Along similar lines of analysis, Berelson suggests that exposure to mass media "is more effective" when communications specialize, and when there are "*new or unstructured issues*" being communicated.[35] In a chapter titled "Uses of Mass Communication by the Individual," E. Katz et al. note that the starting point for an analysis of the effects of mass media is the "media consumer."[36] This approach also "postulates that gratifications can be derived, not only from media content, but also from the very act of exposure to a given medium, as well as from the social context in which it is consumed."[37]

In brief, the authors argue that people select and use media to fulfill psychological and social needs, rather than being passive receptors to media communication. The aforementioned conditions that facilitate the effects of mass media approximate the conditions that were present in the 1850s as the baseball public began to take shape. During this time, little public information was available about baseball, although the circulation of newspapers was increasing and specialized sports periodicals were emerging. Issues over the playing and organization of the game were largely *unstructured* until the end of the 1850s. Nevertheless, the press was becoming a forum for the codification of baseball issues and their debate as baseball entered the 1860s.

The expansion of baseball was enhanced by the ability of the press to communicate the growth and diversity of the game. Gossip and personal experience were no longer sufficient to adequately communicate the increasing complexity of the expansion of baseball to interested others. What was needed was a common frame of reference. The press fulfilled this need. In the 1860s both the sport and metropolitan press carried baseball tables, box scores, and statistics. This gave baseball reporting a systematic character and contributed to its uniform identity.[38]

The hub of baseball activity was New York City. In 1850 the city had a population of 696,115 and a combined daily newspaper circulation of 153,621. In 1880 the population had increased to 1,911,686; however, the combined daily newspaper circulation increased from 22 percent of the population to approximately 43 percent of the population from 1850 to 1880.[39] Reportage of baseball games on a regular basis (daily or weekly) did not take place until the latter part of the 1850s. But as interest in baseball increased, a desire for information about the game also grew. The baseball public was open to the influence of sports reporting. This does not mean that other communication networks were not influential in shaping ideas toward baseball, but sports reports were an influential factor in forming ideas about the game.

The Baseball Spectacle and Rule Changes

When baseball is analyzed from the standpoint of a spectacle, a number of diverse dramatic elements are brought together which are fundamental to the propagation of the image of professional baseball.[40] These elements consist of demonstrations by players of skill, courage, judgment and strategic innovations in the context of an emotionally charged collectivity. Here expressions of club or city allegiance and gambling interest take the form of partisan rooting and outbursts of derision or acclaim for one team (or player) or another. It is within this interactive complex that collective meanings in baseball were fostered and apprehended, and thus reported in the press.

Some rule changes in baseball's early days contributed to making the game a more exciting contest. At first players advocated rule changes to enliven the game, but as spectators became more numerous, they too exerted an influence over rule changes, in accord with their entertainment inclinations.[41] Voigt is aware of the influence of spectators on the rules of the game. He notes that in the 1860s, "probably because of the heightened spectator interest, the rules of the game underwent changes."[42] Seymour also notes that the "long process of rule refinement [made] the game increasingly palatable to spectators...."[43] Novak, writing on baseball, is aware of the relationship between the entertainment aspects of the game and the format of the game. He writes:

> [Baseball is] orderly, reasoned, judiciously balanced, incorporating segments of violence and collision in a larger plan of rationality, absolutely dependent on an interiorization of public rules. It also depends on a balance of power between pitchers and hitters [and] on the delicate interplay between fielders at each position.... A slight change in the weight of the ball or its composition, in the material used for bats, in heights or distances, can alter the character of the game dramatically, giving decisive edge to one factor or another.[44]

The balance between pitchers and hitters that Novak refers to is equivalent to a balance between offense and defense from a dramatic standpoint. Too much of either and the viewing of the game became tedious. This suggests that spectators are inclined toward lively contests that fulfill their entertainment expectations.

Gregory Stone, writing about American sport, makes a similar point. He observes that "with the massification of sport, spectators begin to outnumber participants in overwhelming proportions, and the spectator, as the name implies, encourages the spectacular—the display."[45] In brief, Stone asserts that spectators come to dominate how the game is played. This also suggests that there is a relationship between the format or the rules of the game and the influence of the entertainment inclinations of the spectators. Contemporary critics of baseball have claimed at times that baseball games are getting progressively longer because of the frequent conferences between the pitcher and players and because of the time-consuming movement of the pitcher, such as "pawing the dirt, wiping his forehead, tying his shoe, pattin' the resin bag."[46] From the standpoint of the spectator, these movements are not essential to the playing of the game. They detract from the potential of a steady flow of action. In the early 1850s a batter could swing at only those pitches that he liked. He was also able to call for balls to be thrown either high or low. Balls and strikes were not called at this time. Therefore the game was often a struggle between pitcher and batter with the batter having the advantage. But in the late 1850s and early 1860s the rules were changed permitting balls and strikes to be called. This had the effect of creating a new balance between offense and defense. It also had the effect of increasing the tempo of the game. No longer could a batter force a pitcher to throw just the right pitch by interminably waiting him out.[47]

In 1865 the umpire could call balls and strikes against the batter. Thus, whether a batter was to be called out or to take a base was more quickly determined. The balance between offense of the batter and the defense of the pitcher continued to vacillate, with the pitcher gaining the advantage in the early 1870s. At this time, the number of "bad pitches necessary for a batter to take his base [increased] from three to nine."[48] However, the batter was still "allowed to call for a high or a low strike zone."[49] Pitchers continued to gain an advantage as the decade wore on, and by the mid–1870s pitchers were permitted to throw overhand instead of underhand.

The importance of maintaining the interest of spectators by changing the rules would seem to have played a part in a rule change in 1857 which specified that a contest would be decided by the club that scored the most runs over nine innings, instead of the first club to score twenty-one runs or twenty-one "aces." Matches that depended on the first team to score twenty-one runs often resulted in a short playing time and one-sided victories. This had the effect of producing boredom on the part of players and spectators. However, a nine-inning game resulted in the prolongation of the uncertainty of the outcome of the game, thereby helping to maintain the interest of the spectators.

Baseball Strategies

Changes in rules pertaining to offense and defense stimulated the unfolding drama of the baseball spectacle, but equally important was the introduction of strategic innovations.[50] They helped to underscore the skill of players and further animated the baseball spectacle. Harry Wright was one of the leading players and strategic innovators of his time. He introduced the practice of "backing up his outfield mates on the fielding of hits; also it was Wright who urged an outfielder always to throw a base ahead of the runner."[51] Joe Start, one of the early star players, at first base, is reputed to have introduced the tactic of playing off first base, in an effort to be in a better position to field balls hits between first and second base.[52]

Aiding the development of specialists at playing positions was the introduction of baseball guides. Manuals on how to play the game started to appear in the 1860s. *Beadle's Dime Base-Ball Player* (1860) and *DeWitt's Base-Ball Guide* (1868) provided additional vehicles, other than the press, for the dissemination of technical information on the finer points of playing the game of baseball. Ideas about the special skills needed at different playing positions were part of baseball knowledge in the 1860s. At this time it was known that the catcher should be positioned a few feet behind the batter instead of the earlier practice of staying as much as twenty feet in back of the batter and catching the ball on the bound. Playing positions in the infield and outfield were thought to need special talents in the 1860s. Seymour points out: "Infielders were expected to have strong, accurate throwing arms, and to be 'plucky' enough to handle hard-hit balls.... It was understood that the quickest, most agile man should be the short stop."[53]

Outfielders were required to have strong throwing arms. They were aware of the possibility of relaying throws and how to position themselves in regard to batters. Stealing bases was becoming more common. Tagging up after a fly ball and attempting to advance to another base was also engaged in. More astute players devised "trick plays."

Dick Pearce, a shortstop, one of the stars of the Atlantics, developed the art of bunting, that is, tapping the ball lightly in front of home plate and then quickly running to first base before the infielders recovered from the surprise. George Wright is also believed to be one of the first players to intentionally drop an infield fly in order to turn it into a double play.[54] Baseball players and others in the 1860s personified achievement and a "recompense for the crushing and sordid inertia of daily life, a triumph over the obstacles that society sets in the way of valor."[55]

The Appeal of Baseball

The appeal of baseball to the fan on one level was simple: it provided a diversion from the dreary, repetitive, long working hours that occupied most of their existence. But on another level we might speculate that the attraction of baseball, other than the spectacular elements discussed earlier, was due to a vicarious identification with the rising status of players in American life. In the 1860s players began to symbolize success. Writing about baseball, Barth tells us:

> City people saw plays that they could remember afterwards because of the way specific events built up to a memorable moment — the sudden skillful triumph over an adversary. By making intense competition against an opponent its essential feature, baseball seemed to legitimize and extol each spectator's daily struggle for success.[56]

The decline in the status of the wage earner in mid-nineteenth-century America suggests, in a paradoxical manner, an additional basis for the mass appeal of baseball. As the status of the worker declined, the status of the baseball player rose, because participation in baseball, whether indirect (as spectators) or direct (as participants at any level), afforded middle-class men a vicarious or a real means of compensation for lost opportunities to display their skill and initiative.

Historians have recognized that with the displacement of the small entrepreneur, artisan, mechanic, and to a lesser extent, craftsman, there was a corresponding loss of status for these occupational ranks and a general decline in the status of wage earners.[57] In New York City and Brooklyn, by mid-century, the factory system had almost completely replaced handicraft production.[58] Skilled craftsmen felt the repetitive thrust of mechanization as they were confronted with new modes of work that required relatively little ability or training.[59] The monotony of the mechanized modes of production stifled the creativity and sensitivity of the worker and abrogated his independence. In a chapter on "Hireling Laborers," Rodgers discusses the idea that "the worker owned his own toil, that a man's efforts were his to exert and the successes his to be repeated."[60] But the "dignity" of work was mostly applied to the "self-employed." He observes:

> In the expansive, insistently democratic antebellum North, the word "servant" slid into a term of reproach. "Employee," the term that eventually filled the gap, was still a foreign import, hesitantly spelled and its implications resisted. Antebellum manufacturers preferred to talk of "operatives" and "factory hands," just as Yankee farmers invented the term "help" for their servants and hired men, as if the evasive labels would rectify the anomaly of dependence in a society in which self-employment was the moral norm.[61]

Miller also writes about the loss of status of labor during this time:

> With the triumph of mechanization and the replacement of the craft shop by the factory, the artisan lost his earlier position in the community. Instead of selling his product he was selling his labor.... As more and more workers became mere wage-earners, the general dignity of labor diminished.... Mechanics employed in factories began to consider themselves as wage slaves in a very real sense.[62]

The desire to raise one's occupational status and the belief that "manual labor is disreputable ... skewed the urban economy by placing a special premium on white collar positions. Craftsmen had to be imported from Europe ... because Americans all wanted to be clerks, professionals or bosses, or to drive something."[63]

In a series of articles in the *New York Times* in the late 1860s, the conditions of "Our Working Classes" were assessed."[64] In an attempt to explain the numerous outbreaks of strikes and the increase in trade unions, the author of the series points out that the small workshops are "far less common than they were before the war."[65] Furthermore, "the small manufacturers thus swallowed up have become workmen on wages in the greater establishments...."[66] The loss of independence by the mechanic and the artisan and the lowering of these workmen to the status of "wage earners" was depicted in the *New York Times* as:

> a system of slavery as absolute if not as degrading as that which lately prevailed in the south. The only difference is that there agriculture was the field, landed proprietors were the masters and negroes were the slaves while in the North manufacturers are the field, manufacturing capitalists threaten to become the masters, and it is the white laborers who are to be slaves.[67]

Callois notes that part of the attraction of the spectator to the spectacle is his vicarious identification with the athlete, vis-à-vis his athletic performance. He goes on to point out that in competitive athletic contests such as football, boxing, and wrestling matches:

> These are dramas whose vicissitudes keep the public breathless, and lead to denouements which exalt some and depress others. The nature of these spectacles remains that of an *agon*, but their outward aspect is that of an exhibition. The audience is not content to encourage the efforts of the athletes or horses of their choice merely by voice and gesture. A physical contagion leads them to assume the position of the men ... just as the bowler is known to unconsciously incline his body in the direction that he would like the bowling ball to take at the end of its course. Under these conditions, paralleling the spectator, a competitive *mimicry* is born in the public, which doubles the true *agon* of the field of track.[68]

Voigt, writing about the commercialization of baseball in the 1860s and 1870s, observes: "In the short space of ten years the sport rose to commercial proportions; and in such a brief span people accepted the professional players as skilled performers and took for themselves the role of vicariously participating onlookers."[69] Dunning has suggested that "one of the motives for consuming soccer in Britain may be a desire to compensate for the fact that one's own work offers few opportunities for the expression of physical skill, hence one vicariously experiences the high level of skill displayed by the athletes."[70] Men like James Creighton and Harry Wright exemplified a high level of playing skill, were accorded recognition by the press for their abilities, and undoubtedly, represented to many in the baseball public the status of successful "artisans."

The Rowdy Behavior of the Baseball Audience

Adding to the baseball spectacle was the unruly and, at times, riotous behavior of the baseball audience. These outbursts were reported in the press starting in the 1850s. In a match between the Excelsiors and Niagara baseball clubs in 1857, a reporter noted:

> Some of the Niagara's friends did not behave as gentlemen should. Whenever the Excelsiors were about to strike — such remarks as shanks, shanghai, and other words not quite as decent as the above. In several instances, when the Excelsiors had the bat, on their making a strike and reaching the first base, their ears would be saluted by the word foul, sung out in a loud tone, by one of the Niagara's friends: the consequence would be, that the Excelsior thinking it was the decision of the referee, would hasten back — no sooner would he get half back to first base, and the consequence was the Excelsior was out. Common politeness, at least, required some effort on the part of the Niagara club to stop such proceedings; but they were looked to in vain.[71]

The following year, a reporter, commenting on a "Great Base Ball Match Postponed," (the clubs are not specified) observed:

> The assembly was one of the most respectable in character composed in the main of staid citizens, it included business and professional men of various callings. There was a sparing admixture of a baser element but not loud enough to affect the applause or the spirit of the occasion. One individual was somewhat disorderly for a time but was quelled by the remark, are you a ball player too? This was deemed a bitter reproach and served its purpose.[72]

The same year, in a letter to the editor of the *Spirit of the Times*, a reader complains about the noisy behavior of the players. He remarks:

> A single circumstance should be brought to notice in your journal, and that is the incessant fire of directions and commands issued in no inaudible voice to bystanders, by one of their players to the rest of the field. The Babel their grounds presents on practice days is bad enough, but it is clearly more reprehensible in match games, when not a voice should be raised by the captains.[73]

In a report of a game between the Atlantics and Gothams, in the season of 1858, a writer for the *Spirit of the Times* states:

> There was an immense crowd of spectators on the ground, completely surrounding the players at all points, and materially interfering with the progress of the game; and as the sympathies of the majority were strongly in favor of the Brooklyn play-

ers, it caused the New Yorkers to feel that they had but a poor site for a fair field, and they expressed themselves to that effect.⁷⁴

In an article in 1860 announcing an upcoming "match for the Championship" between the Excelsiors and the Atlantics, concerned about the "disorderly conduct" of spectators, a writer for the *New York Clipper* states:

> No fears need be entertained in regard to disorderly conduct whatever the excitement the game may create, as the Excelsiors as proprietors of the grounds enclosed, they will promptly remove any person who may act in an objectionable manner.⁷⁵

Despite the writer's assurances, one of the first spectator riots occurred at the final game of a three-game series between the Atlantics and Excelsiors. In the first game, the Excelsiors were victorious over the Atlantics, 23 to 4. In the second game, the redoubtable Atlantics came back to beat the Excelsiors 15 to 14.⁷⁶ In the third game the Atlantics, who were the betting favorite of the crowd, were behind 6 runs to 8 in the sixth inning. According to Spalding, from the sixth inning on, "the toughs began a crusade of blackguardism that became so unbearable that ... captain Leggett of the Excelsiors took his players from the field...."⁷⁷ The match was agreed to be called a draw by the team captains. The two teams never played again, and the championship of Brooklyn for 1860 was not resolved.⁷⁸ In reference to the aforementioned game, it was reported in the *New York Clipper* that the Atlantics had "issued a card to the dailies defending the actions of 'the rowdy crowd' and criticizing the press for their stressing the rowdy behavior of the fans."⁷⁹ But the writer for the *Clipper* points out: "The reference to the press is in bad taste, for it is to the press that they are mainly indebted for the present popularity of the game. Once let the press be silent on the subject and baseball will soon be obsolete except as a boys' game at ball."⁸⁰

Contributing to the boisterous behavior of spectators and, at times, their interference in games, was the lack of grandstands, or even enclosures, to clearly separate the playing area from the spectator area. In the early days of baseball, spectators stood by the foul lines.⁸¹ Games were played on open fields, making it difficult to charge admission or to clearly separate players from spectators. Before the advent of grandstands, an enterprising owner of the grounds where the Union Base Ball Club of Brooklyn played, William Caymmer, decided to enclose his baseball grounds and charge admission. In 1862 he enclosed the Union and Capitoline grounds in Brooklyn with a fence and constructed a clubhouse for the players. These early enclosed baseball parks did not have a grandstand, but had a wooden shed with benches provided for the ladies. There were also benches spread throughout the grounds, making it possible to seat approximately one thousand five hundred people.⁸²

Even after grandstands were constructed, spectators were known to interfere with the playing of the game. In a game played between the undefeated Cincinnati Red Stockings and the Atlantics, which resulted in the first loss in two years to the Cincinnati club, fans were reported to have impeded the progress of play of one of Cincinnati's outfielders, thereby contributing to the defeat of the Red Stockings. In a description of the game in the *Cincinnati Commercial*, a writer observes: "Start struck a ball to right field into the crowd, far over McVey's head, and made third on it. In pushing the crowd aside to get to the ball, McVey was kicked at by a scoundrel who had previously tried to kick the ball further off."[83] This interference permitted the runner to advance to third base, where he was advanced home by a hit. The Atlantics won the game 8 to 7 in the eleventh inning.

Spectators interfering with the play of the game, boisterous shouting on their part, and at times riotous behavior among them, can be, in part, attributed to their gambling on the outcome of baseball matches. However, rowdy behavior on the part of spectators can also be linked to factors other than their pecuniary self-interest. What appears to be involved is that the norms guiding deportment at the ball field were similar to the ones that guided audience deportment at the theater. It was not uncommon among theatergoers at the time to express their dissatisfaction with a performance by issuing "catcalls and hisses."[84] Perhaps the norm of free expression among theater audiences carried over to the ball field and contributed to rowdy behavior. Furthermore, the baseball spectacle provided the urban dweller with an opportunity to lose himself in public. It afforded the middle-class merchant, shopkeeper, artisan, mechanic, and professional an opportunity to vent their emotions in the anonymous but, nevertheless, emotionally charged setting of the baseball spectacle. Sennett believed that for the European men at mid-nineteenth century, "going out in public" provided an opportunity for "losing yourself in public"— getting away from the "repressive and authoritarian features of respectability which were supposed to be incarnate in his person, as father and husband in the home."[85] Perhaps American men did not feel the burdens of respectability as much as Europeans did — going to a baseball game and becoming part of the assemblage was a novel way to lose yourself for an afternoon.

Club Rivalries

Another reason for the rowdy behavior and partisan rooting of spectators was the intense rivalry that arose between baseball clubs. Baseball matches provided urban residents with an opportunity to demonstrate "civic pride and identification with the local club" by shouting encouragement or by booing derisively.[86] The press encouraged rivalries by making invidious comparisons between clubs, or chauvinistically referring to the superior playing ability of a club. One of the earliest of city rivalries, which presaged an interborough rivalry, was between Brooklyn and New York. In an article about baseball in the *Brooklyn Eagle*, it was noted that: "Nowhere has the National Game of Base Ball taken firmer hold than in Brooklyn, and nowhere are there better players."[87] In a report on a game between the Excelsior Club of Brooklyn and the Empire Club of New York, a writer for the *Brooklyn Eagle* notes the superiority of Brooklyn's club: "The Empire is one of the best of the New York Clubs, but it would stand but a poor chance with several of our Brooklyn Clubs. If we are ahead of the big city in nothing else, we can beat her at base ball."[88]

Clubs from Boston, Washington, Troy, Philadelphia and Cincinnati provided an additional basis for rivalry with clubs from New York and Brooklyn. Coextensive with club rivalries was an increase in the number of matches played by leading clubs.[89] The Empire Club of New York played in no more than ten matches per season before 1860, but in 1864 they played in twenty-two "first-nine matches."[90] The Brooklyn Atlantics, one of the leading clubs of the 1860s, had played in "seven first-nine matches" in 1861.[91] But in 1864 they played in twenty matches, winning nineteen of them.[92]

Volatile eruptions at baseball games continued into the 1860s and throughout the rest of the century. Yet the press gave less attention to boisterous behavior of spectators than it had done in the late 1850s. Perhaps the attention the press gave to the rowdy behavior of spectators was, at first, due to the marked differences between the lack of emotional restraint present at baseball matches as compared to the decorum exhibited by spectators at cricket matches. This comparison was implicit in the writing of Henry Chadwick. From the late 1850s, sportswriters, principally Henry Chadwick, reported on the boisterous and, at times, rowdy behavior of spectators. The *New York Tribune* in 1857 declared that players and spectators should be "respectable."[93] Voigt notes that Chadwick believed that "baseball's growth should be rationally guided in the direction of elevating the sport in a gentlemanly manner."[94] It was important to Chadwick that baseball be kept "respectable."[95] He also advocated that players should play the game "quietly" and not "needle" the opposing team with jibes.[96] It seems that by the late 1860s, Chadwick and other members of the press had accepted the rowdy behavior of baseball spectators and consequently reported less on it.

The rise, side-by-side, of the baseball public, the baseball audience, and the baseball spectacle was essential to the transmutation of baseball from a boys' game into a commercial enterprise. The aforementioned collective entities constitute a framework in which knowledge about the game was fostered, and consequently they were important in forging the image of professional baseball.

The concept of a public has been discussed as a theoretical precursor to positing the notion of a baseball public — both of these share similar collective

V. The Baseball Public and the Spectacle of Baseball

features. But the analytical utility of the concept of public is limited, because it is too inclusive. It covers too broad a spectrum of interests and behavior to be relevant to the problem at hand. The utility of the idea of a baseball public resides in its ability to focus attention on one segment of the public, having specific features which are subject to specific processes in the construction of baseball meanings. Thus, it is a more viable construct than the concept of a public.

The knotty problem of untangling the multiple ways in which baseball was consumed in relation to the formation of knowledge about the game has been broached by making distinctions between direct and indirect consumption of baseball. Although people both attended games and read about them, I believe the distinction between the baseball audience and the baseball public is a useful one in that it draws attention to the ways in which baseball was consumed. Furthermore, it sensitizes us to the possibility the knowledge could be gained about baseball in one way or the other.

Essential to the rise of the baseball public was an extended chain of social and occupational networks. People who played or watched baseball also belonged to assorted groups, such as occupational groups, political and social clubs, volunteer fire companies, and recreational clubs. It was through the circulation of attitudes, rumors, speculation, and sports news in these social domains that the baseball public was formed and ideas about the game were nurtured. But most important, it was the press that carried baseball news and played an essential part in the formation of ideas about baseball.

Baseball perceived as a spectacle helps explain the popularity and rapid expansion of baseball clubs in the late 1850s and 1860s. Being part of a lively and spontaneous audience, where individual pride and community allegiance were vested in the outcome of the contest, proved to be an irresistible attraction to many. Stone asserts that spectators come to dominate the play of the game, thereby emphasizing the "spectacular — the display." This suggests that there is a relationship between the format or the rules of the game and the influence of the entertainment inclinations of the spectators. The implementation of playing strategies had an effect on the growth of baseball as a spectacle similar to that of rule changes: both helped to dramatically enliven the entertainment appeal of baseball. Although it can never be precisely known what meanings were apprehended by the baseball spectator or the motivation that spurred their attendance at games, it is likely that many spectators vicariously identified with star players, particularly the skill and daring exploits on the field. Perhaps middle-class men identified with certain players because their skillful play symbolically connoted lost opportunities to display their own skill and recapture their lost pride in craftsmanship. Another aspect of the allure of baseball inhered in the novelty of being part of a public assemblage where behavior ranged from the issuance of polite applause to ringing denunciations directed at players, umpires, and, on occasion, other spectators. At times the spectator's emotions boiled over, thus creating a boisterous throng; however, this appears not to be a common occurrence. Surely boisterous behavior must have displeased a segment of the audience, but it also must have exhilarated equal numbers of those present who could at the same time give full expression to their emotions and still preserve their anonymity. What a delight for the work-constricted merchant, the alienated craftsman and the overburdened clerk, to get away for an afternoon and lose himself in the baseball audience by watching and reacting to adults at play.

In the formative years of the baseball public, the press was the only quasi-official source of information about baseball, until the advent of the *Baseball Guide* in 1860. The semi-structured nature and the changes occurring within organized baseball made it imperative for those interested in baseball to follow the game in the press. The press helped establish and influence rule changes (e.g., fly rule) by editorial suggestions and a consistent advocacy for reform. It is also likely that they helped codify the rules by serving as an informal arbiter of disputes among people who would defer to the written word. From this standpoint, the press reinforced both direct experience of baseball and indirectly guided discussion which was freely exchanged in the saloon, workplace, and sporting club.

The growth of the cities of New York and Brooklyn, and the expansion of baseball to other cities, established a basis for inter city rivalries. Much of the partisan rooting and rowdy behavior of spectators can be traced to these rivalries. But gambling on matches also added to the inherent tension of the baseball contest and consequently fueled outbursts of rowdy behavior by spectators. Although drinking is infrequently mentioned in the press before the 1870s, consuming alcoholic beverages at games undoubtedly added to these outbursts.

Baseball in the 1860s was well on its way to becoming a form of staged conflict. To complete the journey, organized baseball needed to bring out into the open monetary compensation to players in the form of salaries. Money and sport, at this time, were uneasy bedfellows, often maligned, but nevertheless a necessary element in the completion of baseball's journey to professional status. The circus atmosphere associated with baseball matches, the introduction of controversial playing practices, and the throwing of matches led to an aura of disrepute surrounding baseball. We turn in the next chapter to the basis for this.

VI

The Disreputable Image of Baseball

For most of the 1850s, commentaries on baseball in the press were praiseworthy; at times, however, mild rebukes were directed toward certain aspects of the game. At the beginning of the 1860s, generally positive views of baseball gave way to increasing criticisms of the game. Censure was directed at a variety of practices undertaken by players and clubs. Criticism also focused on the alleged corrupt behavior of players and umpires. The actions in baseball that drew the most ire from sportswriters were the following: substitution of players, exhibition matches, revolving (players changing from one club to another), admission charges, championship matches, rowdy behavior, salaries, gambling on matches by both spectators and players, and the alleged fixing of matches. The focus of this chapter will be on setting forth representations of commentaries in the press on substitutions, exhibitions, gambling and corruption, and championship matches in baseball. Given this, we would like to know what the public sentiments were toward paid athletes in the first half of the nineteenth century. How did these sentiments affect views toward baseball? How did baseball maintain its popularity despite harsh criticisms of it? Before addressing these questions, an overview of professional athletics and their moral status at mid-nineteenth century provides a background for a better understanding of public sentiments toward professional baseball.

Professional Athletics of the Early Nineteenth Century

Sports in which athletes were paid or received prize money were not extensive in America during the first half of the century. However, they did exist and the following were the most popular: thoroughbred racing, pugilism, rowing, pedestrianism (foot-racing), cricket, harness racing and baseball.

The moral status of paid athletes was an ongoing topic of interest to writers at mid-century. Writing in the 1860s, Henry Chadwick, commenting on professional athletics, said:

> Now, as with the lawyer or physician whose professional status is degraded by the actions of pettifogger and quack, so it is with the professional athlete whose reputation necessarily suffers from the conduct of the class who lower their occupations by degrading associations, dissipated habits and, too frequently, dishonest practices. With the higher class of professionals, whose working capital is based upon mental talent, the black sheep of the flock are the exception and not the rule. With those, however, who excel in physical attributes, the contrary is, unfortunately, the rule; and, hence the term professional which in one case is an honor, in another is too frequently applied as a title almost the very reverse of honorable.[1]

In reference to the integrity of professional athletes at mid-nineteenth century, a sports historian observes:

> When professionals and spurious amateurs who played for money on a part-time basis invaded athletics, many genuine amateurs abandoned the field. Sometimes the integrity of sports declined: because professionals derived their income from competition, many did not hesitate to assure success by prearranging, either by giving or taking bribes, the outcome of contests. By the 1870s, fraud and dishonesty had become so commonplace that a reporter for the *New York Times* sneeringly referred to "that class of crimes known as athletic sports."[2]

Although having a relatively untarnished reputation in the 1830s, thoroughbred racing was reputed to be corrupt in New York (the leading center of turf racing) by the end of the 1840s. Often "gamblers and professional turfmen increasingly assumed control over the sport and the 'better class' either withdrew or were driven from the track."[3] Studying the growth of sport in New Orleans, another sports historian quotes from a *Spirit of the Times* story which notes that jockey Abe Hawkins had his membership revoked at the Metairie Jockey Club "for plain, positive, and palpable dishonesty—in plain terms, 'throwing off' a race which he had already won by sawing his horse around."[4] A writer, commenting on thoroughbred racing during the 1850s, remarks:

> As racing went on in the North, it began to attract a new element, professional gamblers who cared more for money than for horseflesh. In 1856, probably for the first time in America, a newspaper, according to *The Annals of American Sport*, admitted that to the opening of the Long Island racing season ... had come out in its strength, this racing world — this huge agglomeration of gambling and fraud, of weakness and wickedness ... men whose interest in [sporting events] is the interest of "sharps" and "gamblers."[5]

Pedestrianism was a popular sport in America from the late 1820s into the 1880s.[6] It was also considered to be a disreputable activity.[7] The sport was dominated by professional runners and walkers who competed over varying distances ranging from ten to fifteen or more miles and varying periods of time, ranging from one hour to as long as six days.[8] The "peds," as they were

VI. The Disreputable Image of Baseball   95

called, "earned their livelihoods by betting and by charging admission to their exhibitions."[9] Spectators also wagered on the outcome of these contests—heavy betting was common. Because the peds competed for money, "participation by respectable middle and upper-middle class citizens" was precluded.[10] In a brief article in the *New York Clipper*, there is mention of a race between "Shepard" and "Soda Bill." The writer goes on to point out that Soda Bill lost the race. It states in part: "The results completed, the backers of Soda Bill ... immediately assailed him with unmeasured abuse, and charged him with throwing the race off intentionally."[11]

Two years earlier, the *Spirit of the Times* mentioned the arrest of "Roguish Pedestrians" John Stetson, John Pratt and Thomas Wood (also known as "Mundy") for "conspiracy and cheating" in a foot race.[12] Apparently the arrests of Stetson, Pratt and "Mundy" only briefly interrupted their nefarious careers. In 1860 the *Brooklyn Eagle* noted, "Stetson and Mundy get up a race with an understanding who shall win, and Pratt bets with the spectators, always of course placing his stakes in favor of the runner who has arranged to come out ahead."[13]

Contributing to the disrepute of paid athletes were bare-knuckle boxing contests. These contests, although condemned and legally outlawed, were popular throughout the nineteenth century. From the 1820s, starting in Southern plantations, interest in prizefights grew. The press frequently criticized and denounced the prize ring. Betts notes that in 1835 the *New York Sun* suggested that "if any law can be framed by our legislature that may aid in putting down this disgraceful practice, we hope it may be adopted."[14]

During the 1850s and 1860s, the more reputable press often ignored prizefights. But sporting journals gave considerable space to ring activities. *The Spirit of the Times* and the *New York Clipper* regularly published accounts of matches. Although condemning prize fights, publications like *Harper's Weekly* and the *New York Times* still reported the results of major contests, due to the enormous interest in these matches. An editor for *Harper's Weekly*, commenting on a fight between John C. Heenan and John Morrisey, points out: "There was nothing heard of—up town, down town and in the country—but the great prize fight.... The prize fight was, we venture to assert, the only topic discussed that morning in back parlors, counting-rooms, and offices generally throughout the city—to say nothing of bar-rooms, and places of like character."[15]

Two years later in *Harper's Weekly*, in reporting on the Tom Sawyers and John C. Heenan prize fight, the editor had this to say: "We believe prize-fighting is a degrading, brutal, and shameful practice; a natural nucleus of black-guardism and we do not believe that pugilism is in the least degree calculated to do good, which can hardly fail to do evil."[16] Continuing his denunciation, the editor went on to point out:

> The idea of the prize ring is a manly institution, and that prize fighting has a tendency to improve the physical quality of the race, will not bear scrutiny. Nothing can be manly whose inevitable fruits are ruffianism, cheating, drunkenness, debauchery, idleness, and profanity. Did anyone ever hear of a prize fight which did not bring forth these fruits?[17]

Harness racing was a favorite outdoor pastime in New York in the 1830s, and the city was recognized as the "premier city in the breeding and training of trotting horses."[18] As the sport grew, "cries of foul play on New York tracks were already heard as early as the 1830s."[19] In the next two decades the sport press asserted that the "fixing of races was a common practice."[20]

The association of professional athletics with behavior that was considered morally opprobrious emerged in the press. Betts makes this connection when he suggests:

> For years, the association was drawn in the press and impressed on the public mind that contaminating influences in professionalism were due to the gambler and the rowdy.... In the years when commercialized sport first struggled for recognition the pioneer sponsors were the saloon and the poolroom.[21]

Of course, the saloon and the poolroom connoted questionable characters, riff-raff, rowdies and toughs. It was difficult for professional athletics to disassociate itself from these connotations in the public's mind. Not only did boxing matches take place in saloons, but enthusiasts of the "turf" and the baseball diamond also frequented the saloon and the poolroom. Odds on races were wired into countless betting parlors, and baseball fans eagerly awaited scores at their neighborhood cigar store or local saloon.[22] The saloon and the poolroom were meeting places where sport enthusiasts gathered. The bookmaker, the "pug," the baseball player, and others, all met to exchange information, to bet, and to be seen. Writing about the rise of baseball in Chicago, a sports historian notes the connection between paid athletes and corruption. He remarks that "despite all the trappings of upper-class splendor, both [horse] racing and billiards came to be associated with the work of gamblers and thieves."[23]

A distaste for professional athletics in the first half of the century helped to engender negative attitudes toward sport journals. Berryman observes:

> The literature of sport was often viewed as being vulgar and rather disreputable by a substantial portion of the general American reading audience. Sporting magazines suffered from an association with tavern-life, gambling and general smoking-room stories, just as drama suffered because of its early relationship with prostitution.[24]

The opprobrium toward professional athletics also made reporting on sports an act of "bad taste" and called into question the morals of the person writing about sport. Consequently, those who wrote about sport often used a pseudonym to protect their real identity.[25]

VI. The Disreputable Image of Baseball

Inherent in the professional system was the fear of fraud by athletes, since the primary goal of professional athletics was centered on winning in order to maximize his profit. What "guarantees" existed that would prevent the athlete from manipulating the contest to his benefit?[26] It was thought that the only way the public could be assured of honest contests was through the auspices of the "better class"; therefore, to a certain extent, a "class bias" existed toward professional sport.[27]

The aura of disrepute surrounding paid athletes can also be traced to the legacy of Puritan values that equated pay for play with gambling. Writing about baseball in the late 1860s, Spalding recognizes the resistance of Americans toward the commercialization of baseball and the belief that it would bring untoward features. He observes:

> First, that portion of the public—and it was at that time probably in the majority—who believed that Base Ball was simply an ordinary form of outdoor sport, a pastime, like cricket in England, to be played in times of leisure, and by gentlemen, for exercise, and only incidentally for the entertainment of the public, had to be reckoned with. This class felt that the game would suffer by professionalism.... It meant, they thought, the introduction of rowdies, drunkards and dead-beats....
>
> Another class to be dealt with was the gambling element, and this opposition was not to be lightly considered. They had so long been a controlling influence, that anything threatening their ascendancy was sure to meet with stubborn resistance.[28]

It is not surprising that professional baseball would also be subject to the same associations that paid athletes were subject to, considering the disapprobation directed at professional athletics. Nevertheless, organized baseball did not immediately plunge into paying salaries to players. The movement toward salaried players was gradual. But it was not an evolutionary unfolding stemming from one change begetting another. It was rather a hesitant, uneven movement, stemming from a fear of being cast in the same light as professionals that prompted the gradual introduction of the early forms of compensation, such as sinecures, exhibition matches, sharing of gate receipts, etc. However, it was not just the fear of censure by the baseball public, but it was resistance from those within organized baseball who espoused the play ethic that buffeted and temporarily thwarted the ascension of pay-for-play.

Substitution and Revolving: Disreputable Practices in the Transformation of Baseball

One way in which the increasing focus on victory in the late 1850s manifested itself was in the practice of a team "substituting," for a game, some of its players of average ability with players from another team who were known for their exceptional playing ability. The ostensible purpose of this practice was the potential of gaining a competitive edge. The practice drew criticism from the press. One of the early reports of player substitution appeared in the *Spirit of the Times* in 1856. It was noted that a "Mr. Pinckey, a superior player of the Union Club of Morrisania," had played as a substitute for the Gothams in their match against the Knickerbockers. The writer of the account went on to say:

> It did not appear that he [Pinckey] had resigned from the Union, the presumption prevailed that he entered the Gothams for the purpose of this match. We do not know this matter in the way of census, but to suggest that the facility with which good players might be retained at the mere cost of an initiation fee for any important match. A rule ought to be adopted to prevent such objections in the future.[29]

In a letter to the editor of the *Spirit of the Times* the following year, the writer complains about "substitution in matches." The writer states, "I take the liberty to condemn the practice of substituting players from other clubs to play matches."[30] The Baseball Convention earlier in the year had adopted a rule requiring that only "regular members be allowed to play and they should have been members of the club at least thirty days prior to the game."[31] In addition, the rule (Section 27) prohibited substitution of players after the game had started "unless for reasons of illness or injury."[32] Despite the rule, the practice of substitution continued into the 1860s.

Another practice, called "revolving," grew out of substitution and had its roots in the increasing competitive nature of baseball games. Revolving denoted the practice whereby a player would break an agreement to play with one team and "revolve" to another team for a playing season, or the remainder of a season — the inducement being money or other remuneration. The practice of revolving drew even more strenuous objections in the press than criticisms directed at the practice of substitution. The *Brooklyn Eagle*, in a veiled reference to revolving, noted in 1866 that "so many changes have been made among the players that it is now a difficult matter to know where to place some."[33] A writer for the *Brooklyn Eagle* in 1870 had this to say about "Revolvers":

> The rivalry between professional clubs never was carried to such a high pitch as it is at present, and while in many respects it is an excellent thing for the game it has brought into being a class of players known as Revolvers who are bringing contempt upon themselves and upon the game.[34]

In the same year, the *New York Times* was also critical of revolvers. An editorial writer stated:

> Of course, all professionals have a right to better their positions at the close of each season, by changing from one club to another, and several first-class players have done so this past winter, and without loss of reputation. But the class known as revolvers change from one club to another, getting all they can out of each, and breaking regular engagements and written contracts without hesitation and with impunity.[35]

The following year the *Spirit of the Times* pointed out:

> If the system of revolving, which is a most pernicious one, be not treated in a proper spirit and crushed out at once, it will do a great deal of harm to this beautiful game, as no club will be certain of the services of any of their players in any important match.[36]

One reason for the stronger opposition toward revolving than toward substitution was that the latter involved the temporary transferring of services of a player for a single game, whereas the former practice was ostensibly for the remainder of the agreement between the new club and the player. From the perspective of the baseball public, their disfavor shown both practices was rooted in the following logic: substitution denoted the potential of a team to gain a competitive edge for a single match, therefore it connoted poor sportsmanship. Revolving was morally opprobrious because it involved the breaking of an agreement and the transferring of allegiance from one club to another.

Gambling and Corruption in Baseball

A great deal of the negative sentiments expressed toward baseball in the press of the 1860s can be traced to gambling by spectators and the alleged collusive gambling practices by players. Expressions in the press of these practices ranged from a mild rebuke to stinging denouncements. Clubs were accused of deliberately losing matches in order to lengthen a series, thereby increasing their share of gate receipts, or of losing a match in a series to increase the betting odds so that players might make a betting coup. However, by the late 1860s, the press had recognized that wagering by *spectators* on baseball was an integral part of the baseball spectacle.[37] But the press still consistently denounced betting by *players* on matches. What follows is an attempt to trace the diversity of reportage concerning gambling on baseball in its formative years.

The introduction of gambling into baseball is not surprising given the penchant for both English and Americans to indulge in it when a contest was afoot. Gambling on cricket was widespread in America, and with the growth of baseball, it was a certainty that baseball would follow cricket as a vehicle for gambling. The propensity to wager on the outcome of baseball games was spurred by the introduction of match play between clubs and the increasing interest of spectators in the outcome of games in the early 1840s. These elements created a dynamic environment where competitive impulses among players and spectators alike were nourished. It was short step from rooting for a club to expressing enthusiastic support by placing a friendly wager. With the introduction of the box score in 1845, bettors could better gauge the probability of one team triumphing over another by establishing a statistical record. It also provided a clearer distinction between baseball as a boy's game and one played by gentlemen.

One of the early reproaches toward wagering by players appeared in *a New York Clipper* account of a game played between the Eagles and the Gothams in 1860:

> Sec. 30 of the rules and regulations reads—"No person engaged in a match, either as umpire, scorer or player, shall be either directly or indirectly interested in any bet upon the game.... Now, we respectfully ask ball players whether the rules are to be adhered to the letter or violated with impunity, as they were on the occasion of this match. The heavy betting by outsiders on the result of ball matches is sufficiently injurious to the interests of the game without adding the still worse custom of allowing players in matches to indulge in it, especially when there are rules expressly prohibiting it.[38]

The press in the first half of the 1860s occasionally related the quest for victory and intense rivalries between clubs with the amounts wagered. In an editorial in 1863, a writer for the *Brooklyn Eagle* decried the "objectionable affects" due to the heated rivalry between clubs and the "evils arising from encouragement that is also given to the gambling spirit by the opportunity afforded by betting in large amounts."[39] A year later, in an account of a match between the Atlantics and the Mutuals, the *New York Clipper* focused on the behavior of the spectators and the umpire, giving rise to the suspicion that wagering on the match resulted in the umpire favoring the Mutuals in order for their backers to overcome the betting odds. The writer describes the playing of the match as skillful up until the sixth inning. At this point the Atlantic Club led by a score of 23 to 10. But, "in the last innings, the Mutuals made a dash to save such of their friends from loss who had accepted offers of bets that the Atlantics would beat the Mutuals by a score of two to one, and by their efforts in batting they managed to secure six runs, the totals at the close of the game being 26 to 16."[40] If you were betting with the Mutuals, you would have won your wager, since the final score was not in the ratio of two to one.

It might be argued that it was the superior play of the Mutuals that enabled them to score enough runs to cover the odds against them. However, this possibility is undermined by the description of the behavior by the umpire:

> Colonel Fitzgerald of Philadelphia acted as umpire and did his duty creditably and impartially as far as his decisions on points in the field were concerned, some of them being excellent, but owing to a natural feeling of hesitation likely to characterize the action of anyone placed in the position he was, he failed to exact a strict observance of the sixth section of the rules, and thereby permitted the pitchers to indulge in too much of last year's style of delivery.[41]

Although not explicated by the writer, the reference to "last year's style of delivery" suggests a change in the rule that occurred after the season of 1863. The new rules permitted the umpire to award a base-on-balls, if in his judgment enough balls were tossed outside of the strike zone. By not invoking the new rule, the umpire could conceivably permit an unlimited number of pitches without penalizing the pitcher. Strategically this would facilitate more opportunities for the Mutuals to score more runs and, therefore, benefit their backers.

In the latter half of the 1860s, the press commented on the increasing amount of money wagered and the deleterious impact gambling was having on baseball.[42] In a report of a match between the Philadelphia Athletics and the New York Mutuals, a writer for the *New York Mercury* scorns the amounts of money wagered on the match. He goes on to say:

> But whether 20,000 or 10,000 the fact was made apparent that the spirit of gambling has increased and made captives of a large portion of the fraternity — on those who claim to have a leading influence over prominent clubs, and in this fact, we perceive the little cloud foretelling the storm that will wreck the game....[43]

In the same year, a writer for *Harper's Weekly* expresses his displeasure with clubs gambling on baseball:

> So common has betting become at base-ball matches that the most respectable clubs in the country indulge in it to a highly culpable degree, and so common has been the tricks by which games "sold" for the benefit of gamblers that the most respectable of participants have been suspected of their baseness.[44]

Publications like *Harper's Weekly* were quick to condemn all aspects of gambling, while publications like the *Spirit of the Times* saw no great harm in spectators wagering on a match. A writer with this viewpoint argues for gambling on baseball:

> Does every uncertain event, and every such event offer an opportunity for those disposed to make a wager condemn it as immoral? And now to take the practical rather than the argumentative side of this subject, what is it that makes base-ball, or any other pastime popular with all classes? Just this: if one cannot play it himself, he can bet his money and thereby enjoy the excitement more keenly than even the players themselves. Have the patrons of base-ball attained higher moral conceptions of right and wrong than those of the turf, aquatics, quoits, cricket, and in fact all others that special immunity from the practice must be vouchsafed, then, or the game be stamped with their stigma?[45]

One aspect of organized baseball during the 1860s that helped fuel rumors and suspicions of corruption was the inconsistent play of some of the more prominent teams. A writer for the *New York Clipper* is perplexed by the inconsistent play of the Atlantics and other clubs. He writes:

> The Atlantics of Brooklyn have been the champions for some time. Well, they go to Newark to play the Eurekas by whom they are defeated. The Athletics of Philadelphia also played a match with the Eurekas and beat them badly; they also played a match with the Unions, of Morrisania, and beat them too. They next play the Atlantics, of Bedford, and meet with a reverse. Then the Atlantics go to Philadelphia to play a second game with the Athletics, and this time the Atlantics are

beaten almost out of sight. Right on top of this, the Unions of Morrisania play a second match with the Athletics, and the Athletics are vanquished by a score of 42 to 29. We confess that we cannot understand it. Do all these clubs play as good as [*sic*] they can play in each and every match, or do they purposely "throw off" for betting purposes? We are afraid that "money" has much to do with this base-ball muddle....[46]

Similar reasoning is applied by the press when the Washington Nationals lose to the Forest City Players. During the season of 1867, the Washington Nationals undertook a tour of the western part of the nation. They won nine of their ten matches, but their last two games gave impetus to one of the early controversies in baseball which focused on selling of a game and the debasing influence of gamblers. On July 25, the Nationals lost to the Forest City Players of Rockford, Illinois. The loss was taken by local papers as a signal which presaged a victory for the vaunted Excelsiors of Chicago over the Nationals in their last match. Before the game, the *Chicago Times*, in a challenging tone, said:

> When the Nationals shall have lived among us a few days, imbibed pure water from the clear depth of Lake Michigan, breathed the healthy breezes from the prairies, and taken a few lessons in base ball playing, they will begin to realize how profitable has been their trip to the Northwest.[47]

The Nationals beat the Excelsiors by 49 to 4. The one-sidedness of the score and the "rumors spread by disappointed gamblers" evoked charges in the press that the Nationals had "thrown" the game to the Forest City Club as a means to set up a betting coup for their match with the Excelsiors.[48]

Shortly after accusing the Nationals of perpetrating a "regular confidence game" and of "unfair conduct," both the *Chicago Tribune* and the *Chicago Republican* printed retractions.[49] In a letter to the editor of the *Republican*, Frank Jones, the president of the Nationals, states:

> It is false that we travel around the country for gambling purposes; it is false that the game with the Rockford club was "thrown"; it is false that our nine is a "picked nine," and, lastly, it is false that noted gamblers accompany our club, or that such a class is in any way countenanced by the National club.[50]

The above declaration by Jones is probably true. The Nationals had a reputation in the association for discouraging gambling. In the Nationals' playing field, a sign was prominently posted which read "betting positively prohibited."[51] Another circumstance lends credibility to Jones's statement. The pitcher for the Forest City club that defeated the Nationals was Albert Spalding, destined to become one of the great pitchers of his day, but his pitching prowess was not widely known at this time.

Inconsistent play by clubs again prompted the press to charge that the "fix" was in. The *Brooklyn Eagle*, in 1867, reported on a "match for the championship"[52] between the Atlantics of Brooklyn and the Athletics of Philadel-

VI. The Disreputable Image of Baseball

phia. Playing in Philadelphia, the Atlantics lost the match 28 to 8, much to the surprise of the *Eagle* reporter, since in their preceding contest, the Atlantics had decisively won. The reporter points this out by noting:

> After the splendid display they made in their last game with the Athletics, many risked their money on the belief that the Athletics were not capable of winning a ball from the Atlantics.... It is rumored here that the Atlantics lost this game purposely, that the Philadelphians might be induced to risk their money more freely on their favorites. Whether this is true or not we do not know.[53]

After noting that the Atlantics were missing two key players because of injury and that this "may have had the effect of lessening the confidence of the nine,"[54] the writer goes on to say: "It is also rumored that certain betting members of the Atlantics who had not gone with the club were telegraphed not to bet on the nine and that they commenced hedging on the money they had already bet on the Atlantics. This is a given for what it is worth."[55]

The press argued that since clubs shared in gate receipts, it was in their best interests to lengthen a series. It was thought that a club would deliberately lose a match in order to establish a betting coup on a future match with the same club. The press also charged that some clubs were controlled by gamblers and that if corrupt practices continued, baseball would be ruined. A writer for the *Brooklyn Eagle* decries the dangers posed by gambling and gamblers. He states:

> An evil has crept in which every season becomes greater, and which unless it is checked must degrade the game in public estimation to the level of horse racing and other gambling pursuits. We refer to the practice of gambling, which has become as open and prominent on the ball grounds at champion matches as on the race course. Some of our most noted clubs seem to be given over to the control of gamblers.... The public will no longer have the interest they once took in the game knowing that the players are merely striving to decide bets and that the result may have been arranged before hand. Ball matches have been sold as shamelessly as similar transactions on the turf. The players representing the most renowned clubs have allowed themselves to be beaten that gamblers might win the money of those who held a misplaced confidence in the honor as well as the skill of the players.[56]

The disreputable image of people in organized baseball, based on gambling, continued into the 1870s. A writer for the *Spirit of the Times* raises the possibility of players banding together to conspire to lengthen a series of games for their "pecuniary" gain. He states:

> Most matches are made the best two in three, and some clubs who play only to make money will contrive by collusion with their opponents, to bring about a third game on every series, when if they choose, they could win in two straight games. It is this growing evil of throwing games for pecuniary motives that is bringing baseball into disrepute.[57]

In an article for the *New York Times*, the writer in his review of the baseball season of 1870 notes:

There is no doubt that professional baseball playing is an established institution, but in order for it to be permanent some changes are necessary in its management, for the general impression from the past season in regard to the conduct of professional clubs, has been that it has been characterized by too much of the Hippodrome principle, and that professionals have played too much into the hands of regular gamblers. Be this as it may, there is no questioning the fact that at present some professional Players and their clubs are in bad odor with the public.[58]

Writing about baseball in the early 1870s, Albert Spalding, one of the stars of the game, states:

Gambling, in all its features of pool selling, side betting, etc., was still openly engaged in. Not an important game was played on any grounds where pools on same were not sold. A few players, too, had become so corrupt that nobody could be certain as to whether the issue of any game in which these players participated would be determined on its merits. Liquor selling, either on the grounds or in close proximity thereto, was so general as to make scenes of drunkenness and riot of every day occurrence, not only among spectators, but now and then in the ranks of the players themselves. Many games had fist fights, and almost every team had its "lushers."[59]

Spalding also quotes at length from *Beadle's Dime Base-Ball Player* of 1873, in which Henry Chadwick had this to say about the practice of "pool selling": "When the system of professional ball playing as practiced in 1872 shall be among the things that were, on its tombstone — if it have any — will be found the inscription, 'Died of Pool-Selling.'"[60] Chadwick goes on to note that pool-selling replaced the direct form of wagers made between parties, but it introduced a greater "evil." He observes:

Since the introduction of pool-selling at Base Ball matches, pools amounting to over $20,000 have been known to be sold on a single match, and it has been in the power of parties knowing the aggregate amount of money invested, and who also knew which club the larger amount was invested on, to so manipulate things as to make the contest terminate just as the special ring of the day desired it should. What benefit therefore pool-selling yielded in supplying a regular responsibility in the payment of bets in the place of the previous loose way of staking money was more than offset by the great temptations to fraud the knowledge of the amounts invested on the favorite club afforded and which the pool business admitted of. But, aside from the special evil of the system referred to, the very existence of the betting mart on the ball field has been found to be demoralizing in the extreme.[61]

By 1875, the idea that professional baseball was corrupt was well established in the press, but to what extent corruption existed, and to what degree it prospered in specific clubs, could not be known then or now. A writer for the *New York Clipper* recognized the disrepute in which baseball was held. He also recognized that perhaps a minority of people in baseball were prone to corruption. He argues:

As a general thing any professional baseball club will throw a game if there is money in it. A horse race is a pretty safe thing to speculate on in comparison with

VI. The Disreputable Image of Baseball

an average ball match. Thus far there is but one solitary instance in which players have been openly convicted of "throwing" or "selling" a game of ball. There have been charges made, suspicions formed, and circumstantial evidence of fraud at sundry times. There may, too, have been instances in which a very small minority of the players of the professional association clubs have become so interested in bets or pools on the game they played in as to unfit them for faithful service for the time being; but taking the great majority of professional ball-players into the estimate, we can confidently assert that there is no sport in vogue in which so little of the element of fraud prevails as in the baseball arena....[62]

Up until the 1860s, the only substantiated act of collusion among players to fix a game occurred in 1865. Harry Wright, one of the first professional managers (Cincinnati Red Stockings), writing in late 1860s, succinctly summarizes the scandal:

> The first instance on record of a game purposely lost by collusion of the players happened September 28, 1865, when the Eckfords defeated the Mutuals by 28 to 11, to the great surprise of the spectators. Subsequent events, however, showed that this game was sold by three Mutuals, Duffy, Wansley and Devyr, who were expelled, the first name being reinstated and playing short stop for the Chicago club in 1870 and 1871.[63]

The evidence was established by a letter in which Devyr admitted that Wansley had offered him $300, of which he claimed to have received only $30, to throw the game. The three players were expelled by the Mutuals. In 1867 Devyr was reinstated.[64] Both Duffy and Wansley were also reinstated in 1869 and 1870, respectively.[65]

In an attempt to shed light on the stream of corruption accusations appearing in the press, Adelman suggests that sports writers of the 1860s were prone to allege corruption when clubs that were ostensibly favored to win did not, because they did not have a well-established concept of an "upset."[66] Sportswriters did not recognize that the deleterious physical effects of playing an increasing number of games, the tedium of road trips, and the "general drudgery of numerous contests" would result in upsets.[67] But by 1869 the press began to become more tolerant of the losses by clubs that were expected to win.[68] Attempts to explain the inconsistency of play are still with us. A contemporary sportswriter recognizes the inherent difficulty of maintaining motivation to play well. He points out:

> For all the talk about giving 110 percent of effort, the mathematical, biological, psychological fact is that an athlete does not have more than 100 percent to give, even under ideal conditions. When the conditions are less than ideal—when there are four games in four cities in five nights after overnight flights, rushed meals at odd hours, little time for preparation, and nagging injuries—it is unreasonable to expect maximum effort from every player in every game.[69]

Although the extent of corruption in early baseball cannot be accurately determined, it seems that deliberate attempts to throw games were confined to a small number of clubs and players.[70] In an account of a championship match between the Mutuals and Eckfords, which the Mutuals lost 31 to 5, a writer for the *Spirit of the Times* speculates on how the "bad play" of some members of a club might influence the other players:

> The Mutuals aided the Eckfords in their big score by a display of muffinism and wild throwing the like of which they have not shown this season before.... The result has a damaging look to the Mutuals, if not also to the Eckfords, which no explanation can set away with those people who predicted the result beforehand. Having witnessed the game, we state our conviction to be that it was a fair struggle taken altogether but that some palpable bad plays were made by the Mutuals toward the close. This was the consequence of dissatisfaction and bad temper only; for it is well known that where one or two members of a nine repeatedly show bad play, the rest become disheartened and frequently manifest their disinterestedness in the proceeding by becoming particeps criminis to the whole.[71]

The Championship of Baseball: The Quest for Supremacy

Charges of corruption in baseball and questions concerning the reputation of the game were often made in the press, in the context of reports on "Championship Matches." A brief explanation of the inception of championship games, and their structure and impact on the baseball public, will provide an additional perspective in explaining the formation of the image of professional baseball. A systematic description of the origin, emergence, and the structure of the baseball championship has not been undertaken by baseball historians.[72] However, a thorough analysis of the "championship system" has been undertaken by Adelman.[73] He dates the start of the "championship system" in 1861, but notes that the National Association of Base Ball Players did not establish "any formal rules to determine the championship club."[74] The championship was "created" by "ball clubs, the press and the public."[75] Adelman also observes that it was not until 1871, with the inception of the "first professional league ... that some form of systematic scheduling was created to annually define baseball's best."[76]

The Fashion Race Course Series of 1858 was tantamount to being baseball's first championship. Although the series was promoted as an all-star contest, it essentially determined which city, New York or Brooklyn, had the best baseball club.[77] However, the press in 1860 dubbed the first match of what turned out to be a three game series between the Excelsiors and Atlantics as the "Match for the Championship."[78] The Excelsiors won the series.

Shortly before their celebrated tour, the Excelsiors engaged the Atlantics on July 20, 1860, and decisively beat them by the score of 23 to 4.[79] On their return home from Baltimore and Philadelphia, a second match was arranged between the two clubs. On August 10, 1860, the second match was played. To

VI. The Disreputable Image of Baseball

the surprise of many, the redoubtable Creighton of the Excelsiors was beaten in a close contest. The score was 15 to 14 in favor of the Atlantics. This was the first defeat for the Excelsiors since their tour of New York.[80] The victory by the Atlantics prompted a third match which generated a great deal of enthusiasm and "partisanship as the time for the last game drew near, until it had become very bitter. It permeated all grades of society. Schoolboys, clerks, merchants, manufacturers, workingmen, and members of all the learned professions were profoundly interested."[81]

Spectators strongly supported the Atlantics and betting on the game was widespread.[82] In the third game the Excelsiors took the lead and at the end of the fourth inning, they were leading by a score of 8 to 4. But "from this time on the toughs began a crusade of blackguardism that became so unbearable as the game progressed that at the end of the sixth inning, with the score standing 8 to 6 in favor of his team, Captain Leggett, of the Excelsiors, took his players from the field...."[83] The team captains, in a brief verbal exchange, agreed to call the match a draw and left the question of the championship undecided. The two clubs never played again before they were disbanded in 1871.[84]

In October 1861, the Silver Ball Match was held in Hoboken between representative players from the best clubs of Brooklyn and New York. The match was initiated by Frank Queen, the editor of the *New York Clipper*. He offered a silver ball as a trophy to the club whose players scored the greatest number of runs. The trophy went to Pearce, the Atlantics' catcher.[85] From the standpoint of championship, it was the all-stars of Brooklyn, not a single club, that were recognized as champions.

The Eckfords of Brooklyn, due to their superior play over the Atlantics in 1862 and their unbeaten season of 1863, were acknowledged as the championship club.[86] The Atlantics, because of their unbeaten seasons of 1864 and 1865, reigned supreme during these years.[87] The Philadelphia Athletics were the championship club in 1866.[88] In a three-game series with the Atlantics, the Mutuals of Morrisania were victorious and the champions of 1867.[89] The following year, Frank Queen offered a "Gold Ball to the winner of the championship."[90] Because the two clubs contesting for the championship, the Atlantics and the Mutuals, "did not play a tie-breaking game," the championship "went undecided,"[91] although it appears that the Athletics of Philadelphia claimed the championship for the season.[92] In the next three years, chronologically, the following clubs were recognized as champions: the Cincinnati Red Stockings, the Atlantics and the Athletics.

The structure for the championship in the aforementioned years was ambiguous and it was not until 1871 that a formal structure was introduced by the National Association of Professional Base Ball Players. The championship would be decided by the club winning three out of five games in a

Championship game played between the Atlantics of Brooklyn and the Mutuals of New York at the Elysian Fields in Hoboken, New Jersey. The contest was undecided, ending after five innings because of a storm. Atlantics were leading 13 to 12. Woodcut courtesy John Thorn.

championship series.[93] Much of the criticism of baseball in the press throughout the 1860s was attributed to the undesirable consequences which attended championship contests. Gambling and rowdy spectator behavior were seen as the outcome of intense excitement generated by attempts for supremacy. In an editorial in the *New York Clipper* in 1866, under the heading "Championship Base Ball Matches," the writer had this to say: "We scarcely know what to make of our championship base ball matches of late, for they resemble very much those hippodrome affairs which our turfmen are in the habit of indulging in for money making purposes.[94]

The following year, under the headline "Base-Ball Championship," *Harper's Weekly* observed:

> Have we not of late had something too much of these "championship follies"? It was natural that prize fighters and men of such ilk should run into beastly extremes and become champion bruisers and gamblers, but it is not pleasant to witness young gentlemen ... or to see young collegians animated in the pursuance of their sport, other than a generous rivalry, condescending to bet upon their respective fellow students as so much favorite horses....[95]

The editorial writer goes on to castigate gambling by young men and then turns his wrath on a match for the championship. He states: "Even in the last match for the championship between the Atlantics of Brooklyn and the Unions of Morrisania, there have been vague hints of treachery and trickery, and the players who lose, come forth from the contest without honor to be told of 'stained escutcheons' and similar unpleasant things."[96]

VI. The Disreputable Image of Baseball

In an editorial in the *Brooklyn Eagle* in 1868, previewing the upcoming season, the writer had this to say about championship matches:

> For years, the *Eagle* has argued against championship matches: it argued, first, that these games were inducing betting, gambling, the buying of players and the system of gate money. Having argued against these matters, it has had the mortification of seeing these evils which it has predicted come into full force. The whole interest seems to have settled upon the question — Who will be the champions this year? What a mistake.[97]

In 1869, an editorial writer for the *New York Times* comments more approvingly on championships:

> All sports have their championship contests, and though the system is anything but productive of good to the game, custom seems to sanction the efforts of base-ball clubs to become the champion organization of the country. At any rate, the leading matches of each season are those in which the ownership of the "whip pennant" seems to be the great end in view, and this season the battles in the championship arena bid fair to be of extraordinary interest and greatly exciting in their character.[98]

The press in one breath would condemn the idea of playing for the championship and then in another breath would suggest ways in which the championship could be better implemented.

The uniqueness of baseball was recognized by a writer for the *New York Times* in 1870. It was "entirely unlike any game of ball previously known and took the title of our National Game."[99] The writer goes on to stress that the "trouble" with baseball has risen from playing "match games for the championship."[100] But earlier in the year the *Times* was endorsing ways in which the championship should be decided. An editorial writer notes:

> One of the great professional events of the coming season will be the grand Tournament which will take place early in September on the Capitoline Base-Ball Grounds, Brooklyn, the object of the tourney being to settle the question of the championship for 1870. In this tourney the four clubs who hold the leading position at that time will be the contestants, and the games played will be six, one each day, thus having a gala week of first-class play. The club which wins three of the six games will be the champion. The four clubs which have lost the fewest series of games — best two out of three — up to September will alone enter the lists.[101]

Henry Chadwick, commenting on championships, demonstrates his understanding of the inherent contradictions in the quest for supremacy:

> The desire to excel, though an incentive to exertions for the promotion of the most virtuous ends, is also the motive which sometimes leads to results quite the reverse. A club may desire to excel as gentlemanly exponents of the game, while another may care only to win the emblem of success no matter by what means attained. This is the difference of the motives governing amateur and professional organizations. With the one the incentive is to earn the reputation of being the most courteous, liberal and manly experts known in baseball; with the other to gain the championship ball or belt is the main object in view, and that is only sought as a means to an end, pecuniary success being the real incentive.[102]

The Impact of the Championship on Baseball

For most of the 1860s, the press was critical of the quest for the championship. However, toward the end of the sixties and into the early seventies, the press was less consistent and less rigorous in its condemnation of championship matches; equivocation rather than righteous indignation marked their commentaries. The realization of economic self- interest on the part of the press from increased interest in reading about baseball, widespread betting on baseball, and the popularity of championship games, contributed to a softening of views in the press toward championships.[103] Clubs contesting for the championship provided an emotional context in which symbolic meanings were collectively constructed. Championship matches highlighted the symbolic importance of competitive striving, displays of skill, and the significance of victory, all of these were intimately related to vicarious identification with players by the baseball public. A strong sense of community and national pride surrounded the winner of the championship pennant. Consequently, the diverse moral and structural issues which were raised concerning having a championship were overshadowed by the quest for the championship. Furthermore, it is likely that the criticism of baseball in connection with championships acted as a "stimulus" to the growth of baseball.[104]

The Moral Image of Baseball

By the 1870s, baseball players were recognized as skillful and the recipients of monetary remuneration. These characteristics were known through direct observation and reports in the press. However, it cannot be said that an unambiguous moral image of organized baseball existed at this time. Events in baseball and the opprobrium directed toward professional athletics precluded this. The lack of a clear moral image of baseball is derived from a collective process which was primarily dependent upon the influence of the press for the formation of ideas within the baseball public. In this context, a complex of interrelated symbols and moral ideas was created in accord with events occurring in baseball. This resulted in a moral ambivalence toward organized baseball. Previously established negative attitudes toward professional athletics influenced the views of both the press and the baseball public in reference to practices such as compensation, benefit matches, sharing gate receipts, and salaries. In addition, substitution, revolving, and real or alleged acts of corruption added to the "moral framework" by which actions in baseball were judged.[105] Valuations by the baseball public, while primarily dependent upon the press, were also influenced by group interactive processes. Here the exchange of opinions, the imparting of information, and the spread of gossip all contributed to the construction of meanings pertinent to the moral image of baseball. While these processes were fundamental, other factors were also instrumental in engendering an ambivalence toward baseball.

In this period, praise and condemnation of baseball waxed and waned in the press. The vacillation was due in part to events such as championship matches, the substantiation of collusion among three players to throw a game, baseball tours, particularly the Cincinnati Red Stocking tour, and the rise of star players. These events and other similar ones served as a basis for the fluctuating sentiments for and against baseball expressed in the press. Alternating views of baseball were also related to sportswriters' inclinations to cry "fix" when inconsistent play appeared, particularly in championship matches. Their skepticism turned into a generalized suspicion. However, a lack of proof of fraudulent acts, with one exception, and a growing cognizance of the "glorious uncertainties" of playing baseball helped temper their suspicions.

The commercialization of baseball was another factor that played a part in clouding the moral image of the game. The momentum of commercial interests gave rise to a self-fulfilling prophecy: playing for money debases and corrupts people in baseball. Thus, commercialism amplified and tended to "deviantize" actions and events in baseball.[106] Notwithstanding this tendency, the baseball player did not have a "master status" as a deviant.[107] His disreputable actions had not yet hardened into a deviant identity.[108] His status was a dual one. In Klapp's formulation he was both hero and villain.[109] Following Klapp's reasoning, this duality emanates from roles and values that both the hero and villain share. Both roles depend upon agility of thought, aggressive action, and the ability to confront and overcome obstacles. Thus, the baseball player could be viewed simultaneously as hero and villain depending upon reportage of events in baseball and subsequent group interactive processes. The consequence of this was a state of structured ambivalence. Ambivalence did not prevent the baseball public from supporting baseball.

From a social-psychological perspective, it is plausible that the baseball public was able to reduce "dissonance" between negative projections of baseball and the irresistible attraction of the game.[110] The capacity of the baseball spectacle to evoke emotional reactions and the intense interest engendered by the press helped the baseball public suspend and transcend moral judgments against the game.[111] This did not mean that the baseball public was not ambivalent toward baseball, but when it came to taking action they supported baseball in the following ways: attendance at matches; the purchase of sport periodicals, baseball guides, newspapers, and sporting equipment; and purchase of stock in new professional clubs.

African-Americans in Baseball: The Early Years

The processes of affirmation, negation, and disassociation of ideas related to baseball were fundamental to the etching of the image of professional baseball in the press and the baseball public. Taking into account that these collective processes were occurring in the antebellum and Reconstruction periods, it is pertinent to ask whether the press attempted to disassociate white *organized* baseball clubs from "Negro" baseball clubs and whether these clubs affected the emergence of the image of professional baseball. It is difficult to shed light on answers to these questions because information about Negroes in baseball in the antebellum period is limited. One sports historian tells us, "Nothing is known about the earliest Negro clubs."[112] Another sports historian makes a similar point: "Little information exists about blacks who played on white teams in the 1870s."[113] Notwithstanding the paucity of data, there is enough information to suggest that because of racial discrimination, Negroes were excluded from *organized baseball* before and after the Civil War. However, Negroes played baseball in the 1840s, and by 1859, they established a number of clubs. Some of these were the Unknown of Weekville, the Henson, and the Monitor. They were followed by the Uniques and the Union. Both of these clubs were from Brooklyn. In the late 1850s, in Albany, the Bachelors were formed, followed by the Excelsior, the Pythians, and L'Overture formed in Philadelphia.[114] In the early 1870s the Blue Stockings of St. Louis and Chicago and the Uniques of Chicago were formed.

The exclusion of Negroes from organized baseball stems from the Nominating Committee of the National Association of Base Ball Players, who in 1867 declared:

> It is not presumed by your Committee that any club who have applied are composed of persons of color, or any portion of them; and the recommendations of your Committee in this report are based upon this view, and they unanimously report against admission of any club which may be composed of one or more colored persons.[115]

In 1868, *Beadle's Dime Base-Ball Player* noted that the object was "to keep out of the convention the discussion of any subjects having a political bearing, as this undoubtedly had."[116] The status of Negroes in baseball was certainly political in 1867, but it was likely that the reason for excluding them was racial discrimination rather than a political consideration. Seymour has pointed out that the reason for exclusion of Negroes was cloaked in evasive language. The Nominating Committee gave this reason: "If colored clubs were admitted there would be in all probability some division of feeling, whereas, by excluding them no injury could result to anybody, and the possibility of any rupture being created on political grounds would be avoided."[117]

Although Negroes were excluded from organized baseball, they started their own teams and played against each other. In October 1867, the *Brooklyn Daily Union* announced a series of games to be played by the Excelsiors of Philadelphia, a Negro team, with two other Negro clubs: the Uniques and the Monitors of Brooklyn. The *Daily Union* reported:

VI. The Disreputable Image of Baseball

> These organizations are composed of very respectable colored people, well-to-do in the world ... and include many first class players. The visitors will receive all due attention from their colored brethren of Brooklyn; and we trust, for the good of the fraternity, that none of the "white trash" who disgrace white clubs, by following and brawling for them, will be allowed to mar the pleasure of these social colored gatherings.[118]

The *Daily Union* reported unfavorably on the first of these games. It noted that the Excelsiors defeated the Uniques by the score of 42 to 37 and also commented that a "pretty rough crowd" attended the game. The writer goes on to say, "The contest was in no way creditable to the organizations" and "in fact put us in mind of the old style of nines which used to prevail among the white clubs."[119]

Unfortunately, due to limited number of press reports in this period about Negroes and organized baseball, it is difficult to address the notion that the press disassociated itself from Negro baseball clubs or whether the press tried to negate reports of Negroes playing baseball. It appears, nevertheless, that for the most part, the press ignored Negro baseball at this time. And when they did report on it, the patronizing tone of the report suggests an undercurrent of racism. Whatever other reports exist in the press, we may speculate that if the writers did not attempt to negate Negro baseball, they were certainly unlikely to embrace it.[120]

Substitution, revolving, and championship contests evoked the scorn of sportswriters, but the most vitriolic attacks came when the press suspected there were fraudulent practices underfoot. It is difficult, if not impossible, to separate those instances where it is likely that fraud was practiced and those situations where incompetent play was simply the culprit. In this period of time (1850–1870), the most that can be said is that while corruption did exist, it seems it was practiced by a small minority of players and clubs. Despite the difficulty of establishing the reality of fraud then or now, the baseball public, while ambivalent toward the baseball player and baseball, still supported the growth of the game. This should not be too surprising. Parrington has noted America's fondness for the sharpster and an underlying desire for the "human race ... to be humbugged."[121] Therefore the duality of the baseball player represents just another cultural anomaly.

Moreover, it is likely that the furor in the press over gambling by players, and suspicions of fraudulent play, contributed to the popularity of the game by intensifying interest in the outcome of particular matches. Sensationalism has usually had an irrepressible effect upon people's interest in public events.[122] Recognition by the press of the widespread interest in wagering on baseball contributed toward a modification of their views toward people betting on matches. This softening by the press of their views on gambling by spectators may have contributed to the duality of the image of professional baseball.

The upshot of these conflicting ideas about baseball was that the baseball public was able to accommodate to a duality in which the baseball player was both hero and villain. The vacillation of negative and positive valuations in the press helped determine and sustain a state of structured ambivalence, but did not prevent the support by the baseball public of the professional game.

VII

Compensation and Image in Professional Baseball

Paralleling the formation of the skillful image of the baseball player in the press, another representation of the player emerged: the player as a recipient of monetary compensation. From the 1860s until the present, the question of monetary compensation has been a dominant issue in baseball reportage. Today the question is: are players being paid too much? In baseball's infancy, the question was whether or not players should be compensated at all. However, players were compensated. The forms of compensation ranged from indirect payments through "benefit matches" and the sharing of gate receipts, to direct payment (although covert), no-show jobs, and later salaries.[1]

The objective of this chapter is to explore and analyze the various representations of compensation to players in the press. These representations of compensation were crucial to the formation of the image of professional baseball. Therefore, we would like to know when and under what conditions compensation to players started. What were the key issues involved in compensating players? Were changes in the social and occupational background of players an impetus to the payment of players? What effect did compensation to players have on the image of professional baseball? How did the press define amateur and professional baseball? What was the image of professional baseball?

Precursor of Direct Payment to Players: The "Benefit Match"

In the first half of the decade of the 1860s, direct payment to players in the form of salaries appears to have been a limited practice. It is difficult to determine who the first players were to be paid. Since the practice was covert, data are not available to make an accurate determination. However, baseball historians have suggested that James Creighton was the first salaried player, possibly receiving payments starting either in 1859 or 1860, with Al Reach being the second to receive payment in 1863.² Another form of compensation, the "benefit match," was more prevalent in the early 1860s than the payment of salaries to players.³ This practice started in the early 1860s, apparently following the established practice of holding benefit matches for cricket players. Generally, benefit matches were post-season games, arranged between all-star teams formed for the purpose of honoring prominent players. In baseball, a benefit match was also referred to as an "exhibition match" or a "social game" (a semantic device used to circumvent the prohibition against compensation by the NABBP).⁴ These games were usually announced in the press where the names of participating players were given. Admission proceeds from these contests were donated to the persons being honored.

The press was often critical of benefit matches in cricket and baseball. A writer for the *Spirit of the Times,* in an editorial on a cricket benefit match, remarked that players who were "announced" in the press as participants did not appear and, because of this, the game was delayed until late in the afternoon when a sufficient number of players arrived to constitute a match. The writer also states:

> The affair was a total failure, and such, we predict, will be the result of any future attempt to build up a system of begging, under the specious guise of a benefit. If men cannot afford time for play, they had better forego the pleasure; and if any club thinks it necessary to employ a player, let him be paid, and paid handsomely, too, but do not reduce him to a level with a beggar, by sending him round with his hat in his hand from house to house and from man to man, begging for fifty cents.⁵

It should be noted that some cricketers were paid salaries at this time; therefore, the gist of the above quotation is directed toward the ambiguity of the status of players who received compensation through benefit matches rather than receiving outright salaries. Apparently, following the practice of benefit matches in cricket, James Creighton and Dick Pierce, two prominent baseball players, were honored by a benefit match in 1861. What follows are the announcements and subsequent reports of the playing of the match which appeared in the *Brooklyn Eagle* and the *New York Clipper.* Starting in October 1861, an article appeared in the *Brooklyn Eagle* under the heading of "Benefit Matches." The writer stated:

> We understand that there is some talk of a match, between the pick nine in the Silver Ball Contest, and the Brooklyn Side, to play with a pick nine selected from the Exercise, Excelsior, Atlantic, Enterprise, Hamilton and Eckford clubs, this match is to take place on the seventh of November, on the St. George's ground at Hoboken. The price of admission is to be ten cents and is for the benefit of Creighton and Pierce. Who won't go.⁶

The following day the *Eagle* carried another story about the upcoming benefit match. A writer noted:

VII. Compensation and Image in Professional Baseball 117

In yesterday's *Eagle* a paragraph stated that a match was talked of, for the benefit of Messrs. Richard Pierce, of the Atlantics, and James Creighton, of the Excelsior Club. We have not as yet learned the full particulars regarding the arrangements. The gentlemen for whom the benefit is gotten up, are well known to the Base Ball Fraternity, the names of Pierce and Creighton being names of players not to be forgotten, the latter noted for his superior pitching.... [The] two are to share the proceeds, and to judge from the large circle of their acquaintances, the proceeds will amount to something handsome.[7]

Several days later, another article appeared in the *Eagle* in reference to the Creighton and Pierce benefit game. It advocated the upcoming match on the basis that the aforementioned players, because of their service to the game, should be honored. After noting the names of the teams and players who would be playing, the writer goes on to point out:

The St. Georges are going, we believe, to charge Messrs. Creighton and Pierce one third of the amount raised for the use of their grounds. Now by the time one third has been deducted from the proceeds, and numerous other little items paid for, unless the capital amounts to something large, we are afraid the whole proceeds will not amount to enough to pay the expenses of going and coming, much less aiding them this winter. The affair deserves patronage, and we hope those who have witnessed the many matches these two gentlemen have participated in, will not grudge to pay the ten cents demanded of them for admission. If he does he is no true ball player and we can hardly credit the rumor about the St. Georges charging for the ground. As no intoxicating liquors will be permitted to be sold, school boys will find a trip over to witness the match not only beneficial but also pleasant.[8]

The *Eagle* reported the results of the match. The "first nine" won over the "second nine" 17 to 7.[9] The report was critical of the failure of "announced" players who "failed to be present" and was generally disparaging of the idea of benefit matches.[10] An editorial in the *New York Clipper*, in reference to the match, sounded a similar note:

Indeed from the comparatively slim attendance of spectators, we should judge these benefit matches do not find favor in the ball playing community, free contests being the order of the day among them. There were no less than ten players absent out of the two nines originally appointed to play, among them every member of the Eckford Club.... Had the two nines, originally named as the contestants been present it might have been different; as it was, however, there was no object in view, of sufficient importance, to act as an incentive to extra effort on the part of those engaged in the match, and hence it turned out to be a comparatively tame affair. Matches between rival clubs, or between selected nines from separate localities in which the trapping is simply the ball used on the occasion; and the incentive, the honor derived from a credible victory are legitimate affairs yielding interesting and exciting contests; but when we depart from these, and bring other influences to bear, in which self interest, in a pecuniary point of view is likely to become prominent, an element is at once introduced that is undoubtedly injurious in its results, to the best interests of the game.[11]

Although the benefit or the exhibition match continued throughout the

1860s, the press continued its criticism of the practice, focusing its ire on the promoters' motives for these games. An editorial in the *New York Clipper*, commenting on a benefit match, the writer pointed out:

> The result was not quite as satisfactory to those who had been induced to put in an appearance as spectators by the attractive announcement of "a grand match between the Atlantic nine and a pick nine of New York and New Jersey." The real object, however, was far the less praiseworthy, it being no more nor less than a speculation for the pecuniary advantage of those of the club who seemed to think that the sole end and aim of base ball is to make money.[12]

In addition to the injunction against player compensation, the above editorial is also critical of the raising of the admission price from ten cents to twenty-five cents and the danger of baseball being subverted by corruption. The editorial writer goes on to state:

> Benefit matches are another thing, they are altogether a different matter. In fact, it is neither more nor less than making base ball a business instead of recreation. By and by, the game — if this rule is carried out — will be played according to regular Hippodrome tactics of certain turf parties and we shall have our matches marked by just such discreditable scenes as we have had to record on one instance already this season.[13]

The practice of exhibition and benefit matches continued throughout the 1860s and into the early 1870s. So did criticisms of them continue. In a *New York Times* editorial, a writer's charges of corruption are directed toward the practice of the benefit match:

> The most proficient players in the country, adopting the game as a profession, are now employed by many of the clubs at salaries ranging from one thousand to two thousand five hundred dollars a season. They relinquish all other business, and even travel throughout the country, giving exhibitions of their skill. Although nominally known as "match games" these are strictly exhibitions as circus performances. The clubs not only contend for the amount received for the admission of spectators, but in many instances they are accompanied by "friends" not only willing but anxious to make wagers upon the results, which they are pretty sure to win.[14]

Despite the criticisms directed toward the practice of benefit and exhibition matches in the press, one of the consequences of these reports was that they had the implicit effect of introducing the following idea to the baseball public: skillful players should be compensated for their playing ability and for the time and effort needed to be a first-class player. The need to devote full-time to baseball is discussed by an editorial writer for the *Spirit of the Times*: "A first class organization in these days of ball-playing cannot be sustained by men dividing their time between business and pleasure. To play ball for pleasure is no longer a part for a man holding a prominent position in a prominent club."[15]

Henry Chadwick noted the superiority of "the regular trained profes-

VII. Compensation and Image in Professional Baseball

The first enclosed baseball field, built in 1862 in Williamsburg, Brooklyn. The grounds provided a grandstand for several hundred people and a clubhouse for three clubs. It was the home field for the Brooklyn Eckfords and the Mutuals of New York. The Atlantics of Brooklyn also played there. Woodcut courtesy John Thorn.

sional nines, who, as professionals, necessarily had more time for practice, and practice is the chief element of success in a base ball nine."[16] The continuation of benefit matches and the introduction of admission charges occurred side-by-side with the willingness of the baseball public to pay admission to see skillful play.[17] The willingness of people to pay for something they formerly had for free did not go unnoticed by those in a position to gain from this.

Admission Charges and Sharing of Gate Receipts

The emergence of direct compensation to players was facilitated by the revenues generated by charging admission to baseball games. With the exception of the 1858 Fashion Race Course game and benefit matches, games were free. Until the early 1860s, playing areas were large open fields in relatively unpopulated areas of the city. Under these conditions it was not feasible to charge admission unless the grounds could be enclosed, thereby barring a view of the game from spectators. Perhaps due to the limited success of benefit matches, William H. Cammayer, in 1862, decided to turn his skating pond into a baseball field. He fenced off the grounds, graded the field, provided rudimentary seating, and constructed a clubhouse. He permitted several teams to play on the ground, free of charge, for the right of charging ten cents admission to games. One of the teams was the Unions. After one season they persuaded Cammayer to permit sharing of gate receipts with them. Before long, sharing gate receipts between teams and owners of the playing fields became a common practice. Cammayer's playing field became known as the Union Ball Grounds. It was located in the Eastern District of Brooklyn.[18]

The Capitoline Grounds, located at Nostrand Ave., Brooklyn, New York, was the location of a game that was dubbed the 1866 championship match between the Brooklyn Atlantics and the Philadelphia Athletics. The Atlantics won 27–17. Woodcut courtesy John Thorn.

In the early spring of 1864, an article appeared in the *Brooklyn Eagle* noting: "Messrs. Weed and Decker will open their grounds at Bedford — hitherto occupied solely for skating purposes in winter — as ball grounds."[19] These grounds became known as the Capitoline Grounds in the Western District of Brooklyn. One of the teams that played at the Union Grounds was the Atlantics. They obtained permission to play on Cammayer's enclosed field. As Cammayer's receipts grew, the Atlantics, like the Unions, demanded and succeeded in gaining a share of gate receipts in 1864. The practice of sharing gate receipts continued throughout the 1860s. In 1867, "the price of admission to Brooklyn's enclosed ball fields rose from a dime to a quarter."[20]

The sharing of gate receipts was reported on throughout the 1860s. One favorite theme raised in connection with this practice was the throwing of a game in order to lengthen a series, thereby increasing the amount of money to be shared by the players. In an editorial for the *New York Clipper*, a writer comments on the deliberate extension of a championship series between the Brooklyn Atlantics and the Philadelphia Athletics:

> In view of the fact that the gate money was to be divided between the two clubs in this game, and that if the Atlantics had played to win this game they would have closed the series, but by the success of the Athletics another profitable match would

be afforded them, there are hundreds who will not believe otherwise than that the Atlantics did not care to win the game. When clubs descend to playing ball for gate money they must expect to be suspected of just such corrupt doings as marks the Hippodrome trotting races.[21]

In the same issue of the *New York Clipper*, an editor comments on a dispute over the sharing of gate receipts between the Atlantics and the Athletics. The writer points out:

In dividing the proceeds of the match on October 22nd, the expense incurred in putting up this fence was deducted by the Athletics before coming to "sharing terms." To this the Atlantics, very properly, we think, objected insofar as the fence enclosed the Athletics' ground in which the Atlantics had no interest. The Atlantics refused to accept any of the money if this extra expense was put on them mutually with the Athletics—hence the deadlock as to the third game. It should be remarked, however, that while the Athletics paid the expenses of the Atlantics to Philadelphia, the Atlantics did not pay the Athletics' expenses to New York, as they should have done. Be this as it may, a third match will have to be played before the public will believe that the whole affair is anything else than a "hippodrome arrangement."[22]

The theme that money corrupts, that teams would deliberately lose a match in order to extend a series of games into a third game, was an idea that was repeated throughout the 1860s and at other times in baseball's history. In connection with attempts to lengthen a series, a writer for the *Spirit of the Times* remarks:

Most matches are made the best two in three, and some clubs who play only to make money will contrive by collusion with their opponents, to bring about a third game on every series, when if they choose they could win in two straight games. It is this growing evil of throwing games for pecuniary motives that is bringing baseball into disrepute.[23]

Sinecures: An Indirect Form of Player Compensation

Another indirect form of compensation during the decade of the 1860s was the practice of providing sinecures for star players. These no-show jobs were made possible through corrupt city government, as in the case of the Mutuals of New York, under the auspices of Boss Tweed, or through local merchants who were baseball fans. Under the ownership of William Marcy Tweed from 1860 through 1870, the Mutuals were reputed to have placed many of their players on the city payrolls, especially the "street-cleaning department." Tweed, at this time, held several high positions in city government and his influence was widespread.[24]

Throughout the 1860s, the forms of compensation were diverse. Some players received direct compensation in the form of salaries; other players were placed in "no-show" jobs or positions where little work was required. Albert Spalding, one of the early stars of the game, recalled a typical pattern of recruitment and covert compensation to players in the 1860s. He describes how senior baseball clubs would draft the best players from their junior teams by inducing them to play with offers of covert compensation.[25] Spalding tells of going briefly to Chicago in 1867 "ostensibly to accept a clerkship in a wholesale grocery, but really to become a member of the Chicago Excelsior Base Ball Club."[26] However, because of the failure of the grocery company, he returned to Rockford, Illinois, to play with the Forest City Club. There he "received employment in the insurance office of A.N. Nicholas, secretary of the club."[27]

Spalding goes on the say that at this time "professionalism of every kind was tabu."[28] However, as far as the National Association of Base Ball Players (NABBP) was concerned, "the rule prohibiting salaries was nevertheless a dead letter. Most clubs of prominence, all over the country, had players who were either directly or indirectly receiving "financial advantages from the game."[29]

The Adoption of the Rule Prohibiting Compensation to Players

Although various forms of player compensation were practiced in the 1860s and possibly in the late 1850s, they were in direct contravention of an NABBP rule passed in 1859 which prohibited all forms of compensation to players. The rule was amended shortly afterward to include a prohibition against having other club members pay the club membership dues for a player who is in "arrears."[30]

In an article in the *New York Times,* dealing with the opening of the baseball season in 1869, the writer briefly reviews the 1859 Association rule against compensation:

> The original idea in introducing this rule was to exclude the class of professionals similar to those employed by cricket clubs from taking part in matches .... The prohibitory clause was not the result of any special opposition to playing baseball for money so much as to keep contests out of the hands of trained professionals.[31]

The writer goes on to remark on the inequality of having teams with "trained professionals" playing against "amateur organizations." He states:

> As the prohibitory rule in question during this time still continued in force, the result was the introduction of a series of practices by leading clubs to evade the rules, and, as a matter of course, the arrangements made did not redound to the credit of either the clubs or players engaged in it, as it placed them in a false position, the clubs ostensibly having an equal footing with regular amateur organizations, while in reality they enjoyed the playing advantages of having trained professional nine.... And the National Association, seeing that something must be done to save the game from losing its popularity ... repealed the law prohibiting professional players from taking part in match games.[32]

VII. Compensation and Image in Professional Baseball

The reason for the adoption of the rule and the subsequent amendment has not been explained by baseball historians. However, an editorial and an editorial reply, appearing at this time, indicate that covert compensation to players may have been the reason for the adoption of the rule. The following excerpts from this editorial and reply in the *Spirit of the Times* shed some light on the reasons for the adoption of said rule. They also illustrate arguments for and against compensation to players:

> What can it matter in the long run whether a player in a match shall receive directly or indirectly compensation for his services from the club for which he appears.... If, from any circumstances, personal or pecuniary, a lover of the sport cannot afford a day to travel from his home to play a match of cricket or base ball, and his brother members of the club are able and willing to remunerate him for his time and expenses, why should they not be permitted to do so?[33]

Seven days later, the *Spirit of the Times* printed a reply to the above editorial. The letter was from Francis Pidgeon, one of the members of the rules committee that had drafted the rule barring compensation to players. Pidgeon writes:

> My object in sending this communication is to give you the reasons why the Committee on Rules of the National Association of Base Ball Players thought it necessary to recommend the passing of Section 36 of Rules and Regulations.... As to compensation: you mistake the object of the rule entirely when you attribute the passing of it to snobbish inclinations; on the contrary, quite the reverse. We will suppose, sir, you belong to a club composed mostly of mechanics; that you had shared their victories and defeats, and became attached to them, and they to you, by those friendly ties, the existence of which is one of the charms of ball playing; how would you like to see those you depended upon to uphold the name and fame of the club bought like cattle; or if not bought, would you like to see the bribes repeatedly offered to them, to desert their colors? These things have occurred, and it was thought best to nip them in the bud and it was done without one dissenting voice.[34]

The above reply to the editor suggests that players were compensated and perhaps offered money to move on to another club before the season of 1859. The fact that the association passed a rule prohibiting compensation suggests that the practice of covertly compensating players and paying for their expenses was not an uncommon practice at this time. Furthermore, the editorial suggests that the earliest form of compensation was possibly thought of as a subsidy rather than compensation for services.

Some Issues Surrounding Salaries

The editorial and editorial reply, quoted above, constitute the opening round of a continuing controversy over compensation to players. The controversy took on greater ideological and symbolic significance in relation to the two dominant orientations to playing baseball when salaries were paid to players. Viewpoints in the press that opposed compensation, for the most part, were based on the idea that monetary compensation undermines the moral and ethical behavior of people playing baseball. This position often was associated with the fear that as baseball became a business the interests of gamblers would prevail, resulting in the collusion of players and gamblers for the purposes of defrauding the baseball public. Another argument against compensation was based on the idea that a team that had paid players had an unfair advantage over a team that did not. On the other side of the compensation issue, stories suggested that compensation to players raised the standard of playing, and since payment of players was a *fait accompli*, a separation of players into those who received compensation and those who did not would raise the dignity of the game by precluding covert payments.

The opening salvo in the press against players receiving direct compensation in the form of salaries may have started with an editorial in the *New York Clipper* in 1865. The writer states in part: "Section 38 of the rules must be adhered to or good bye to the welfare of baseball, and it cannot be as long as baseball is played for money, whether in this form, benefits or any other of the plans adopted to infringe the rule in question."[35]

A more specific charge against direct compensation to players appeared in 1866, when it was alleged that "four players of the Philadelphia Athletics received payment for playing."[36] The allegation was made in an article which the writer said in part:

> Of course it is unknown how far any club in this vicinity may be guilty of this practice [paying players] as no specific charges have been made, although there are some pretty loud whispers heard occasionally. The Athletics, however, have not escaped so easily. Col. Fitzgerald is after them with a sharp stick. He charges them directly and openly with paying four of their first nine.[37]

The writer goes on to note, "It seems hardly possible that a club of gentlemen, as the Philadelphians have been and are considered, should be guilty of a practice so injurious to the interests of the game, and so directly contrary to its rules and regulations."[38] From 1866 the issue over payment to players was discussed more openly. One of the leading opponents against direct payment to players in the 1860s was the sportswriter and member of the NABBP Rules Committee, Henry Chadwick. He points out:

> Suffice it to say this committee is unanimous in their determination to put a check upon the growing evils connected with the game which the experience of the season of 1866 has so plainly developed. The hiring principle received due attention and the facilities for changing from one club to another will be greatly abridged.[39]

VII. Compensation and Image in Professional Baseball

In 1868, Chadwick attacked the compensation of players through sinecures. He notes:

> Why, Sir, this season choice sinecures have been kept in New York City Municipal offices, especially to accommodate the professionals of the Tweed Base Ball Club, if you know which club that is. Clerkships in tax offices, inspectorships of streets, sewers, docks, and other city places have been at the disposal of Directors and Managers of the leading professional organizations of that city; and what with salaries from these positions and a due share of gate money, with occasional presents from those who win their little piles of stamps on the big games, the arrangement between the professionals and the aforesaid Directors has been mutually agreeable.[40]

Chadwick changed his position in the early 1870s and advocated payment to players. Nevertheless, he was always quick to criticize the abuses connected with compensation to players. In the latter part of the 1860s, the controversy over payment of salaries to players was often contained in a recurrent theme: separation of amateurs from professionals.[41] One of the early calls for separation appeared in an article in 1866, in the *New York Clipper*. In the article the writer, in addition to calling for separation of players, points out the desirability of having "professionals" being engaged to teach the game to college students. The article also notes that the professional cricket players are the "most honest and worthy men of any class of our citizens."[42] The writer concludes by urging separation of players at the next convention. He goes on to say: "A complete stop will be put to the system of hiring players to win matches, and this is the evil that is doing the most mischief in the future welfare of the game."[43]

The advocacy of the separation of amateurs from professionals was also an attempt to resuscitate the dwindling interest in games played by less skillful teams. An editorial writer in the *Brooklyn Eagle* advocates the following:

> Let us have two classes, since it must be; one that goes the whole length of betting, informs the betting fraternity, and let *them* play in the presence of that most despicable class of our community — the betting fraternity, and let us have another class of gentlemanly players, whose matches, the gentlemanly and honorable portion of the community, who rejoice in the recollection of their glorious juvenile days, when they played base-ball, can attend without the fear of losing their watches and their pocket books. There are enough good players among gentlemen, in New York and Brooklyn to form a nine that will vanquish any professional nine in the country.... We advocate the sweeping away of all restrictions, in a pecuniary point of view, upon players. Let them make all the money they can; "let them play for place, position and emolument" and if we have gentleman players, and we know we have them, let them step forward, and from the *bastard* ball players, let them wrest all their ill-got honors.[44]

Later in the year, a similar plea was made by a writer in an editorial appearing in the *Spirit of the Times*. It states in part:

> Since the play of last season and the present has drawn the line so wide between professional and social clubs, why not consolidate the first class players of the social organizations into one club, and let them strive for supremacy over the professionals? Something of this kind must be done or the institution of base-ball will die out....[45]

However, the following year a writer for the *Spirit of the Times* had this to say in regard to "the professional question":

> It does not appear that the paying of men to play ball has interfered with the game. Nor that it has brought the game to be a mere vehicle for betting, as was prophesied last spring. Nor has it robbed the game of its interest. Under professionalism we have seen a club organized, trained, disciplined and victorious in sixty-one encounters and we have yet to hear a charge made against its integrity.[46]

After the close of the 1868 season, the NABBP recognized that there was a class of players called "professional" and that they should be separated from the "amateurs." Reports of this resolution were carried in the press. A writer for the *New York Herald* noted:

> For the general public, however, it may be stated that the National Association, at its last meeting, drew a line which divides professionals from amateurs. There need be no more subterfuges resorted to with the idea of leading people to believe that players are not professionals and do not play ball for pecuniary considerations. No person thinks ill of an actor or an acrobat who receives a regular salary for his performance, and certainly a professional ball player should be as honored and as honorable as any other performer.[47]

Earlier in the year, the *New York Clipper* reported on the adoption of the new "amendment." The writer states in part:

> The most important amendment made to the rule was that of striking out the whole of the section prohibiting professional players from taking part in match games, and substituting a rule officially recognizing professionals as a class of players distinct from amateurs.... Since 1860 the professional system has been practically in vogue, though ostensibly all were amateur players, that is, all were unpaid for their services. But it is well known that nearly all the leading clubs—certainly all the prominent aspirants for the championship—employed professional players and the fact that the rules prohibiting the custom were mere dead letters and that also it was almost impossible to frame a law on the subject that could not be evaded.... The new rule says: "All players who play base ball for money, or who shall at any time receive compensation for their services as players, shall be considered professional players; and all others shall be regarded as amateurs."[48]

Player Compensation, Socio-Occupational Background and the Professionalization of Baseball

The impact of compensation to players and the changing composition of the socio-occupational background of players on the professionalization of baseball have not been specifically taken up by baseball historians Voigt and Seymour. At times, these historians do comment on the changing class

VII. Compensation and Image in Professional Baseball

composition of players and payment to players, but their comments are unclear insofar as how these elements bear on the professionalization of baseball. In discussing direct payment to players in 1866, Voigt observes: "This kind of remuneration for skilled players suggested that the time was not far off when young men of modest circumstances would see in a professional baseball career a chance to make something of themselves."[49] Voigt also remarks: "The professionals were often from lower status backgrounds, as indeed were the first ranked amateurs. The latter group served as a sort of a training ground for the recruitment of future professionals."[50] The observations of Voigt seem to suggest that baseball was an avenue of upward mobility with implications for status attainment in the latter part of the 1860s.

Seymour is even less specific when he comments on professional baseball and its relationship to social class and payment to players. Seymour observes: "A game can remain amateur only as long as a privileged minority plays it as an aristocratic diversion. Once those who must earn a living devote themselves to a game, it ceases to be just a pleasurable pastime, and becomes instead a serious affair."[51] Like Voigt, Seymour has not specifically identified the payment of money to players and their social background as factors which contributed to the professionalization of baseball. By their commentary, both historians imply that the payment of money to players and the changing social class composition of players were responsible for the rise of professional baseball.

Before we attempt to assess the effect of payments to players and the changes in their socio-occupational backgrounds on the professionalization of baseball, the analyses of Adelman and Riess on the socio-occupational background of baseball players will be instructive. Adelman has researched and reconstructed the occupational backgrounds of baseball players in New York and Brooklyn between 1850 and 1870.[52] He categorizes the occupational structure of baseball players into four groupings. They are: (1) "Professional High White Collar" (PHC). This group includes professional men and merchants. (2) "Low White Collar Proprietor" (LWC). This group includes shop owners and artisans. (3) "Skilled Craftsmen" (SC). This group includes masters, journeymen, and apprentices. The last category is (4) "Unskilled Workers."[53] The data are derived from players listed in "box scores," in newspapers and the *Baseball Encyclopedia*. The names derived from the foregoing sources were compared to names in "city directories," to determine the occupations of the players.[54]

During the period from 1856 to 1860, as compared to the previous five years, Adelman finds that there was a shift from PHC toward a greater representation of LWC and SC.[55] Clerks, professionals, and merchants comprised sixty-three percent of the players between 1850 and 1855. In the next five years they made up only forty-nine percent of the players. PHC constituted thirty-eight percent of the players between 1850 and 1855. However, between 1856 and 1860 their representation declined to twenty percent.[56] Thus, PHC made up one-fifth of the players, while LWC and SC constituted three-fifths of the players. Baseball was moving from a sport that was heavily represented by upper-middle-class men in the first half of the decade to one where the middle and lower-middle class ranks constituted the majority of players in the latter half of the 1850s.

Adelman also finds that in New York, between 1855 and 1860, there was an increase in the "proprietor class" in several clubs. These clubs were "composed mainly of men from the city's Fulton and Jefferson meat, fish, and poultry markets."[57] Thus, in the five years prior to the Civil War, "clerks and food industry people together made up a third of the active participants" in organized baseball.[58] "However, unskilled workers, roughly a third of the work force in each city, were virtually absent from the diamond game."[59]

Adelman concludes that baseball before the Civil War "was dominated, at least on the playing field, by clerks, a select group of proprietors, and especially skilled craftsmen."[60] He goes on to observe that these players, because of their manual occupations, were in "better physical condition,"[61] which contributed to their "dominance on the playing field."[62] He asserts that these players were drawn from particular occupational ranks that had a sporting heritage. Traditionally men had participated in fencing, bear-baiting, harness racing, and playing rackets. It is likely that they admired "physical prowess and skill."[63] Ademan goes on to note:

> The ability to excel at a physical skill or sport brought prestige and possibly influence among one's peers and within ones community.... The demonstration of physical skill in the game was therefore doubly rewarding, providing the players with prestige within the local community and within the growing community of baseball players and fans. It was the search for fame, before the search for fortune which attracted these workers to the sport.[64]

The occupational structure of New York and Brooklyn ball players between 1866 and 1870 was similar to the pattern of the previous ten-year period. Small proprietors, managers, lower level officials, sales and kindred workers, and skilled craftsmen constituted seventy-five percent of the members of the teams in the neighboring cities. Although involvement came mainly from middle and lower middle-class groups, still, approximately twenty-five percent of the players were drawn from the more high-ranking occupations. Only "one percent of the members of the New York and Brooklyn ball clubs were unskilled laborers" during this time.[65] With the onset of the acknowledgment of payment to players, Adelman suggests there was a slight change in the occupational structure of those teams that chose to be identified with payment to players. He estimates that sixty percent of these players come from the "artisan class,"[66] and "nearly forty percent of professional teams

VII. Compensation and Image in Professional Baseball   129

came from the middling group, most of whom held jobs as clerks or similar occupations."[67]

Riess has studied the ethnicity, salaries, residence, and occupations of retired baseball players between 1871 and 1882.[68] His findings are that players of the National Association of Professional Base Ball Players (NAPBBP, established in 1871) were "mainly of English descent," but were also German and Irish.[69] He points out that "only a handful from other ethnic groups, including one Cuban and two Jews," were members of the NAPBBP.[70] He goes on to note that seventy-five percent of the players (233) were born in America and six percent (20) were foreign-born. The birthplace of fifty-eight others could not be determined. Of the 233 professional baseball players studied by Riess, eighty-six percent came from cities. The players were mainly from the Northeast, particularly Brooklyn, New York, Philadelphia, and Baltimore. Out of the twenty-three teams that belonged to the NAPBBP, eight of them played in the aforementioned cities.[71] The age of professional players in the early 1810s was below thirty, with the average age being twenty-five.[72]

Income was relatively high for these professional players. The Chicago team of 1872 had three men who were paid $2,500 and four players who earned $2,000. Other less prestigious teams also paid relatively high salaries. Riess notes that "the New Haven franchise paid an average salary of $1,600 in 1875."[73] For the most part, salaries ranged from $500 to $2,500.[74] Out of the 207 ex-professional baseball players identified in Riess's study, 15.4 percent were classified as "High White-Collar" ("professionals, managers, high officials and major proprietors"); 45.5 percent were classified as "Low White-Collar" ("clerks, sales and kindred workers, semi-professionals, petty proprietors, managers and low officials"). "Blue-Collar" workers ("skilled, semi-skilled and service, and unskilled") comprised 37.7 percent, while farmers made up the remaining 1.4 percent.[75] The findings of Riess tend to confirm Adelman's conclusion that baseball in the 1860s was predominantly middle class, although the number of semiskilled and unskilled men who played for clubs was increasing.

The Cincinnati Red Stocking Team of 1869–70

The organization and tour of the Cincinnati Red Stocking team of 1869 contributed to the controversy over payment to players. The Red Stocking team was baseball's first team to acknowledge that their starting nine were paid players and that they would embark on a national tour. Baseball had long been established in Ohio, with the Gotham Baseball Club having been organized in 1852.[76] The formation of the Cincinnati Red Stocking team was due in part to the efforts of a young lawyer named Aaron B. Champion. The establishment of the Union Cricket Club of Ohio at the end of the Civil War exposed him to baseball.[77] In 1866 Champion organized and presided over the Cincinnati baseball club.[78] The first two seasons of play the team was organized on an amateur basis, but in 1868 the team took on four paid players to meet the challenge of the Buckeye Base Ball Team and other clubs. The Cincinnati baseball fans, after the defeat by the Washington Nationals in 1867, "were determined to have a winning team even if it meant paying players."[79]

Champion assigned two directors to the club. They were George B. Ellard and Alfred Gosham. They were instructed by Champion to find the best players. They did. One of these players was Harry Wright. He had previously come to the Union Cricket Club as manager in 1865 for the salary of $1,200. In 1867, for the same salary, he accepted an offer to manage and play with the Cincinnati club. By the end of 1868, Wright had obtained five men who would play on the great team of 1869. He added five more men, rounding out the team to ten players. They were Doug Allison, catcher; Asa Brainard, pitcher; Charles Gould, first baseman; Charles Sweasy, second baseman; Fred Waterman, third baseman; George Wright (brother of Harry Wright), shortstop; Cal McVey, center field; Andy Leonard, right fielder; Harry Wright, left field; and Dick Hurley, substitute.[80]

Wright believed that rigorous training and discipline were crucial to the fielding of a first-class team that would be commercially viable.[81] Champion, who was "publicity minded," arranged for Henry Millar, a writer for the *Cincinnati Commercial*, to accompany the team and send back reports to the "excited home folks."[82] Before starting off on their tour, the Reds won their first seven games at home. Traveling east, they added ten more victories before coming to New York and Brooklyn. On June 14, 1869, playing before a crowd estimated at 8,000 spectators, they triumphed over the powerful Mutuals, 4 to 2. They went on to play the best teams of the day. In the season of 1869 they were undefeated, winning fifty-six games and tying one.[83] As the team began to compile victories, the more respected periodical journals took notice. In 1869 and 1870 *Harper's* published a picture of the team. In September 1869, the Reds toured the West by train, playing in California and other states.

The following season the Cincinnati team started another impressive string of victories. They won their first twenty-seven games. However, on the Capitoline Grounds in Brooklyn, their consecutive number of wins was ended by the Atlantics of Brooklyn, who defeated the Reds in eleven innings by the score of 8 to 7.[84] The *Cincinnati Commercial* called it "the finest game on record."[85] The report of the game is both a tribute to the Cincinnati baseball team and to baseball. It reads in part:

> Since 1868, the noted Red Stocking Nine of the Cincinnati Club has escaped defeat in every game they have played up to June 14, 1870, and during the interim they have earned a reputation any club might feel proud of, not only for their masterly display as willful experts in the game, but also for their fair and manly efforts to

VII. Compensation and Image in Professional Baseball 131

win for the honor of victory, aside from any temptations offered by the dollar and cent influence in the form of extra gate money, contests, or "betting ring" arrangements. On their third eastern tour, they entered the metropolis victorious in every encounter since they left home and in their first match with the Champion club of New York City they came out of the conflict victorious, after having given our citizens a model display of the beauties of baseball.

On Tuesday, June 14th, however, they for the first time met their equals in the field, and after a game played in masterly style on both sides in a majority of innings they were obliged to succumb to the superior play of their opponents; but it was a defeat they had no need to be ashamed of, for never before in the annals of the Atlantic Club did the Brooklyn Nine make so fine a display of fielding and scientific batting....[86]

After their defeat to the Atlantics, the Reds also lost to the Philadelphia Athletics and to the Chicago White Stockings later that year. After these defeats, "interest fell off sharply both at home and abroad."[87] With the announcement by Harry Wright that he planned to join the Boston team in 1871, the Cincinnati team management decided to disband under pressure of its stockholders. In November of 1870, the new president-elect of the Cincinnati club announced that he would not field another salaried team because of "outbreaks of jealousy among players and stockholders," but would field an amateur nine for the season of 1871.[88]

Despite the demise of the Red Stockings (they were reorganized in the mid–1870s), they had demonstrated the superiority of carefully selected paid players, and had influenced the formation of other teams on a commercial basis. In 1870, eleven teams existed that either paid players outright or permitted players to share in gate receipts.[89]

The successful tour of the paid players of the Cincinnati Red Stocking team gave proponents of "professional" baseball an additional argument to further their advocacy of hiring players. *The New York Clipper* reports on a meeting held for the purpose of reorganizing the Boston team on a "professional" basis for the season of 1871. One of the club's executives, Ivers W. Adams, had this to say:

> There is really not the slightest reasonable objection which can be made to professional baseball playing pursued in its integrity; on the contrary, much can be said in its favor.... Not a breath of suspicion, not a blot upon the fair escutcheon of the Cincinnati Club can be charged.... The fact is, if the admirers of the game in the city desire to see base ball played as it should be, they must look to a well-managed professional nine to gratify them ... amateurs ... cannot spare the time or attention to attaining the success at the command of a well-organized professional nine....[90]

In his remarks, Adams also dwells on the aesthetics associated with the performance of paid players and goes on to attempt to disabuse "people" of the "erroneous notions" connected with "professional" ball playing. He states:

> It is only through the medium of a disciplined, well-trained, professional nine that the fielding beauties of the game can be fully presented. In the field meetings of

such a nine, managed with a view solely to developing the attractive features of base ball and presenting to the pleasure-seeking public an exciting out-door sport, free from the objectionable surroundings and evils connected with nearly every other of our great public sports.... It is about time that the erroneous notions which some people have got into their heads that professional ball playing means gambling and rowdyism and to have anything to do with that class of ball players is to countenance betting ring contests, and "hippodrome" matches for gate money, should be given up as a mistaken idea.[91]

Player Compensation and the Image of Professional Baseball

The introduction of diverse forms of compensation to players (especially direct payment to them) helped to symbolically polarize those orientations that either espoused playing baseball for money or for fun. Gusfield's analysis of the legal prohibition of the sale of alcoholic beverages and the repeal of the Volstead Act in the United states theoretically parallels the conflict that arose in baseball. He observes that drinking became a symbolic "focus for the conflict between Protestant and Catholic, rural and urban, native and immigrant, middle-class and lower-class in American society."[92]

Similarly, money became a symbolic focus for the conflict between the two different orientations to playing baseball. For those who clung to the belief that baseball should be played as a polite form of social recreation, payment indicated that the player was "an object of oneself," and this was in itself a "degrading act."[93] Organized baseball from this standpoint was contaminated and, therefore, could no longer provide an effective vehicle for conspicuous leisure for those who desired it for that reason. On the other hand, playing baseball for money symbolized consummate skill, a vocational commitment, and esteem within the baseball public. However, earning money also signified occupational work rather than a social form of esteemed leisure.

The introduction of diverse forms of compensation to players in organized baseball coincided with an earlier trend that saw the diminution of upper-middle and middle class men from the ranks of organized baseball. The depletion of professionals, merchants, shop owners, and artisans, starting in the 1850s, was primarily due to the changing nature of the game, which was epitomized by increasing competition and a growing emphasis on victory. Voight and Seymour imply that the professionalization of baseball was due to the influx of working-class men who were attracted to baseball due to economic and social opportunities as a means to advance themselves.[94] If I have interpreted these historians correctly, their scenario is incorrect for the following reasons. Payment to players before the late 1860s was covert, and the practice of indirect compensation was only for a selected few. Therefore, it

VII. Compensation and Image in Professional Baseball 133

is doubtful that the lure of financial gain was the principal reason that prompted young men to enter baseball in the 1850s and 1860s. It is more likely that baseball afforded a temporary romantic excursion before taking on the rigors of a "real job."[95] Or, as Chadwick suggested, the lure of playing before "three or four thousand" people was an "enticement."[96] Voigt's and Seymour's references to pecuniary gain and upward mobility as reasons for young men entering baseball are more applicable to the 1870s than the 1860s.

Adelman, writing about the reason for youths entering baseball in the 1870s, supports this contention. He observes:

> While middle class youths, like skilled craftsmen, were attracted to professional baseball by the high salaries, the evidence suggested that they were less likely to view the sport as a career. Star players ... stayed in the sport for the big money. The average white-collar ballplayer, however, remained in the sport only briefly because of the uncertainty of paydays from time to time, the drudgery of travel, and the low prestige of the profession.[97]

In the late 1850s and into the 1860s, it was not so much that organized baseball was taken over by pecuniary-minded members of the "lower classes" who wanted to use baseball as a means for upward mobility, as Voigt and Seymour imply.[98] But it was primarily a repudiation of organized baseball by upper-middle and middle-class men, and secondly it was the formation of junior clubs and clubs which were formed mostly of workingmen, that contributed to the changing socio-occupational composition of players in baseball.

At this time, those men who espoused the play ethic became disenchanted with the direction in which baseball was heading and consequently withdrew from organized baseball. The resignation of James Whyte Davis, one of the oldest members of the Knickerbockers, suggests that some members of the club were relinquishing their membership because of a growing disenchantment with various practices, especially the practice of compensation to players.[99] Davis resigned from the Knickerbockers because they consented to play in a match where admission was to be charged, even though the club refused to partake in a sharing of the gate receipts. In his resignation letter, Davis stresses that the practice of charging admission had "desecrated time honored principles of playing Base Ball for health and recreation merely."[100]

As competition amongst clubs grew, the older clubs (Eagle, Empire, etc.) began to establish "junior organizations" whose purpose was to provide recruits for the senior clubs.[101] Since members of the junior organizations were usually under the age of twenty-one, it is reasonable to assume that their youth permitted a relaxation of the requirement that candidates for membership be of a "certain social standing" and be able to "meet the various financial obligations which membership entailed: dues, fees, purchase of uniforms, and assessments to cover deficits in the treasury."[102] However, it is likely that the overriding consideration was their playing ability.

The lessening of restrictive admission policies for junior organizations accompanied a similar flexibility within senior clubs' admission policies. Adelman notes that, in response to a greater emphasis on victory, the Excelsiors took on players "whose economic and social standing were less well off" than previously admitted members.[103] Seymour also remarks that "even the Knickerbockers were paying less attention to the social status of new members and more to their ball-playing ability. They stopped bothering to record the occupations of recruits, and required them to show what they could do in a few games before "being accepted."[104] In the latter part of the 1850s, the formation of baseball clubs that were mainly composed of shipwrights, mechanics, butchers, tradesmen and other manual occupational groups helped to change the socio-occupational composition of organized baseball. In brief, increasing competition and the importance of victory were fundamental reasons which contributed to both the disenchantment and withdrawal of those players who espoused the play ethic, and opened the door for the entrance of players from lower socio-occupational backgrounds. Payment to players was only a concomitant to a process underway, and not in itself a primary reason for professional baseball.

The 1870s: A Time for Decisions in Organized Baseball

In the beginning of the 1870s, baseball faced a time when unrest and instability pervaded the game. At the center of the unrest was indecision amongst many clubs as to whether they should fully endorse payment to players and field a paid nine, or resist the pay-for-play movement and field an unpaid nine, or some combination thereof. At the close of the 1870 season, an article describing this state of uncertainty in organized baseball appeared in the *New York Clipper*. The writer noted:

> Before the ball season of 1870 was brought to a finale the various professional clubs were becoming partitioned, dismembered, cut and slashed.... The wildest statements have been made with an air of truth well calculated to mislead parties who have not made themselves acquainted with all the minutiae by which our national game is run. The players according to these mis-statements are to undergo a general change.... Professional clubs are to be transmogrified into amateurs and vice versa.... Joint stock concerns are to be made out of some, with a cash capital of thousands of dollars, and much more of the same sort. For a few of these reports there may have been some little foundation, but in a general sense they are destitute of truth, having their origin in the lively imagination of gentlemen who write for the papers. It is entirely too early to say, with any degree of accuracy, what our clubs intend doing, or what changes our professional players contemplate.[105]

VII. Compensation and Image in Professional Baseball 135

The following year, an article in the *Brooklyn Eagle* bespeaks of the uncertainty besetting the Atlantics, one of the more prominent clubs of the time. The writer states in part:

> There is a division in the ranks of this club at present which is anything but advantageous to its interests. A large party of the old members of the club, now that nearly all the old members of their professional nine have joined other organizations, are in favor of the club playing upon an amateur basis, at least for the present season.... On the other hand there is a party desirous of having the club take the field on a co-operative basis, as hitherto, and raising the best nine they can from volunteers, and go in for gate money receipts. Between the two parties nothing has as yet been decided.[106]

In the same edition of the *Brooklyn Eagle*, a brief notice announced that the Excelsior Club "Will take the field early this spring, with the strongest amateur nine they have presented for some years past.... They have plenty of means at command and to make them independent of gate-money receipts; either to help pay for grounds or to pay expenses on tours; and they intend running their club on an entirely independent and regular amateur basis."[107]

Contributing to the confusion in baseball at this time was the distinction made by the National Association of Baseball Players (NABBP) in 1868 whereby "amateurs" and "professionals" were separated into distinct categories, and the collapse of the NABBP in 1871.[108] Writing about the impact of the separation between amateurs and professionals on organized baseball, a reporter for the *New York Times* comments:

> This radical change in the status of clubs and players has already had an immensely beneficial effect on the amateur organizations throughout the country — the results, in fact, being the kindling of quite an amateur revival.... With the amateur revival will come increased interest in the contests of professional clubs, as now all their efforts to excel can be made openly and honorably, which before was not exactly the case, inasmuch as they had to violate express laws of the game to play professional nines.[109]

The foregoing optimism for an amateur revival was short lived. In 1871, the National Association of Base Ball Players was replaced by the National Association of Amateur Base Ball Players. This occurred after the former association called two meetings and failed to get a quorum at either meeting, due to the irreconcilable differences between representatives of the pay-for-play movement and those who opposed it. The new association took on the rules of the old association, maintaining the prohibition against compensation; however, the question of gate receipts produced heated debate amongst club representatives. Some teams threatened to withdraw if gate receipts were prohibited. A compromise was reached which permitted clubs on tour to collect gate receipts.[110] Not to be outdone, ten clubs met, also in 1871, and formed the National Association of Professional Base Ball Players. By the end of 1870, twenty clubs had paid players.[111]

As the terms amateur and professional baseball took on more definite meanings, the influence of amateur baseball on the baseball public declined. Part of the reason for this was the superior play of the professionals, but in addition, the instability of the amateurs, due to unresolved problems within their circle, contributed to their demise as a power in baseball. It was thought that both the newly formed amateur and professional associations would thrive side-by-side, but this was not to be. The best players moved to the professional clubs. Stimulated by press and telegraph reports, the activities of the professionals overshadowed the amateurs, and soon, they dominated baseball. Within a short time, the amateur association declined and disbanded. Referring to the future of commercial baseball, a writer for the *Sporting Times*, in 1870, offered a prognosis: "To what extent this business of professional playing may grow is not easy to see. The public interest in the game is evidently on the increase, and the press year by year is forced to devote a continually increasing space to the reports of important matches. It is a means of livelihood which is peculiarly fascinating to those who dislike the routine of office or mercantile life...."[112]

The *New York Clipper*, in an 1870 an editorial, writer commented on the declining power of amateur baseball in the NABBP:

> A glance at the present position of affairs shows the existence of laxity in the observance of the rules and regulations of the game established by the National Association and neglect of their duties by regular members of the association anything but advantageous to the best interests of baseball, or creditable to the majority of the leading clubs belonging to the association.... Now within the past four years the singular anomaly has been exhibited in the business of base ball legislation of a decided and marked control being held of the majority by the minority; or, in other words, some twenty odd professional clubs managed to gain possession of the power in the Annual Convention of the National Association to rule the representatives of ten times the number of amateur organizations.[113]

The above writer goes on to accurately predict that the NABBP would cease to exist if the rules governing representatives by state delegates were not amended to give equal representation to those states that were underpopulated insofar as baseball clubs were concerned. The article is alluding to the ability of the relatively large number of professional baseball clubs in New York State, compared to other states, to exert discriminatory influence over amateur clubs.

Attempts by the Press to Define the Terms Amateur and Professional

The press did not use the terms amateur or professional to describe the playing of organized baseball in the 1850s. Neither did the first association of baseball clubs refer to themselves as an amateur association. They were

VII. Compensation and Image in Professional Baseball 137

named, simply, the National Association of Base Ball Players. The press this time referred to players as "gentlemen" and the playing of baseball was noted as a "manly pastime" or a "noble pastime."[114] Since there was only one category of player and one overarching orientation to playing baseball, there apparently was no need to invoke the term amateur. But as the game of baseball changed, so did the descriptions used to refer to it. Prior to 1865 the term amateur is infrequently used; however, it can be found in editorials in the *Brooklyn Eagle* in 1864.[115]

One of the early references to the changing description of playing baseball appeared in a report of a match between the Empire and Star Clubs in 1863. Although the writer does not use the terms amateur or professional, his contrasting use of the terms "seriousness" and "fun" is tantamount to the use of the ideas of professional and amateur. He states:

> A commendable feature of this game was the thorough good humor that characterized the proceedings throughout on both sides. We have been so accustomed of late to see ball matches played with a degree of earnestness and seriousness that would lead one to think that the contest was a business of the first importance rather than a recreation, that it was quite a treat to see the contestants on this occasion play as if they enjoyed themselves and had come on the ground to have some fun.[116]

In the latter part of the decade of the sixties, the press used the terms amateur and professional more frequently. The *Brooklyn Eagle*, in a lengthy editorial in 1868 called for a separation of clubs into "two classes." The editorial writer states:

> Let those clubs which propose to win the championship, at the risk of honor and respect, notify the association that they are candidates for the championship; and those clubs which propose to make base ball the game of the gentlemanly youth of America, say that they will play the game in its purity; not for gate money, not for telling purposes, not for the empty honors of championship, but for the honor, the reputation and the manliness of the club to which they belong, and the honor, the reputation of the players themselves. Let us have *two classes,* since it must be, one that goes the whole length of betting, and forms the betting fraternity, and let *them* play in the presence of that most despicable class of our community — the betting fraternity, and let us have another class of gentlemanly players whose matches the gentlemanly and honorable portion of community who rejoice in the recollection of their glories.[117]

Later in the year, the *Spirit of the Times* used the term "social clubs" instead of amateur in reference to merging amateur and professional baseball.[118] In the same year the National Association of Base Ball Players defined a professional and also repealed the 1858 prohibition against professional players from taking part in match games between association clubs. In its place, it adopted the rule which separated clubs into "two distinct classes." The *New York Times* reported this the following year: "All players who play base ball for money, or who shall at any time receive compensation for their services as players shall be considered professional players, and all others shall be regarded as amateur players."[119]

The *New York Times* defined the difference between amateur and professional in the following way:

> The distinction is that one class is compensated for their services on the field, either by regular salary, a division of gate money receipts, or by appointment to sinecure public office or to private positions as clerks, etc. The amateurs, on the other hand, pay for their privileges in the form of club fees and dues, and they play ball chiefly for its attendant excitement and recreative exercise.[120]

The article goes on to point out that there are "not less than a thousand regularly organized ball clubs," but out of these there are "thirty professional clubs." The clubs in New York and Brooklyn which were professional were: Atlantics, Eckfords, Mutuals, and Unions.[121] A definition of amateur and professional baseball clubs was also put forth by the New York State Association.[122] The definition was printed in an article in the *Brooklyn Eagle*. It stated: "Any player who by reason of superior ability to play ball, is recompensed by place, pay or emolument is a professional."[123] In the same article, readers' suggestions to amend the above definition were incorporated. One reader suggested adding to the above definition the following: "But the act of receiving gate money when its use is devoted to the club and not to the players shall not make the club a professional club."[124] Another reader took the opposite view by suggesting that any player who receives gate money should be declared a professional.[125]

Conflicting ideas such as these and the ambiguity surrounding whether or not some clubs were professional further obscured a clear distinction between amateur and professional. Although the press would eventually come to support professional baseball, they, at first consistently and then intermittently, would be highly critical of professional baseball and supportive of amateur baseball.[126] The revival of the terms "honor" and "manliness," used during the previous decade to describe baseball, were equated with amateur baseball, while professionals were relegated to a "despicable class."[127] However, the press was not always consistent in its support or condemnation of amateur or professional baseball. A *New York Herald* editorial, early in 1869, supported the idea of professional baseball, by comparing public performers with baseball players. The writer suggests that "no person thinks ill of an actor or an acrobat who receives a regular salary for his performance, and certainly a professional ball player should be honored as any other performer."[128] But later in the year, the same paper extols the qualities to be gained from joining an amateur club, which "presents an advantage to the youth of this country. In their association, the members are almost unconsciously trained in the system of legislation. Business is conducted on the same plan as in the legislative and corporate bodies throughout the country, and the members of the clubs become fitted with the proper performance of their duties as sovereigns."[129]

Compounding the confusion over the definition of amateur and professional baseball, the press also recognized the existence of hybrid forms of baseball clubs.[130] In an article assessing whether or not clubs would be organized as amateur or professional, a writer for the *Brooklyn Eagle* refers to the Excelsior Club as an "out and out amateur club," and depicts those clubs that are ostensibly amateur, but who also partake in the division of gate receipts, as "half-breeds."[131]

The *Spirit of the Times* defended the practice of amateur clubs' sharing in gate receipts. An editorial writer remarks that although amateur clubs "have an interest in the money taken ... this goes toward defraying their travelling expenses, and the balance, if any, goes into the treasury to buy the uniforms, bats and balls...."[132] A writer for the *Brooklyn Eagle*, addressing the amateur/professional question, takes a different viewpoint. The writer states:

> The question seems to hinge upon the question of gate money and remuneration by place and emolument. It appears plain that he who receives any benefit, whether by place, pay or emolument, as a player should be called a professional. But upon the matter of place there may be a question raised. If a player, by the influence of the club which he joins, obtains a position where he receives pay greater than the services he renders would warrant, in a commercial point of view he would be a professional player but if his services are commensurate with the pay he receives, he hardly could be called one. Still the fact remains that were it not that he could play ball well, that influence would not be exerted in his favor. This is a delicate question for the National Association to decide and its decision will be awaited with some anxiety.[133]

On one level, the quarreling over what constituted amateur or professional baseball can be related to the conflict between ideological interests of the amateur and the commercial aspirations of the professionals. From a different standpoint, the moral symbolism of the amateurs clashed with the aura of disrepute surrounding the professionals. These conflicts are derived, in part, from the changing values toward work and play in nineteenth century America.[134]

The Image of Professional Baseball

The reporting of monetary compensation to players in the press had a pronounced effect on shaping the image of professional baseball. The practices of pay-for-play grew in conjunction with a more aggressive style of play in the 1860s. However, an amateur orientation to playing still persisted, albeit in a subordinate position, due to the association of the play ethic with lesser skilled players and muffin matches. The persistence of the play ethic in baseball reverberates in the editorial remonstrations against compensation to players quoted earlier. The durability of the play ethic can also be found in the hesitancy of both the press and people in baseball to report on and to acknowledge payment to players.[135]

Part of this reluctance stems from the conventional wisdom of the time that associated corrupt sporting practices with paid athletics. It is also likely that the press was more interested in promoting the welfare of baseball as the national game, rather than attempting to tarnish the image of baseball by reporting payment to players.[136] From an analytic perspective, rather than denouncing payment to players, the press at times tried to negate the underlying disrepute associated with paid athletes by recommending the benefits to be gained by outright payment, to the players. Starting in 1866, the press reported that payment to players was occurring. Later in the decade, stimulated by the success of the Cincinnati Red Stocking team, clubs began to acknowledge that they were paying players. This new openness on the part of clubs and the 1868 resolution by the NABBP to separate amateurs from professionals contributed to a brief period of indecision on the part of a number of prominent clubs, as to whether they would reorganize and pay players or continue without paid players. Underlying much of the indecision and controversy over payment to players was the belief that money corrupts.

The construction of the image of professional baseball was dependent on a collective process that would permit the mass distribution of knowledge about baseball from which generalized ideas about the game could be formed. Face-to-face communication also played a part in this process, although it was not a substitute, nor could it be thought of as being equivalent to the collective phenomenon of mass communication. From this standpoint, the interactive relationship among the baseball spectacle, the baseball audience, and the baseball public was fundamental to the generation of ideas about baseball. However, it was the reporting of baseball matters by the press that played a key part in the formation of the image of professional baseball, particularly their attempts to negate or to affirm ideas that would impede or promote the growth of baseball.

Much of the interest in baseball stemmed from the dramatic aspects of the game. A sport philosopher, commenting on the dramatic appeal of sports, notes:

> The drama is an art form developed with spectators in mind. It is perhaps in the drama that sport reaches its closest affinity with art as process. The audiences at athletic contests behave similarly to those at dramatic stage productions; there is applause for performers who are skillful as well as overt manifestations of disapproval for poor performances.... The attitudes and experiences surrounding stage and arena are also similar in that we take pleasure and delight in exciting performances which deliver an organized sequence of action executed with skill.[137]

The drama in baseball was engendered by the unfolding of inning-by-inning play, daring catches, close plays, and strategic innovations, which all helped to accentuate the inherent uncertainty of the baseball contest. At times these dramatic elements contributed to the overflow of emotions, resulting in outbursts of boisterous rooting and instances of hooliganism among spectators. It is also likely that the gambling interests of the spectators played a part in their unruly behavior. A great deal of this was reported in the press, transmitting the excitement and vitality of the game for the vicarious consumption of the reader. It gave baseball a new dimension: the cognitive experience of a baseball game was translated into print. Baseball now had a sense of permanence. It was recorded as a public event, providing the fan with a reference source for discussion and a guide to performance standards. This helped shape the baseball public's generalized expectations of playing performance. The baseball guide, *Beadle's Dime Base-Ball Player*, was an especially important source for a variety of information pertaining to playing skill. Articles on rule changes, advice on how to implement playing strategies could all be found in *Beadle's*.

The first baseball guide offering readers a compendium of information about baseball including rules and regulations, changes in rules, descriptions of games played in the previous season, team rosters, etc. Woodcut courtesy John Thorn.

Consistent, skillful plays, and recognition of it by the press and the baseball public, were benchmarks in the movement of baseball toward professional status. Although skillful play was present in the 1860s, organized baseball had not yet achieved consistency in playing performance. When lapses in play occurred, the press was quick to report on these departures, often reacting with moral indignation and occasionally alleging matches were "fixed."

Toward the end of the 1860s, sport writers began to understand that inconsistent play could be attributed to chance and other factors, rather than deliberate attempts by players to "fix" games. By the 1870s, despite occasional inconsistent play, the baseball public came to associate a high level of performance with professional baseball players.

Concurrent with the molding of generalized expectations of playing performance and underlying the spectacular elements of baseball were changes in the playing rules. Rule changes were, in part, the result of actions taken by those who advocated a more competitive style of play and serendipitous innovations of players (e.g., the curve ball). The introduction of the fly rule, changes in the number of balls and strikes, and substitution of players bespeak of people's intentions in baseball to develop a more aggressive style of play. Since baseball was a form of entertainment, changes in rules were inextricably tied to the implicit demands by spectators for a more exciting brand of baseball. Although it cannot be firmly established, it is reasonable to assume that people in baseball were aware of the entertainment inclinations of spectators and took this into consideration when rule changes were implemented.

It is even more reasonable to assume that in the 1860s, when admission was charged and gate receipts shared, there was greater awareness among people in baseball of the entertainment function of the game. When admission was charged and when gate receipts were shared with players in the 1860s, baseball players can be said to have started to work at play.[138] The domains of work and play interpenetrated each other and converged on the playing field. This was largely due to a more lively competitive style of play and rising standards of playing performance. In order to meet these standards, players were required to devote full-time to baseball. Physical training, practicing in intra-squad matches, and heeding the coaching lessons of men like Harry Wright, were all part of the regimen of first class clubs. Furthermore, players had to perfect specialized techniques required for different playing positions and had to be able to absorb the lessons of innovative strategies. Playing baseball was as coercive as work. Play was now rationalized in the context of a highly competitive game, and because of this, working at play was made to look like play. The convergence of the domains of work and play in baseball also symbolically transmuted values that were usually associated with the workplace and symbolically transferred them to the playing field.

The press in the 1860s implicitly recognized the convergence of work and play in baseball. One of their criticisms was that baseball was becoming too serious. Closely related to this criticism and perhaps underlying it was the disavowal of the professional for his "exclusive development of one skill, instead of developing a variety of skills."[139] According to this argument "the professional games player was just like a trained seal."[140] Henry Chadwick's critiques of baseball echoed similar sentiments. In one of his arguments against the professional game, he criticized it because players had to give up other interests in order to succeed.[141] This is not surprising considering Chadwick's English origin and his consistency in espousing the English sports ideal. The English feared that the self-interest of professional athletes was greater than their concern for the integrity of the contest. Americans also shared this fear. Chadwick's writings in the late 1860s reflect this concern. He thought that professionals would succumb to the practice of a club deliberately stretching a, series in order to gain more gate money.[142] Chadwick also reproached professionals for unduly emphasizing the winning of games. He believed that players should be more interested in playing in a "gentlemanly fashion" rather than playing for money.[143]

The image of professional baseball was not a stable entity. Events occurring within baseball, and the reportage of them in the press, precluded this. Baseball was alternately condemned and praised by sports writers. Toward the end of the 1860s, and the beginning of the 1870s, organized baseball was in an unstable condition. The question as to whether or not clubs would organize either as amateur or professional dominated all other issues. Contributing to this condition was the confusion emanating from the diverse composition of the more prominent clubs. Some clubs considered themselves to be either amateur or professional and were organized as such. Other clubs were composed of both amateur and professional players. The press referred to this combination as "half-breeds," while the clubs that were all professional were called "out and outers."[144]

Complicating the organizational decision on the part of the baseball clubs was the conflicting moral valuations associated with amateur and professional baseball. Perhaps unwittingly, the rhetoric of the press, which drew invidious distinctions between the two, helped clarify the moral context in which a choice could be made. The use of phrases like "two classes" and "social organization" connoted the moral worth of amateur baseball, while the phrase "despicable class" denoted the disrepute associated with professional baseball. Whatever the impact was of these invidious distinctions on the decision-making process of people in organized baseball, the fact is that many of the prominent clubs either remained or turned professional by the early 1870s. From an ideational perspective, these distinctions helped in an interdependent fashion to delineate and bring into sharper focus the image of professional baseball. By the early 1870s, the image of professional baseball was recognizable by the baseball public as a loose configuration of attributes. These attributes were: skillful play, receiving monetary compensation, intermittently being an object of disrepute, and being identified by name as a player who played for a well-known baseball club. Players like Harry Wright, Joe Leggett, and Al Reach were known to play respectively for the Cincinnati Red Stockings, Excelsior and the Eckfords. Their exploits and the efforts of others that followed them did much to establish a basis out of which that enviable "corporate image" that Robert Angell, whom we referred to earlier, said would be "firmly planted in the mind of every American male."

Chapter Notes

Introduction

1. Terms such as an event and phrases like the baseball public will be defined in subsequent chapters.
2. Roger Angell, *The Summer Game* (New York: Viking, 1972), p. 95. Italics mine.
3. *Ibid.*
4. *New York Clipper*, April 24, 1875.
5. *Brooklyn Eagle*, August 3, 1859.
6. Kenneth E. Boulding, *The Image* (Ann Arbor: University of Michigan Press, 1956), p. 77.
7. *Ibid.*
8. *Ibid.*, p. 6.
9. *Ibid.*, p. 64.
10. *Ibid.*
11. *Ibid.*, pp. 164–175.
12. *Ibid.*, p. 164.
13. *Ibid.*
14. *Ibid.*
15. *Ibid.*, p. 172.
16. See Richard H. Brown, *A Poetic for Sociology* (Cambridge: Cambridge University Press, 1977), for a theoretical discussion of using metaphor as an approach to "isomorphism between domains instead of an absolute correspondence" (p. 154). See Brown for comments on the "radical symbolism" of Harold Garfinkel (*Ibid.*, p. 147). See also Harvey Molotch and Marilyn Lester, "News as Purposive Behavior: On the Strategic Use of Routine Events, Accidents, and Scandals," *American Sociological Review* 39, No. 1 (February 1974) for the construction of social reality by news media.
17. See Harold Seymour, *Baseball: The Early Years* (New York: Oxford University Press, 1960), p. 350, for the use of colorful metaphors in baseball. The use of exotic metaphors was more of a phenomenon of the 1870s than the 1860s. Nevertheless, less descriptive prose by writers of the 1860s still aroused great interest among the baseball public. In this connection, Seymour notes that by the 1850s, "Baseball news sold newspapers, and newspapers sold baseball" (p. 32).
18. Werner Cahnman and Alvin Boskoff, eds., *Sociology and History: Theory and Research* (New York: Free Press, 1964), p. 563.
19. *Ibid.*
20. Cf. George Becker's methodological approach in *The Mad Genius Controversy* (Beverly Hills, CA: Sage, 1978), p. 14.
21. A discussion of the sport press will be taken up at a later point.
22. a discussion of corruption in baseball will be taken up at a later point.
23. Popular histories of the beginnings of baseball are plentiful. See ed. Anton Grobani, *Guide to Baseball Literature* (Detroit: Gale Research, 1975), "General Histories," Chapter 6, pp. 41–48.
24. David Quentin Voigt, "Cash and Glory: The Commercialization of Major League Baseball as a Sports Spectacular, 1865–1892" (unpublished Ph.D. dissertation, Dept. of Sociology, Syracuse University, 1962).
25. Melvin L. Adelman, "The Development of Modern Athletics: Sport in New York City, 1820–1870" (unpublished Ph.D. dissertation, Dept. of History, University of Illinois at Urbana-Champaign, 1980).
26. Robert W. Henderson, *Ball, Bat and Bishop: The Origin of Ball Games* (New York: Rockport, 1947).
27. Charles A. Peverelly, *Book of American Pastimes* (New York: American News Company, 1866).
28. Albert G. Spalding, *America's National Game* (New York: American Sports Publishing, 1911).
29. Jeffrey L. Haven, "Baseball: The Origins

and Development of the Game to 1903" (unpublished Ph.D. dissertation, Dept. of Physical Education, Brigham Young University, 1979).
   30. Jacob Morse, *Sphere and Ash: History of Baseball* (Boston: J.C. Spofford, 1888).
   31. Seymour R. Church, *Base Ball* (1902; Reprint, Princeton: Pyne Press, 1974).
   32. Irving A. Leitner, *Baseball: Diamond in the Rough* (New York: Criterion Books, 1972).
   33. Martha M. Seban, "A Theoretical Consideration of the Internal Dynamics of Sport," *Sport in the Sociocultural Process*, ed. Marie Hart (2nd ed.; Dubuque, IA: Wm. C. Brown, 1976), pp. 220–243.
   34. John Thorn, *Baseball in the Garden of Eden: The Secret History of the Early Game* (New York: Simon & Schuster, 2011).
   35. David Block, *Baseball Before We Knew It: A Search for the Roots of the Game* (Lincoln, NE: Canadian Scholars Press, 2005).
   36. The treatment of the professionalization of baseball by historians and other researchers bears a close resemblance to the approach of many contemporary occupational sociologists; both start their inquiry by focusing on the internal events of the occupation under study.

Chapter I

1. See John W. Loy, Jr., "The Nature of Sport: A Definitional Effort," *Sport, Culture, and Society*, eds. John W. Loy, Jr., and Gerald S. Kenyon (New York: Macmillan, 1969) pp. 56–71, for a discussion of the difficulties of defining sport.
   2. Cricket was not popular among Americans in the 1840s. It was popular among English immigrants in the cities of New York, Philadelphia, Richmond, New Orleans, Savannah, and Cincinnati. See John Rickards Betts, *America's Sporting Heritage: 1850–1950* (Reading, MA: Addison-Wesley, 1974), for comments on the playing of cricket by English immigrants, p. 18.
   3. Quoted in Louise Jordan Walmsley's "Sport Attitudes and Practices of Representative Americans Before 1870" (unpublished master's thesis, Graduate School of Education, George Peabody College for Teachers, 1938), p. 43.
   4. This summary of early American recreational pastimes and amusements is based on John S. Lucas and Ronald A. Smith, *Saga of American Sport* (Philadelphia: Lea & Febiger, 1978), Chapter 2.
   5. Thomas R. Davis, "Puritanism and Physical Education: The Shroud of Gloom Lifted," *Canadian Journal of History of Sport and Physical Education* 3, No. 2 (May 1972), p. 7. Italics mine.

6. Betty Spears and Richard A. Swanson, *History of Sport and Physical Activity in the United States* (Dubuque, IA: Wm. C. Brown Company, 1978), p. 44. Italics mine.
   7. Robert Knight Barney, "Physical Education and Sport in North America," *History of Physical Education and Sport*, ed. Earle F. Zeigler (Englewood Cliffs, NJ: Prentice-Hall, 1979), pp. 178–179. Italics mine.
   8. See Lucas and Smith, Chapters 2, 6 and 17.
   9. *Ibid.*, p. 70.
   10. See Johan Huizinga, *Homo Ludens: A Study of the Play Elements in Culture* (Boston: Beacon Press, 1955) for the significance of play in culture.
   11. Cf. Lucas and Smith, p. 102.
   12. Robert Lee, *Religion and Leisure in America* (New York: Abingdon, 1964), p. 163.
   13. *Ibid.*, p. 161.
   14. *Ibid.*
   15. Betts, p. 162.
   16. See David K. Wiggins, "Work, Leisure, and Sport in America: The British Travelers Image, 1830–1860," *Canadian Journal of History of Sport* 13, No. 1 (May 1982), pp. 28–60, for the British view of American attitudes toward work and sport.
   17. *Ibid.*, p. 30.
   18. *Ibid.*, p. 37, quoting W.E. Baxter in *America and the Americans*, pp. 98–99.
   19. *Ibid.*
   20. Wiggins, p. 28.
   21. Lucas and Smith, p. 60.
   22. See Vernon L. Parrington, *Main Currents in American Thought*, vol. 2: *The Romantic Revolution in America 1800–1860* (New York: Harcourt, Brace & World, 1927), pp. 320–330, for a discussion of the views of William Ellery Channing.
   23. Lucas and Smith, p. 70.
   24. Parrington, p. 371. See also Roberta J. Park, "The Attitudes of Leading New England Transcendentalists Toward Healthful Exercise, Active Recreation and Proper Care of the Body: 1830–1860," *Journal of Sport History* 4, No. 1 (Spring 1977), p. 49, for an analysis of the transcendental movement.
   25. Park, p. 35.
   26. *Ibid.*
   27. Lucas and Smith, pp. 88–89.
   28. *Ibid.*, p. 89.
   29. Park, p. 50.
   30. Lucas and Smith, p. 71.
   31. For a discussion of Beecher's views toward leisure and work see Daniel T. Rodgers, *The Work Ethnic in Industrial America 1850–1920*

(Chicago: University of Chicago Press, Phoenix Edition, 1979), pp. 94–99.
32. Ibid., p. 97.
33. Ibid., p. 94.
34. Ibid., p. 96.
35. Ibid., p. 97.
36. Ibid.
37. William G. McLaughlin, *The Meaning of Henry Ward Beecher: An Essay on the Shifting Values of Mid-Victorian America, 1840–1870* (New York: Alfred Knopf, 1970), p. 110.
38. Ibid.
39. Ibid.
40. See Spears and Swanson, p. 119, for a brief discussion of Beecher's views.
41. Rogers, pp. 94–95; Lucas and Smith, p. 108.
42. A more detailed account of the roots of Muscular Christianity is given in the next chapter.
43. Lucas and Smith, p. 109.
44. Ibid., p. 108.
45. Ibid., p. 109.
46. Spears and Swanson, p. 122.
47. Lucas and Smith, pp. 109–115.
48. Rodgers, p. 108
49. Ibid., p. 106.
50. Lucas and Smith, p. 112.
51. Cited by Rodgers, p. 104.
52. Cited in Lucas and Smith, 110.
53. Rogers, p. 109.
54. Ibid., p. 102.
55. Ibid., p. 95.
56. Ibid., p. 102.
57. Lucas and Smith, p. 74.
58. Walmsley, p. 25.
59. Arthur Charles Cole, *The Irrepressible Conflict, 1850–1865*, vol. 7 of *A History of American Life*, eds. Arthur M. Schlesinger and Dixon Ryan Fox (12 vols.; New York: Macmillan, 1934), p. 179.
60. Ibid, p. 182.
61. H.W. Bellows, "Cities and Parks, with Special Reference to the New York Central Park," *Atlantic Monthly* 7 (1861), p. 416, quoted in Cole, p. 182.
62. Cole, p. 184.
63. "Why We Get Sick," *Harper's Monthly* 13 (1856), pp. 642, 646, quoted in Cole, p. 187.
64. Cole, pp. 187–188.
65. Edward Everett, *Orations and Speeches on Various Occasions* (Boston, 1865–1872), III, 407, quoted in Cole, p. 188.
66. T.W. Higginson, "Saints and Their Bodies," *Atlantic Monthly* 1 (1857–1858): 582–595; same author, "Physical Courage," *Atlantic Monthly* 2 (1858): 728–737, quoted in Cole, p. 188.
67. Walmsley, p. 44.
68. Lucas and Smith, pp. 73–75.
69. Jack W. Berryman, "The Tenuous Attempts of Americans to Catch Up with 'John Bull': Specialty Magazines and Sporting Journalism, 1800–1835," *Canadian Journal of History of Sport and Physical Education* 10, No. 1 (May 1979), p. 43.
70. Ibid.
71. Ibid., pp. 48–49.
72. Ibid., p. 49.
73. Lucas and Smith, p. 80.
74. Betts, p. 53.
75. For simplicity this publication is referred to as the *Spirit of the Times*.
76. Betts, pp. 53–54.
77. Cole, p. 217.
78. *American Almanac and Repository of Useful Knowledge* (Boston: Charles Bowen, 1834), p. 96.
79. Carl Bode, *The Anatomy of Popular Culture, 1840–1861* (Berkley: University of California Press, 1959), p. 110.
80. Ibid.
81. *American Almanac*, p. 96.
82. From here on, all those publications which reported on baseball will be referred to as the press.
83. Alfred McClung Lee, *The Daily Newspaper in America: The Evolution of a Social Instrument* (New York: Macmillan, 1937), p. 609.
84. Betts, p. 55.
85. Ibid., p. 62.
86. Seymour, p. 33.
87. Ibid. See also Betts, p. 63, for the assigning of correspondents to sport events.
88. Seymour, p. 33.
89. Christian Karl Messenger, "Sport in American Literature (1830–1930)" (unpublished Ph.D. dissertation, Dept. of Philosophy, Northwestern University, 1974), p. 1.
90. Ibid., p. 14.
91. Leitner, p. 58, quoting the *Sunday Courier*, July 1907.
92. In an article by Chadwick in 1861, he points out that he was covering baseball ten years earlier (1851). Henry Chadwick, *Scrapbooks*, vol. 1, p. 3, Spalding Collection, Rare Manuscript Division, New York Public Library.
93. Voigt, p. 222.
94. Chadwick, *Scrapbooks*, vol. 1, p. 121.
95. John Thorn, "1853: The Baseball Press Emerges," *Baseball* 5, No. 1 (Spring 2011).
96. See Grobani for an extensive listing of baseball guides for both the nineteenth and twentieth centuries.
97. Voigt, p. 221.

98. Chadwick, *Beadle's Dime Base-Ball Player* (New York: Irwin P. Beadle, 1860–1881).
99. Grobani, p. 12.

CHAPTER II

1. See Ralph Nevill, *Sporting Days and Sporting Ways* (London: Duckworth, 1910), p. 146, for stories about 18th- and 19th-century English field sports.
2. See P.C. McIntosh, *Sport in Society* (London: C.A. Watts, 1963), pp. 5–59, for a history of early English sport.
3. Nevill, p. 238.
4. McIntosh, p. 8.
5. Eric Dunning and Kenneth Sheard, *Barbarians, Gentlemen and Players* (New York: New York University Press, 1979), Chapter 4.
6. *Ibid.*, pp. 77, 81.
7. *Ibid.* p. 84.
8. *Ibid.*, p. 85.
9. *Ibid.*, p. 86.
10. *Ibid.*, p. 153.
11. Dunning and Sheard, p. 153.
12. "Horse Racing and Breeding" *Encyclopedia Britannica*, 1959 ed,. Vol. 11, p. 764.
13. Peter C. McIntosh, "The British Attitude to Sport," *Sport and Society: A Symposium*, ed. Alex Natan (London: Bowes & Bowes, 1958), p. 18.
14. *Ibid.*, p. 18.
15. See Dunning and Sheard, Chapters 7 and 8, and also Richard Gruneau, *Class, Sports, and Social Development* (Amherst: University of Massachusetts Press, 1983), p. 53, for the function of amateurism in society.
16. Dunning and Sheard, p. 178.
17. *Ibid.*
18. *Ibid.*
19. *Ibid.*
20. *Ibid.*, p. 181.
21. *Ibid.*
22. Gruneau, p. 134.
23. *Ibid.*
24. Hugh Cunningham, *Leisure in the Industrial Revolution* (New York: St. Martin's, 1980), p. 135. Italics mine. Perhaps the earliest use of the term "amateur" occurred in English pugilism in the late eighteenth century. But it is not clear if the term referred to the participants or the viewers.
25. McIntosh, "The British Attitude to Sport," p. 20.
26. *Ibid.*
27. Eton had several boats as early as 1811, but there appears to be no record of their competing with other schools until 1817 when Oxford and Cambridge began to compete. See "Rowing," *Encyclopedia Britannica*, 1959 ed., Vol. 19, p. 590.
28. Carl Diem, "Yours is the Earth," *Sport and Society: A Symposium*, ed. Alex Natan (London: Bowes & Bowes, 1958), p. 118.
29. *Ibid.*, p. 113.
30. *Ibid.*, p. 119.
31. Frank Cosentino, "A History of the Concept of Professionalism in Canadian Sport" (unpublished Ph.D. dissertation, University of Alberta, Canada, 1973), p. 9.
32. *Ibid.*
33. For an omission of an analysis of the amateur athlete before the Civil War see the following histories of sport: Betts, Dulles, Lucas and Smith, and Spears and Swanson. The lack of amateur athletics in the first half of the nineteenth century is also suggested by the exclusion of the term from the index of an annotated bibliography of more than 1,000 entries on American sports before 1860. See Robert W. Henderson, *Early American Sport: A Checklist of Books* (Cranbury, NJ: Associated University Presses, Inc., 1977).
34. Margaret K. Woodhouse, "A History of Amateur Club Rowing in the New York Metropolitan Area, 1830–1870," *Canadian Journal of History of Sport and Physical Education* 11, No. 2 (December 1980), p. 75.
35. Adelman, "The Development of Modern Athletics," p. 479.
36. *Ibid.*, pp. 480–482.
37. *New York Gazette*, November 10, 13, 1820, quoted in Adelman, "The Development of Modern Athletics." p. 480.
38. Woodhouse, p. 77.
39. *Ibid.*, p. 77.
40. Adelman, "The Development of Modern Athletics," p. 482, and Dulles, p. 142.
41. Adelman, "The Development of Modern Athletics," p. 482.
42. *Ibid.*
43. Woodhouse, p. 79.
44. Adelman, "The Development of Modern Athletics," p. 482.
45. *Ibid.*
46. *Ibid.*, p. 484.
47. *Ibid.*
48. *Ibid*, p. 486.
49. *Ibid.*
50. *Ibid.*
51. *Ibid.*
52. *Ibid.*, p. 489.
53. *Ibid.*, p. 491.
54. Samuel Crowther and Arthur Ruhl, *Rowing and Track Athletics* (New York: Macmillan,

1905), pp. 163–164, as quoted by Adelman, "The Development of Modern Athletics," p. 491.

55. Adelman, "The Development of Modern Athletics," p. 1191.

56. Jennie Holliman, *American Sports (1785–1835)* (Durham, NC: Seeman, 1931), p. 3. See also sports historians Betts (pp. 19–20), McIntosh (p. 84), and Lucas and Smith (pp. 137–139). They have also written about the influence of the British on American sports, but Holliman's analysis is the most extensive.

57. Holliman, p. 5.
58. *Ibid.*, pp. 7–8.
59. *Ibid.*, p. 8.
60. *Ibid.*
61. *Ibid.*, p. 9.
62. See Henderson, *Early American Sport*, p. 62.
63. Holliman, p. 9.
64. *Ibid.*, p. 10. See Bonnie S. Ledbetter, "Sports and Games of the American Revolution," *Journal of Sport History* 6, No. 3 (Winter 1979), pp. 36–37, for a similar view.

65. Barbara Miller Solomon, *Ancestors and Immigrants: A Changing New England Tradition* (Cambridge: Harvard University Press, 1956), pp. 7–8.

66. Stephen Hardy, *How Boston Played* (Boston: Northeastern University Press, 1962), p. 196.

67. Larzer Ziff, *Literary Democracy: The Declaration of Cultural Independence in America* (New York: Penguin Books, 1981), p. 24.

Chapter III

1. For the origin of baseball David Q. Voigt, *American Baseball: From The Gentleman's Sport to the Commissioner System* (University Park: Pennsylvania State University Press, 1983), p. 7; and R. Brasch, *How Did Sports Begin: A Look at the Origins of Man at Play* (New York: David McKay, 1970), p. 33; John Thorn, *Baseball in the Garden of Eden;* and Block.

2. Seymour, pp. 4–5.
3. Block, pp. 25–27 for a refutation of Henderson.
4. Block, pp. 30–31.
5. Henderson, *Bat, Ball and Bishop.*
6. *Ibid.*, p. 132.
7. *Ibid.*
8. *Ibid.*, p. 133.
9. *Ibid.*, p. 134.
10. *Ibid.*
11. *Ibid.*, p. 143.
12. *Ibid.*, pp. 134–135.
13. *Ibid.*, p. 135.
14. *Ibid.*
15. *Ibid.*, p. 136.
16. *Ibid.*
17. *Ibid.*, p. 178.
18. *Ibid.*, p. 145.
19. *Ibid.*, p. 145.
20. Seymour, p. 5.
21. Henderson, *Ball, Bat and Bishop*, p. 51.
22. *Ibid.*, p. 152.
23. *Ibid.*, p. 255.
24. *Ibid.*, p. 158.
25. *Ibid.*, p. 160.
26. *Ibid.*, p. 163.
27. *Ibid.*
28. Leitner, p. 58.
29. Henderson, p. 175.
30. Henderson, p. 186.
31. *Ibid.*, p. 187.
32. See Ronald Takaki, "The Black Child-Savage in Antebellum America," in G.B. Nash and R. Weiss, eds., *The Great Fear: Race in the Mind of America* (New York: Holt, Rinehart, Winston, 1970), pp. 27–44, for the concept of "Black Child-Savage."

33. Stewart Culin, *Games of North American Indians* (New York: Dover, 1975), pp. 561, 708.
34. *Ibid.*, p. 789.
35. The Spalding Baseball Collection, Rare Manuscript Division, New York Public Library, contains one of the largest repositories of primary data on the early history of baseball. The scrapbooks of Henry Chadwick and Harry Wright, and the correspondence and the Club Books of the Knickerbockers are among the holdings in this collection. Unfortunately, other than a box score for a match played in 1846, there appears to be no other first-person accounts describing the activities of the Knickerbockers until 1854.

36. Peverelly, quoted in Leitner, p. 33.
37. *Ibid.*, pp. 340–341. See also Henry Chadwick, *Beadle's Dime Base-Ball Player*, 1860, for a similar account of the beginnings of the Knickerbockers.

38. Harold Peterson, *The Man Who Invented Baseball* (New York: Charles Scribner's Sons, 1973), p. 51.

39. *Ibid.*, p. 55–76. Henderson locates Sunfish Pond at what now would be 27th Street and Madison Avenue, p. 161.

40. Peterson, p. 2.
41. Henderson, p. 163.
42. *Ibid.*
43. *Ibid.*, p. 4.
44. *Ibid.*, pp. 2–3.
45. Club Books, New York Knickerbocker Base Ball Club, 1854–1859, Manuscript Division. New York Public Library.

46. Spalding, p. 67.
47. Edward Pessen, *Riches, Class and Power Before the Civil War* (Lexington, MA: D.C. Heath, 1973), p. 229.
48. Adelman, "The Development of Modern Athletics," p. 265.
49. Melvin L. Adelman, "The First Baseball Game, the First Newspaper References to Baseball, and the New York Club: A Note on the Early History of Baseball," *Journal of Sport History* 7, No. 3 (Winter 1980), pp. 132–135.
50. See Seymour, p. 18, and Leitner, p. 36, for the first match game played.
51. Adelman, "The First Baseball Game," p. 133.
52. *Ibid.*
53. *Ibid.*, p. 132.
54. *Ibid.*
55. *Ibid.*, p. 133.
56. Adelman refers to the Herald, November 11, 1845, to support the gathering of baseball players and cricketers, p. 133.
57. Seymour, p. 15.
58. *Ibid.*
59. Voigt, "Cash and Glory," p. 51.
60. *Ibid.*, p. 27.
61. See Stephen Freedman, "The Baseball Fad In Chicago, 1865–1870: An Exploration of the Role of Sport in the Nineteenth-Century City," *Journal of Sport History* 5, No. 2 (Summer 1978): pp. 42–64, for a discussion on the relationship between voluntary associations and baseball clubs as one means by which native-born middle-class people "utilized the voluntary association to enhance the level of cohesion among its own members; to extend the leadership role of the businessman and the professional man into the social realm; and to promote the spread of 'Victorian' patterns of behavior in a culturally pluralistic environment" (p. 43).
62. Voigt, p. 27.
63. See Adelman, "The Development of Modern Athletics," pp. 226–268, for competition between English cricket clubs in the greater New York area. For the competitive function of cricket among aristocratic men in early nineteenth century England, see Dunning and Sheard, pp. 177–178.
64. New York Knickerbocker Base Ball Club Books, 1859–1860, Rare Manuscript Division, New York Public Library.
65. See the By-Laws, Regulations, and Rules of the Knickerbocker Base Ball Club, Article VII, Sections 1–8, Knickerbocker Club Books, 1854–1859. See also Leitner, p.36 and Seymour, p. 17.
66. Knickerbocker Club Books, 1854–1859, Article IX, Section 1.
67. *Ibid.*
68. Seymour, p, 16.
69. *Ibid.*
70. For the concept of a "status group," see Max Weber, *Economy and Society*, eds. Guenther Roth and Claus Wittich (New York: Bedminster, 1968), pp. 305–306.
71. See Seymour, p. 20, and Voigt, p. 51, for the influence of the Knickerbockers as a model for other baseball clubs.
72. In the 1850s, print media treated the Knickerbockers, for the most part, with respect and admiration. The *New York Herald* noted that "the Knickerbocker is the oldest base ball club now existing in the city and seems to be the most influential" (January 3, 1857).
73. The Knickerbockers adopted uniforms in 1849. The straw hat was replaced with a mohair cap in 1855. Peverelly, pp. 344, 349.
74. Thorstein Veblen, *The Theory of the Leisure Class* (New York: New American Library, 1953), pp. 43¬44. See also Stephen Hardy, Chapter 7, for a discussion of how the sporting club helped in determining and maintaining social status.
75. Veblen, Chapter 3.
76. McIntosh, *Sport in Society*, p. 188.
77. Rodgers, p. 109.
78. For an analysis of American ideas of success, see John G. Cawelti, *Apostles of the Self-Made Man* (Chicago: University of Chicago Press, 1965), pp. 4–6.
79. Dunning and Sheard, p.154.
80. *Ibid.*, pp. 168–176.
81. See Seymour, p. 15; Voigt, p. 52; Peverelly, pp. 340–341; Foster Rhea Dulles, *A History of Recreation: America Learns to Play* (New York: Appleton-Century-Crofts, 1956), p. 187, and Spalding, p. 66, for descriptions of the Knickerbockers as devoted to the pursuit of baseball as a social-recreational diversion rather than a competitive endeavor.
82. Thorn, p. 53.
83. *Spirit of the Times*, March 7, 1857.
84. There is no record of this resolution, but its existence can be inferred from another resolution which was adopted in 1855 to rescind it.
85. Knickerbocker Club Books, 1854–1859.
86. *Ibid.*
87. *Ibid.* Italics mine.
88. Spalding, p. 43.
89. Leitner, p. 3.
90. See Seymour, p. 23, for the idea of the Knickerbockers restricting baseball to their own social class. See also the *Spirit of the Times*, January 23, 1869, for the Knickerbockers' coming from the "mercantile class."

91. For the association of baseball with children and young adults see Adelman, Chapter 6, and Seymour, p. 23. For rejection of match games and the rejection of membership, see Knickerbocker Club Books, 1854–1859.
92. Adelman, "The Development of Modern Athletics," pp. 326–327.
93. Rodgers, p. 109.
94. Cited in Joseph F. Kett, *Rites of Passage: Adolescence in America, 1790 to the Present* (New York: Basic Books, 1977), p. 163.
95. *Ibid.*
96. *Ibid.*
97. John Dizikes, *Sportsmen and Gamesmen* (Boston: Houghton Mifflin, 1981), p. 69.
98. *Ibid.*, p. 222.
99. *Ibid.*, p. 223.
100. Harold Peterson, p. 11.
101. *Ibid.*, pp. 54–55.
102. *Ibid.*, p. 55.
103. *Ibid.*, p. 56.
104. *Ibid.*, p. 57.
105. *Ibid.*
106. Thorn., p. 31.
107. *Ibid.*, p. 26.
108. Quoted in Thorn, p. 60.
109. Spalding, p. 56.
110. *Ibid.*
111. *Ibid.*, p. 57.
112. *Ibid.*, p. 64.
113. Seymour, p. 20.
114. *Spirit of the Times*, March 8, 1856. In reference to the social festivities after a match, Chadwick observes that at the annual convention of the National Association of Base Ball Players in 1859, it was decided to eliminate the social gatherings after games, because the practice "had degenerated into one, seriously detrimental to the interests of the game, owing to the spirit of emulation that arose among the clubs each aspiring to excel each other in expense and splendor of these entertainments" (Chadwick, *Beadle's Dime Base-Ball Player*, 1860).
115. See Adelman, "The Development of Modern Athletics," Chapter 6, for a discussion of the class composition of early baseball clubs.
116. Thorn, pp. 90–92.
117. By the end of the summer of 1856, there were seventeen organized teams, and they played approximately fifty-three games (Spalding, p. 64, and Seymour, p. 24). In 1858 the number of clubs had risen to about fifty (Seymour, p. 24).
118. Spalding, p. 69.
119. Knickerbocker Club Books, 1854–1859.
120. *New York Herald*, December 7, 1855. Unfortunately, there is no information given in the article pertaining to what transpired at this meeting, nor does there appear to be any account of this meeting in the literature, other than a reference by Peverelly, who notes that "prior to 1857, the series of rules prepared by a committee of the principal clubs of New York governed all match games of base ball played by metropolitan clubs" (Peverelly, p. 499).
121. *New York Herald*, December 22, 1856.
122. *Spirit of the Times*, March 7, 1857.
123. *Ibid.*
124. *Spirit of the Times*, September 7, 1857.
125. *Ibid.*, November 8, 1856.
126. *Spirit of the Times*, November 22, 1856.
127. *Ibid.*, December 20, 1856.
128. *Ibid.*, March 7, 1857.
129. *Ibid.*
130. *Spirit of the Times*, April 3, 1858.
131. *Ibid.*
132. Seymour, p. 52.
133. *Ibid.*, p. 24.
134. *Spirit of the Times*, March 20, 1858. Italics mine.
135. *Brooklyn Eagle*, April 6, 1861.
136. Spalding, p. 9.
137. Seymour, p. 43.

Chapter IV

1. Joseph R. Gusfield, "Moral passage: The Symbolic Process in Public Designation of Deviance," *Social Problems* 15, No. 2 (Fall 1967), pp. 175–188.
2. *Ibid.*, pp. 176–177.
3. See Talcott Parsons, *The Social System* (Glencoe: Free Press, 1951), p. 386, for a discussion of "expressive symbols." See also Orrin E. Klapp, *Heroes, Villains and Fools: Reflections of the American Character* (San Diego: Aegis, 1972), for an analysis of a collective consensual process, where symbols and images are created in society.
4. The idea of "manly" is never explicated in the print media when it refers to baseball and cricket. However, the connotation is that manliness is tantamount to courage and physical perseverance. The English term of "pluck" suggests manliness.
5. Morris Mott, "The British Protestant Pioneers and the Establishment of Manly Sports in Manitoba, 1870–1886," *Journal of Sport History* 7, No. 3 (Winter 1980), p. 27.
6. November 7, 1853.
7. November 6, 1853.
8. *Spirit of the Times*, March 7, 1858.
9. *Ibid.*, May 14, 1859.

10. *New York Tribune*, November 21, 1846.
11. *New York Herald*, November 3, 1854. Italics in original.
12. *Spirit of the Times*, December 22, 1856.
13. *Brooklyn Eagle*, July 28, 1858.
14. *Harper's Weekly*, November 5, 1859.
15. *Spirit of the Times*, September 13, 1856.
16. *Spirit of the Times*, January 31, 1857.
17. *Brooklyn Eagle*, August 3, 1859.
18. The use of the term "event" will denote either a series of happenings or a singular occurrence in baseball that was widely reported in print media and an element(s) of the image of professional baseball. Following Lyman's discussion of an event in *Structure, Consciousness, and History*, Richard H. Brown and Stanford M. Lyman, eds. (Cambridge: Cambridge University Press, 1978), p. 86, an event in baseball will also be known as such, because it is "embedded" in the eventful outcomes of a "happening" or "an engagement of happenings" which are bounded by both "rules of irrelevance" and "relevance" which make the reportage of the event count, insofar as it contributes to the image of professional baseball. See *Encounters*, by Erving Goffman (Indianapolis: Bobbs-Merrill, 1961), p. 1926, for a discussion of the "rules of irrelevance."
19. Perhaps, because of increased competition in the 1860s, the term "team" is often substituted for the term "club" in the press.
20. *New York Times*, July 21, 1858.
21. This series presaged a long rivalry between teams from Brooklyn and New York, culminating with the New York Giants and Brooklyn Dodgers in the 1950s. Until the late 1860s, New York and Brooklyn dominated the baseball scene.
22. Seymour, p. 25.
23. *Ibid.*
24. *New York Times*, July 21, 1858.
25. *Brooklyn Eagle*, October 22, 1861.
26. Church, p. 27.
27. *New York Times*, July 21, 1858.
28. *Brooklyn Eagle*, October 22, 1861.
29. Church, p. 36.
30. *Brooklyn Eagle*, April 30, 1860.
31. *Ibid.*
32. Spalding, p. 80.
33. Spalding, pp. 106–107.
34. *Ibid.*, p. 107.
35. The loss to the Forest City team by the Washington Nationals, and their subsequent victory over the Chicago Excelsiors, brought charges from local newspapers that the loss to the Forest City team was a deliberate attempt to set up a betting coup on the part of the Washington team. See Leitner, pp. 77–80, for a discussion of the charges.
36. For references to baseball as a "boy's" game see *New York Herald*, December 22, 1856, and *Spirit of the Times*, January 31, 1857.
37. *Spirit of the Times*, March 7, 1858.
38. If this was the case, why is it that cricket did not become the national pastime? Although cricket preceded baseball, and was popular, it did not have the elements which were conducive to creating an entertainment spectacle. Moreover, the polite, gentlemanly decorum of both the players and the spectators precluded the emergence of spontaneous behavior on the part of either. The length of the game, often two days' duration, worked against the development of tension which was inherent and essential to the format of baseball. In addition, the British origins of the game, the reputed difficulty of playing the game, and the fact that a majority of the players were Englishmen, all worked against cricket's chances of becoming a popular public spectacle.
39. *Brooklyn Eagle*, March 15, 1864.
40. *Spirit of the Times*, December 3, 1859.
41. *Ibid.*, March 7, 1857.
42. *Ibid.*
43. *Ibid.*, July 9, 1859.
44. *New York Herald*, July 5, 1869.
45. *New York Herald*, November 3, 1854.
46. *Spirit of the Times*, July 30, 1859.
47. *Brooklyn Eagle*, August 6, 1860.
48. *Brooklyn Eagle*, July 19, 1860.
49. *Ibid.*, August 19, 1863.
50. *Brooklyn Eagle*, August 17, 1863.
51. *New York Clipper*, June 20, 1874, in Voigt.
52. Chadwick, *Scrapbooks*, I, p. 90, as quoted in Voigt, p. 223.
53. Robert J. Kelly, "Toward a Theory of Competition and Cooperation in Sports as an Indicator of Change in American Life," *Journal of Popular Culture* 4, No. 3 (Winter 1971): p. 611.
54. Jacques Ellul, *The Technological Society*, trans. J. Wilkinson (New York: Vintage, 1967), p. 382.
55. See Richard Sennett, *The Fall of Public Man* (New York: Vintage, 1978), p. 205, for an analysis of the elements that constitute the image of a stage performance by an actor.
56. Kelly, p. 613.
57. See Christopher Lasch, *The Culture of Narcissism* (New York: Warner, 1979), p. 216, for the function of sport in culture.
58. *Brooklyn Eagle*, August 27, 1863. The term "muffin" signifies ineptness. In the *Spirit of the Times*, August 7, 1869, it was defined as follows: "A ball is 'muffed' when it is badly judged as it

falls; it is muffed also if it be not picked up neatly when hit moderately hard; a fielder is also guilty of muffin play if he stops or handles a ball clumsily; or throws it hastily and wildly to any particular point of the field aimed for. Muffinism is simply the result of a lack of skill, practice or judgment in the player, or of all three."

59. Seymour points out that as specialization in baseball increased, those players who were expert at a position were called "artists," p. 61.

CHAPTER V

1. For the use of the term public see Voigt, "Cash and Glory," pp. 115, 190 and 202, and Adelman, "The Development of Modern Athletics," pp. 382 and 406.
2. Ralph H. Turner and Lewis M. Killian, *Collective Behavior* (2nd ed.; Englewood Cliffs, NJ: Prentice-Hall, 1972), p. 179, for the ideas of "distinct publics."
3. For the concept of a public see Herbert Blumer, "Outline of Collective Behavior," *Readings in Collective Behavior*, ed. Robert R. Evans (2nd edition; Chicago: Rand McNally College Publishing, 1975); Robert E. Park, *The Crowd and the Public and Other Essays* (Chicago: University of Chicago Press, 1972); Turner and Killian; L. Benson, "An Approach to the Scientific Study of Past Public Opinion," *Public Opinion Quarterly* 4 (Winter 1967-68): pp. 522-566; and H.L. Childs, *Public Opinion: Nature, Formation and Role* (Princeton, NJ: D. Von Nostrand, 1965).
4. Blumer, p. 38.
5. Ibid.
6. Park, p. 61.
7. Ibid.
8. Turner and Killian, p. 179.
9. Benson, p. 524.
10. Ibid.
11. This does not necessarily mean that conflict was unknown in baseball before the 1850s, but a lack of data has kept scholars from analyzing this period other than making the briefest of comments, which do not indicate the existence of conflict.
12. See Benson, p. 544, on the relationship between public opinion and public policy.
13. Gabriel Tarde, *Communication and Social Influence: Selected Papers*, ed. Terry N. Clark (Chicago: University of Chicago Press, 1969), p. 285.
14. Ibid.
15. Harold D. Lasswell, "The Structure and Function of Communication in Society," *Mass Communication*, ed. Wilbur Schramm (Urbana: University of Illinois Press, 1972), pp. 111-130.

16. See Barry C. McPherson, "Sports Consumption and the Economics of Consumerism," *Sport and Social Order: Contributions to the Sociology of Sport*, eds. Donald W. Ball and John W. Loy (Reading, MA: Addison-Wesley, 1975), pp. 256-258, for the role of the sports consumer.
17. Ibid., p. 245.
18. Cf. Turner and Killian, pp. 179-180, for a distinction between the crowd and the public. See also Park, p. 61, for a similar distinction.
19. See Elias Canetti, *Crowds and Power*, trans. Carol Stewart (New York: Viking, 1966), for a discussion of the crowd.
20. Turner and Killian identify common features that both crowds and audiences share, but subsume the latter under the former. See pp. 145-146.
21. Seymour, p. 327.
22. Adelman, "The Development of Modern Athletics," p. 387.
23. Ibid.
24. May 19, 1883, quoted in Steven A. Riess, "Professional Baseball and American Culture in the Progressive Era: Myths and Realities, with Special Emphasis on Atlanta, Chicago, and New York" (unpublished Ph.D. dissertation, Dept. of History, University of Chicago, 1974), p. 35.
25. November, 1870, quoted in Leitner, p. 102.
26. *New York Mercury*, September 2, 1876.
27. Seymour, p., 328.
28. Ibid., p. 29.
29. see Norman F. Cantor and Michael S. Werthman, eds., *The History of Popular Culture: Since 1815* (London: Macmillan, 1969), and Russell Nye, *The Unembarrassed Muse: The Popular Arts in America* (New York: Dial Press, 1971) for information on the growth of entertainment in America.
30. For a discussion of communication networks see Jay Corzine, "Media Diffusion of Subcultural Elements: Comment on Fine and Kleinman," *American Journal of Sociology* 87, No. 1 (July 1981): pp. 170-173, and Gary Alan Fine and Sherryl Kleinman, "Mass and Specialized Media: Reply to Corzine," ibid., pp. 173-177.
31. See William J. Goode, *The Celebration of Heroes* (Berkeley: University of California Press, 1978), pp. 108-110, for an analysis of the "flow of prestige" among social networks that share interest in a given activity.
32. The historian Arthur C. Cole recognizes the influence of newsprint on Americans. He remarks that "many an American gleaned his education and drew his inspiration chiefly from the printed page" (p. 216). More specifically, Voigt suggests that it was the sportswriter who

helped "sustain the public interest" in baseball (p. 220).

33. Phillip W. Davison, et al., *Mass Media Systems and Effects* (New York: Praeger, 1976), p. 177. Italics mine.

34. *Ibid.*, p. 181.

35. B. Berelson, *Content Analysis in Communication Research* (New York: Hafner, 1972), pp. 534–535. Italics mine.

36. W. Phillip Davison and Frederick T.C. Yu, eds., *Mass Communication Research: Major Issues and Future Directions* (New York: Praeger, 1974), p. 12.

37. *Ibid.*

38. Gunther Barth, *City People: The Rise of Modern City Culture in Nineteenth-Century America* (New York: Oxford University Press, 1982), p. 163.

39. See Alfred McClung Lee, p. 731, for data on newspaper circulation in New York City in the nineteenth century.

40. These elements are dramatic because they constitute a complex whole which conveys vivid emotional meanings to the baseball audience. Cf. Francis W. Keenan, "The Athletic Contest as a Tragic Form of Art," *The Philosophy of Sport*, ed. Robert G. Osterhoudt, Ph.D. (Springfield, IL: Charles C. Thomas, 1973), p. 313, and Benjamin Lowe, *The Beauty of Sport* (Englewood Cliffs, NJ: Prentice-Hall, 1977), pp. 101–104. Voigt suggests that in the 1860s, because of the "leisure" patterns" of Americans, the game of baseball grew into a "sports spectacle," p. 45.

41. Because of the complexity of the phenomenon, it is difficult to isolate the mechanisms by which rule changes in baseball were influenced by the entertainment inclinations of the baseball audience. Notwithstanding this, it seems reasonable to assume that with the increase in the size of the baseball audience, and with an increase in partisan rooting, the influence of the spectator also increased.

42. Voigt, p. 58.

43. Seymour, p. 30.

44. Michael Novak, *The Joy of Sports* (New York: Basic Books, 1976), p. 58.

45. Gregory P. Stone, "American Sports: Play and Display," *Sport and Society*, eds. John T. Talamini and Charles H. Page (Boston: Little, Brown, 1973), p. 83. Italics mine.

46. M. Wylie, *Clear Channels* (New York: Funk & Wagnalls Co., 1955), p. 33.

47. An editor for the *Spirit of the Times* notes that this rule "will save much valuable time and many a drawn game which has been too often frittered away, much to the disgust of parties who have gone into the field for an afternoon's recreation." *Spirit of the Times*, March 7, 1857.

48. Voigt, p. 210.

49. *Ibid.*

50. See Paul Weiss, *Sport: A Philosophic Inquiry* (Carbondale: Southern Illinois University Press, 1969), p. 87 on strategy.

51. Voigt, p. 213.

52. *Ibid.*

53. Seymour, p. 64.

54. Voigt, p. 213.

55. Roger Caillois, *Man, Play, and Games*, trans. Meyer Barash (New York: Free Press of Glencoe, Inc., 1961), p. 122.

56. Barth, p. 180.

57. For the decline of the status of wage earner, see David Montgomery, *Beyond Equality: Labor and the Radical Republicans 1862–1872* (New York: Alfred A. Knopf, 1967), pp. 25–28; Rodgers, p. 31; and Douglas T. Miller, *Jacksonian Aristocracy: Class and Democracy in New York 1830–1860* (New York: Oxford University Press, 1967), p. 153.

58. Miller, p. 118.

59. *Ibid.*, p. 131.

60. Rodgers, pp. 30–31.

61. *Ibid.*

62. Miller, p. 153.

63. Montgomery, p. 34.

64. *New York Times*, February 22, 24, March 2, 5, 17, 24, 1869, cited by Montgomery, p. 25.

65. *New York Times*, February 22, 1869, quoted in Montgomery, p. 25.

66. *Ibid.*

67. *Ibid.*, p. 26.

68. Caillois, p. 22.

69. Voigt, p. 45.

70. Quoted in Ball and Loy, p. 251.

71. *Spirit of the Times*, September 5, 1857.

72. *New York Tribune*, July 20, 1858, quoted in Preston D. Orem, *Baseball: 1845–1881* (Altadena, CA: published by the author, 1961), p. 19.

73. *Spirit of the Times*, July 31, 1858.

74. *Ibid.*, October 30, 1858.

75. *New York Clipper*, July 21, 1860.

76. Seymour, p. 29.

77. Spalding, p. 85.

78. Seymour, p. 29.

79. *New York Clipper*, September 8, 1860.

80. *Ibid.*

81. Henry Chadwick reports that in 1857 he estimated the crowd watching the Athletics of Philadelphia play the Atlantics of Brooklyn to be forty thousand. He also notes that the game was "adjourned after one inning because of the immense crowd surrounding the field." Chadwick, *Scrapbooks*, Vol. I, p. 14.

82. For a description of early baseball parks, see Seymour, pp. 48–49.
83. *Cincinnati Commercial*, June 14, 1870, quoted in Leitner, p. 92.
84. Cantor and Werthman, p. 62.
85. Sennett, p. 23.
86. Seymour, p. 346. For a study of community pride expressed through allegiance to sport teams, see P.E. Frohlich, "Sport and the Community: A Study in Social Change in Athens, Ohio, 1952" (unpublished Ph.D. dissertation, University of Wisconsin).
87. *Brooklyn Eagle*, May 10, 1860.
88. *Ibid.*, September 3, 1860.
89. An indication of the growth of baseball was the increase in the number of clubs and geographical representative delegates to the annual baseball conventions. Spalding points out that at the 1866 annual convention "delegates were present from clubs in New York, Pennsylvania, New Jersey, Connecticut, the District of Columbia, Maryland, Ohio, Massachusetts, Iowa, Tennessee, Missouri, Kansas, Delaware, Virginia, West Virginia, Kentucky, Oregon, Maine" (Spalding, pp. 101–102). There were sixteen delegates to the convention of 1857. Ten years later, there were delegates from 237 clubs (*Spirit of the Times*, March 3, 1857).
90. See Peverelly, p. 375, for an overview of match games played by prominent clubs of New York and Brooklyn in the 1850s.
91. *New York Clipper*, November 16, 1869.
92. Chadwick, *Beadle's Dime Base-Ball Player*, 1865.
93. *New York Tribune*, September 5, 1857.
94. Voigt, p. 221.
95. *Ibid.*, p. 222.
96. *Ibid.*, p. 223.

Chapter VI

1. Chadwick, scrapbooks, Vol. I, p. 28.
2. Dale A. Somers, *The Rise of Sport in New Orleans 1850–1900* (Baton Rouge: Louisiana State University Press, 1972), p. 293.
3. Adelman, "The Development of Modern Athletics," p. 37.
4. *Spirit of the Times*, May 10, 1851, as quoted in Somers, p. 30.
5. Henry Chafetz, *Play the Devil: A History of Gambling in the United States from 1492 to 1955* (New York: Bonanza Books, 1960), p. 262.
6. Spears and Swanson, p. 67.
7. Dulles, p. 190.
8. George Moss, "The Long Distance Runners of Ante-Bellum America," *Journal of Popular Culture* 8, No. 2 (Fall 1974): p, 370.

9. Somers, p. 61. See also Betts, p. 36, for a discussion of "foot racing."
10. Somers, p. 243.
11. *New York Clipper*, July 9, 1859.
12. *Spirit of the Times*, September 5, 1857.
13. *Brooklyn Eagle*, May 10, 1860.
14. Betts, p. 38, quoting *New York Sun*, 1835.
15. *Harper's Weekly*, October 30, 1858.
16. *Ibid.*, May 5, 1860.
17. *Ibid.*
18. Melvin L. Adelman, "The First Modern Sport in America: Harness Racing in New York City, 1825–1870," *Journal of Sport History* 8, No. 1 (Spring 1981): pp. 5–32.
19. *Ibid.*, p. 16.
20. *Ibid.*, p. 17.
21. Betts p. 162.
22. *Ibid.*, pp. 162–163.
23. Freedman, p. 48.
24. Berryman, p. 48–49.
25. Robert E. Riegel, *Young America, 1830–1840* (Norman: University of Oklahoma Press, 1949), p. 410.
26. Adelman, "The First Modern Sport in America"
27. *Ibid.*
28. Spalding, p. 134.
29. *Spirit of the Times*, September 13, 1856.
30. *Ibid.*, November 28, 1857.
31. *Ibid.*
32. *Ibid.*, March 7, 1857.
33. *Brooklyn Eagle*, August 4, 1866.
34. *Ibid.*, March 11, 1870.
35. *New York Times*, April 7, 1870.
36. *Spirit of the Times*, March 11, 1871.
37. Adelman, "The Development of Modern Athletics," p. 414.
38. *New York Clipper*, July 31, 1860. In the late 1850s, gambling on games by players had been expressly forbidden by the NABBP.
39. *Brooklyn Eagle*, August 4, 1863.
40. *New York Clipper*, July 9, 1864. The *New York Clipper* writer has apparently erred in his computation. If the Mutuals scored five runs in the later innings, their total would be fifteen runs instead of sixteen. Notwithstanding this error, it does not negate the point being made: the Mutuals were able to overcome the odds against them, thereby protecting the wagers of their friends.
41. *Ibid.*
42. See letters to the editor from "Old Chalk" (pseudonym) referring to a player of the Nationals by the name of Andy Johnson, being drunk while playing and selling games to gamblers. Chadwick, *Scrapbooks*, Vol. 1, p. 18. Further on in Chadwick's scrapbook there is a

series of clipped-out articles by "Old Chalk." It appears that he wrote a gossip column for the *Morning Programme*, in the form of a letter to a certain "Briggs" in 1868. The articles are critical of Chadwick's position against professional baseball and the practice of subsidizing players of the Mutuals through the municipal payroll. One article (February 28, 1868, no publication cited) by "Old Chalk" accuses Chadwick of monetarily profiting from baseball owners. It states in part: "I don't like to make charges against any man, but if Chad don't make heaps of tin out of clubs they tell big lies about him. I'm going to watch him close this spring, and if I can get hold of anything reliable I'll show him up just as sure as my name is Chalk." See Chadwick's *Scrapbooks*, Vol. I, pp. 18, 21, 23.

43. *New York Mercury*, September 7, 1867.
44. *Harper's Weekly*, October 26, 1867.
45. *Spirit of the Times*, April 25, 1868.
46. *New York Clipper*, November 3, 1866.
47. *Chicago Times*, July 25, 1867, as quoted in Leitner, p, 78.
48. Leitner, p. 79.
49. *Ibid*.
50. *Chicago Republican*, July 29, 1867, quoted in Leitner, p, 80.
51. Voigt, p, 67.
52. *Brooklyn Eagle*, September 24, 1867.
53. *Ibid*.
54. *Ibid*.
55. *Ibid*.
56. *Brooklyn Eagle*, April 10, 1868.
57. *Spirit of the Times*, November 26, 1870.
58. *New York Times*, November 27, 1870.
59. Spalding, pp. 189–190. The above reference to "pools" denotes the practice of "pool selling." This was an organized system of betting, where "the pool-seller gets a fair commission for his travail in keeping the record of the pools sold, in making out the tickets which serve as certificates of the risks taken and seeing that the parties directly interested shall be able to settle their dues as speedily as possible" (*Boston Daily Globe*, July 24, 1877). Before a baseball match, the pool seller, in an auction, would ask for bids on an upcoming contest. The highest bidder had the right to select the club of his choice. Bets on the opposing club were then taken. If the bets and the odds established did not please the first better, he had the option to decline or withdraw his bet. See also Thorn, p. 169.
60. Chadwick, *Beadle's Dime Base-Ball Player*, 1873, quoted in Spalding, p. 190.
61. *Ibid.*, p. 191.
62. *New York Clipper*, April 24, 1875.
63. Harry Wright Scrapbooks, Vol. 2, Spalding Collection, Rare Manuscript Division, New York Public Library.
64. Adelman, "The Development of Modern Athletics," p. 414.
65. Seymour, p. 53.
66. Adelman, "The Development of Modern Athletics," p. 416.
67. *Ibid*. While Adelman's explanation is plausible, it should be mentioned that the press did recognize the "glorious uncertainty of Base-Ball," in reference to losses by the Excelsiors and Atlantics, to the Unions and the Eckfords, respectively. See *Brooklyn Eagle*, July 28, 1862, and September 3, 1866, for the idea of "uncertainty" in baseball. In the celebrated game between the Atlantics and the Cincinnati Red Stockings, in which the Atlantics triumphed in the 11th inning, a writer for the *Brooklyn Eagle* notes that in the 10th inning, the "Reds now thought they had the game certain but it seems there is nothing certain in base ball" (*Brooklyn Eagle*, June 15, 1870).
68. See *New York Clipper*, August 14, 1869, and August 20, 1870.
69. Malcolm Moran, "Striving for 100%, 100% of the Time," *New York Times*, October 29, 1979, p. Cl.
70. Cf. Adelman, "The Development of Modern Athletics," pp. 416–417.
71. *Spirit of the Times*, July 10, 1869.
72. See Seymour, pp. 50, 60, and Voigt, pp. 63–64.
73. Adelman, "The Development of Modern Athletics," pp. 382–383 and 405–408.
74. *Ibid.*, p. 382.
75. *Ibid*.
76. *Ibid.*, p. 408.
77. *New York Times*, July 21, 1858.
78. *New York Clipper*, July 21, 1860. During the formative years of baseball, matches were arranged during the playing season by invitational challenges, usually in writing. Occasionally a series of games was also prearranged.
79. Spalding, p. 81.
80. *Ibid.*, p. 84.
81. *Ibid*.
82. *Ibid.*, p. 85.
83. *Ibid*.
84. *Ibid*. See also Seymour, pp. 29–30.
85. *Brooklyn Eagle*, October 22, 1861.
86. Church, p, 26.
87. *Ibid*.
88. *Ibid.*, p. 34.
89. *Ibid.*, p. 26.
90. Adelman, "The Development of Modern Athletics," p. 407.
91. *Ibid*.

92. Church, p. 34.
93. Seymour, p. 60.
94. *New York Clipper*, November 3, 1866.
95. *Harper's Weekly*, April 26, 1867.
96. *Ibid.*
97. *Brooklyn Eagle*, July 10, 1868. An early baseball historian suggests that "the first series of games for what may be called a championship took place in the years 1857–59." See Morse.
98. *New York Times*, April 10, 1869.
99. *Ibid.*, July 3, 1870.
100. *Ibid.*
101. *Ibid.*, April 7, 1870.
102. Chadwick, *Scrapbooks*, Vol. 1., p. 11.
103. The press was aware of the popularity of wagering on championship contests. See *Spirit of the Times*, April 25, 1868. For the economic relationship between interest in baseball and the press, see Voigt, "Cash and Glory," p. 220, and Betts, pp. 60, 62.
104. See Cunningham, p. 22, for a discussion of how suppression of sport may act as a "stimulus to greater indulgence" in the sport.
105. Orrin E. Klapp, *Social Types: Process, Structure and Ethos* (San Diego, CA: Aegis, 1971), p. 86.
106. See Edwin M. Schur, *The Politics of Deviance* (Englewood Cliffs, NJ: Prentice-Hall, 1980), pp. 5 and 13, for deviant amplification.
107. See Everett C. Hughes, *The Sociological Eye: Selected Papers on Institutions and Race* (Chicago: Aldine-Atherton, 1971), pp. 141–150, for the idea of a master status.
108. See Edward Sagarin, *Deviants & Deviance* (New York: Praeger, 1975), pp. 144–146, for a discussion of the variability of the acceptance of a deviant identity by self and others.
109. Klapp, *Heroes, Villains and Fools*, p. 67.
110. Leon Festinger, "An Introduction to the Theory of Dissonance," *Current Perspectives in Social Psychology*, eds. Edwin P. Hollander and Raymond G. Hunt (New York: Oxford University Press, 1967), p. 352.
111. A similar process occurred when Jackie Robinson entered baseball as a member of the Brooklyn Dodgers in 1947. He "took the first step toward the desegregation of baseball." See Lucas and Smith, pp. 385–386. At first, "he received death threats to himself and his family" and took verbal abuse from players and managers of the St. Louis Cardinals and the Philadelphia Phillies. *Ibid.*, pp. 388–389. However, Robinson was able to transcend those initial negative sentiments toward him by his superior play and was admired by people within and without baseball.
112. Robert Peterson, *Only the Ball Was White* (New Jersey: Prentice Hall, 1970), p. 17.
113. Jules Tygiel, *Baseball's Great Experiment: Jackie Robinson and His Legacy* (New York: Vintage, 1984), p. 13.
114. Thorn, p. 129.
115. Peterson, p. 16.
116. Quoted in Peterson, p. 17.
117. Seymour, p. 42.
118. Quoted in Peterson, p, 17.
119. Peterson, p, 18.
120. See *Early Image of Black Baseball: Race and Representation in the Popular Press, 1871–1890* by James E. Brunson III (Jefferson, NC: McFarland, 2009) for a seminal account of the image of Negroes in baseball. Brunson focuses on the "black image" of baseball in a period slightly beyond the time where the image of professional baseball was already formed. Other than the exclusion of Negroes from organized baseball, it appears that Negroes had little, if any, impact on the *formation* of the image of professional baseball.
121. Vernon L. Parrington, *Main Currents in American Thought*, vol. 3: *The Beginnings of Critical Realism in America: 1860–1920* (New York: Harcourt Brace & World, 1930
122. See "Yellow Journalism and the Sports Page" in Betts, pp. 62–67.

Chapter VII

1. See the *Brooklyn Eagle*, October 31, 1861, for an early reference to a "Benefit Match."
2. Voigt, "Cash and Glory," p. 60, and Seymour, p. 47.
3. See the *Brooklyn Eagle*, October 31, 1861 for one of the early announcements of a "benefit match" in baseball.
4. See the *New York Clipper*, January 23, 1869, for a new rule adopted by the NABBP to prohibit a "social game," a "friendly game" or an "exhibition game" as a means to circumvent the rule against compensation to players.
5. *Spirit of the Times*, November 6, 1847.
6. *Brooklyn Eagle*, October 31, 1861.
7. *Ibid.*, November 1, 1861.
8. *Brooklyn Eagle*, November 4, 1861.
9. *Ibid.*, November 7, 1861.
10. *Ibid.*
11. *New York Clipper*, November 16, 1861.
12. *Ibid.*, December 9, 1865.
13. *New York Clipper*, December 9, 1865. The reference from the *Clipper* to "such discreditable scenes" refers to baseball's first scandal to be substantiated. On September 28, 1865, Edward Duffy, William Wansley and Thomas

Devyr "conspired to throw the game" between their team, the Mutuals, and their opponents, the Eckfords. The Eckfords won the game 28 to 11 (Seymour, p. 53). The term "Hippodrome" was used to connote the arrangement of a contest (usually turf racing) for the "sole purpose of splitting the gate receipts." "With no money depending on the outcome, and therefore with no incentive to win," these contests were susceptible to fixing. See Adelman, "The First Modern. Sport in America," p. 18, for the term "Hippodrome."

14. *New York Times*, July 3, 1870.
15. *Spirit of the Times*, July 24, 1869.
16. Chadwick's *Scrapbooks*, Vol. I, p. 28.
17. Harry Wright, the manager of the Cincinnati Red Stockings (1869) and later manager of the Boston Red Stockings, recognized the public's willingness to "pay to see a good game of base ball" (Seymour, p. 67).
18. Leitner, p. 71. Adelman also sheds light on the financial arrangements between Cammayer and the team using the Union Grounds. He points out that the press reported (*New York Clipper*, April 27, 1867, and *Spirit of the Times*, April 27, 1867) that "the Atlantics would pay Cammayer forty percent of the receipts plus expenses for the use of the Union Grounds. The players probably divided the profits equally, but it is possible that some veterans or star players received a larger share" (Adelman, "The Development of Modern Athletics," p. 408).
19. *Brooklyn Eagle*, May 4, 1864.
20. Adelman, "The Development of Modern Athletics," p. 408.
21. *New York Clipper*, November 3, 1866.
22. *Ibid.*
23. *Spirit of the Times*, November 26, 1870.
24. Seymour, p. 52.
25. Spalding, p. 122.
26. *Ibid.*, p. 130.
27. *Ibid.*, p. 122.
28. *Ibid.*
29. *Ibid.*
30. *Spirit of the Times*, March 19, 1859.
31. *New York Times*, April 10, 1869.
32. *Ibid.*
33. *Spirit of the Times*, March 19, 1859.
34. *Ibid.*, March 26, 1859. Italics mine.
35. *New York Clipper*, December 9, 1865. There appears to be a complete lack of specific charges or a discussion of direct compensation to players before 1865 in the press, with the exception of the 1859 *Spirit of the Times* (April 19, 1859) editorial advocating compensation for "time and expenses" and the subsequent letter to the editor in reply to this editorial. However, indirect compensation, such as sharing of gate receipts and benefit matches, were discussed in the press beginning in the early 1860s.
36. *New York Clipper*, September 3, 1866.
37. *Ibid.*
38. *Ibid.*
39. *Spirit of the Times*, December 1, 1866.
40. *Union*, November 29, 1868, and in Chadwick's *Scrapbooks*, Vol. I, p. 21.
41. The distinction between amateur and professional in the press will be taken up later.
42. *New York Clipper*, December 15, 1866.
43. *Ibid.*
44. *Brooklyn Eagle*, July 10, 1868. Emphasis in the original.
45. *Spirit of the Times*, October 24, 1868.
46. *Ibid.*, November 15, 1869.
47. *New York Herald*, April 4, 1869.
48. *New York Clipper*, January 23, 1869.
49. Voigt, "Cash and Glory," p. 68.
50. *Ibid.*, p. 69.
51. Seymour, p. 47.
52. Adelman, "The Development of Modern Athletics," Chapter 6.
53. *Ibid.*
54. In a personal communication, Adelman points out that there are a number of limitations to his approach: common names were not easily identifiable as baseball players, and the listings in these "directories" discriminated against "lower class" people and heads of households. Furthermore, it could not always be ascertained if the directory listing referred to a father or a son, or if both had the same first names ("The Development of Modern Athletics," p. 331).
55. The number of occupational backgrounds of players examined by Adelman for the period from 1850 to 1855 was sixty-two ("The Development of Modern Athletics," p. 331). During this time there were thirteen baseball clubs that were organized according to bylaws and playing rules. Assuming there were approximately thirty members to a club, the total number of active players in Brooklyn and New York would be almost four hundred. By 1857 there were twenty-four organized clubs. See Spalding, "America's National Game," p. 64, for the number of clubs.
56. By 1860 there were 77 teams. Again, assuming thirty players to a club, there were approximately 1,700 active players at this time. Adelman examined the occupational background of 357 of these players.
57. Adelman, "The Development of Modern Athletics," p. 358.
58. *Ibid.*, p. 361.
59. *Ibid.*, p. 357.

Notes—Chapter VII

60. *Ibid.*, p. 362.
61. *Ibid.*, p. 363.
62. *Ibid.*
63. *Ibid.*
64. *Ibid.*
65. *Ibid.*, p. 445.
66. *Ibid.*, p. 451.
67. *Ibid.*
68. The source of Riess's data comes from *The Baseball Encyclopedia: The Complete and Official Record of Major League Baseball* (New York: Macmillan, 1969), pp, 47–491.
69. Riess, p. 242. The origin of the NAPBBP will be discussed shortly.
70. *Ibid.*
71. *Ibid.*, pp. 242–243.
72. Voigt, "Cash and Glory," p. 202.
73. Riess, p. 243.
74. Adelman, "The Development of Modern Athletics," p. 452.
75. Riess, p. 249.
76. Harry Ellard, *Baseball in Cincinnati: A History* (Cincinnati, Ohio: Johnson & Hardin, 1907), p. 25.
77. Many cricketers and baseball players had playing experience in both games.
78. Voigt, "Cash and Glory," p. 75.
79. Seymour, p. 56.
80. Ritter Collett, *The Cincinnati Reds* (Virginia Beach, VA: Jordan-Powers, 1976), p. 13.
81. Voigt, p. 81.
82. *Ibid.*, p. 82.
83. Seymour, p. 57.
84. Voigt, "Cash and Glory," p. 89.
85. *Cincinnati Commercial*, June 15, 1870, quoted in Voigt, p. 90.
86. *Ibid.*
87. Voigt, "Cash and Glory," p. 91.
88. *Ibid.*
89. *Ibid.*, p. 93.
90. *New York Clipper*, January 28, 1871.
91. *Ibid.*
92. Gusfield, p. 178.
93. See Stanford M. Lyman, *The Seven Deadly Sins* (New York: St. Martin's, 1978), pp. 241–243, for an analysis of Simmel's critique of the social role of money.
94. See Voigt, "Cash and Glory," pp. 68–69, and Seymour, p. 47.
95. Adelman, "The Development of Modern Athletics," p. 454.
96. Chadwick, *Scrapbooks*, Vol. I, p. 14.
97. Adelman, "The Development of Modern Athletics," p. 454.
98. For the use of the term "lower classes" see Voigt, "Cash and Glory," pp. 54–55, and Seymour, p. 23.
99. See letters of resignation, New York Knickerbocker Base Ball Club Correspondence, Rare Manuscript Division, New York Public Library, Vol. I, 1859–1860, and Seymour, p. 49.
100. Seymour, p. 49.
101. Spalding, p. 79.
102. Seymour, p. 16. Unfortunately, little data exist on the *early* formation of junior clubs, and no information appears to be extant on membership requirements of these clubs.
103. Adelman, "The Development of Modern Athletics," p. 346.
104. Seymour, p. 56.
105. *New York Clipper*, December 9, 1870.
106. *Brooklyn Eagle*, March 24, 1871.
107. *Ibid.*
108. Seymour, p. 70.
109. *New York Times*, April 10, 1869.
110. Seymour, p. 70.
111. *New York Clipper*, October 22, 1870.
112. *Sporting Times*, July 2, 1870, quoted in Voigt, "Cash and Glory," p. 94.
113. *New York Clipper*, October 22, 1870.
114. *Brooklyn Eagle*, August 3, 1859.
115. *Brooklyn Eagle*, May 4, 1864, and August 17, 1864.
116. *Brooklyn Eagle*, August 19, 1863. Italics mine.
117. *Ibid.*, July 10, 1868. Italics in original.
118. October 24, 1868.
119. *New York Times*, April 10, 1869.
120. *Ibid.*, April 7, 1870.
121. *Ibid.*
122. This association was formed after the NABBP. It consisted of representatives of baseball clubs from New York State.
123. *Brooklyn Eagle*, November 17, 1869.
124. *Ibid.*
125. *Ibid.*
126. Sport historians, Somers and Adelman, have recognized the ambiguity of the concept of the amateur athlete. Writing about baseball after the Civil War in New Orleans, Somers mentions that "few teams could be strictly classed as amateur. Teams described as amateur clubs played for money and hired vagabond professionals. Amateur players often competed as professionals and then returned to amateur nines. Popular definitions of amateurism and professionalism did little to dispel the confusion. An amateur, while he might occasionally play for money, regularly pursued another occupation, but a professional made a business of pleasure. Teams composed of both amateurs and professionals were described as semi-professional" (Somers, pp. 138, 293). See Adelman, "The Development of Modern Athletics," pp. 392 and 491.

127. *Brooklyn Eagle*, July 10, 1868.
128. *New York Herald*, April 4, 1869.
129. *Ibid.*, July 5, 1869.
130. In the early 1980s, similar ambiguity surrounded amateur track and field. Confusion over what constituted amateur or professional running surfaced in connection with the Boston Marathon. The president of the Boston Athletic Association, Will Cloney, announced that in the prize money would offer in the 1983 Boston Marathon. In this context, he "contends" that a "semantic difference" exists between "being paid and running for prizes." He went on to say, "If you were to say to me, 'Is the Boston Marathon going professional?' my answer is emphatically no. As to paying prize money, under the existing rules of amateurism, that is a distinct possibility.'" *New York Times*, April 19, 1982, p. 69. In response to Cloney's semantic quibbling, the writer wryly notes that the "existing rules of amateurism could have been written by Cole Porter: Anything goes." Ibid.

Since 1983, prize money has been openly acknowledged in all major marathon races. The amount of prize money has been actively publicized by race organizations and has become a key factor in the competition among marathon organizers to attract the best runners for their races.

131. *Brooklyn Eagle*, March 24, 1871.
132. *Spirit of the Times*, November 26, 1870.
133. *Brooklyn Eagle*, March 15, 1869. Similar questions have been raised throughout the twentieth and twenty-first centuries in reference to amateur athletics and whether athletes trading on their position as well-known athletes constitutes a violation of amateur conduct. With the greater commercialization of the Olympics in the twenty-first century, Olympic athletes are rarely criticized for their endorsement of products and services.
134. In the preceding chapters I have often been tempted to substitute the awkward phrase "social-recreational orientation to playing baseball" with the simpler term amateur. However, I have resisted, knowing that the redundant usage of the aforementioned phrase would add to the tedium associated with reading a book already crammed with terminology. At this juncture, I hope the reasons for my reluctance in using the term amateur are evident. In addition to the historical inappropriateness of using the term amateur to convey meanings about antebellum sport, my hesitancy in using the term also stems from contemporary usage and meanings of the term amateur. Today, in highly competitive organized sport, the term amateur is infrequently used. The notion of amateurism has eroded in the 20th and 21st centuries. With the exception of amateur golf and boxing the designation has lingered on. Today's athletes are motivated to perform at increasing levels of excellence, and in many cases they are monetarily compensated. In brief, this was not the case with the Castle Garden Amateur Boat Club Association, the Knickerbocker Base Ball Club of the 1840s, or other like-minded sport clubs before the Civil War; therefore, the use of the term amateur to describe athletic activities of early nineteenth-century sport enthusiasts would have been misleading.
135. Although payment to players was covert, it was common knowledge in baseball circles that the practice was going on. Therefore, it is reasonable to assume that reporters were aware of it.
136. In addition, the growing economic interdependency between the press and baseball may have been an underlying factor in the hesitancy of writers to be more forthright in their reporting. The following quote suggests that the editorial writer for the *Brooklyn Eagle* was aware of covert payments to players as early as 1863. The writer notes: "Ball matches of late years get to be quite serious affairs and some have intimated that ball playing has been quite a money making business, many finding it to pay well to play ball" (August 21, 1863). Cf. Seymour, pp. 41–49.
137. Keenan, p. 313.
138. Chadwick notes that before 1869 the clubs that shared "gate-money" were "the old Atlantic, Mutual, Eckford, Athletic and Philadelphia Clubs of Brooklyn, New York and Philadelphia" (Chadwick, *Scrapbooks*, Vol. I, p. 22).
139. Lincoln Allison, "Batsman and Bowler: The Key Relations of Victorian England," *Journal of Sport History* 7, No. 2 (Summer 1980): p. 14.
140. *Ibid.*
141. Chadwick, *Scrapbooks*, Vol. I, p. 14.
142. *Ibid.*, p. 18.
143. *Ibid.*
144. See the *Brooklyn Eagle*, March 24, 1871, for the use of these terms.

Bibliography

I. Primary Sources

Unpublished Works

Chadwick, Henry. *Scrapbooks*. 26 Vols. Spalding Collection, Rare Manuscript Division, New York Public Library.

New York Knickerbocker Base Ball Club. Club Book, 1854–1859. Manuscript Division, New York Public Library.

New York Knickerbocker Base Ball Club. Club Book, 1859–1860. Manuscript Division, New York Public Library.

New York Knickerbocker Base Ball Club Correspondence. Vol. I, 1859–1860. Manuscript Division, New York Public Library.

Wright, Harry. *Scrapbooks*, Vol. II. Manuscript Division, New York Public Library.

Newspapers and Periodicals

Beadle's Dime Base-Ball Player, 1860–1881.
Boston Daily Globe, 1811.
Brooklyn Eagle, 1858–1811.
Harper's Weekly, 1858–1861.
New York Clipper, 1859–1815.
New York Herald, 1853–1869.
New York Mercury, 1861–1816.
New York Tribune, 1853–1851.
Spirit of the Times, 1841–1811.

Books

American Almanac and Repository of Useful Knowledge. Boston: Charles Bowen, 1834.

Church, Seymour R. *Baseball: The History, Statistics and Romance of the American National Game from Its Inception to the Present Time*, vol. 1, 1845–1871. San Francisco: n.p., 1902. Reprint, Princeton, NJ: Pyne Press, 1974.

Ellard, Harry. *Baseball in Cincinnati: A History*. Cincinnati: Johnson & Hardin, 1907. Reprint, Jefferson, NC: McFarland, 2004.

Morse, Jacob. *Sphere and Ash: History of Baseball*. Boston: J.C. Spofford, 1888.

Nevill, Ralph. *Sporting Days and Sporting Ways*. London: Duckworth, 1911.

Peverelly, Charles A. *Book of American Pastimes*. New York: American News Company, 1866.

Spalding, Albert G. *America's National Game: Historic Facts Concerning the Beginning, Evolution, Popularity and Development of Base Ball*. New York: American Sports Publishing, 1911. Reprint, Lincoln: University of Nebraska Press, 1992.

II. Secondary Sources

Books and Articles

Adelman, Melvin L. "The First Baseball Game, the First Newspaper Reference to Baseball, and the New York Club: A Note on the Early History of Baseball." *Journal of Sport History* 7, No. 344 (Winter 1980): 132–135.

———. "The First Modern Sport in America: Harness Racing in New York City, 1825–1870." *Journal of Sport History* 8, No. 1 (Spring 1981): 5–32.

Allison, Lincoln. "Batsman and Bowler: The Key Relations of Victorian England." *Journal of Sport History* 7, No. 2 (Summer 1980): 5–20.

Angell, Roger. *The Summer Game*. New York: Viking, 1972.

Barney, Robert Knight. "Physical Education and Sport in North America." In *History of Physical Education and Sport*, pp. 171–

227. Edited by Earle F. Zeigler. Englewood Cliffs, NJ: Prentice-Hall, 1979.

Barth, Gunther. *City People: The Rise of Modern City Culture in Nineteenth-Century America*. New York: Oxford University Press, 1982.

The Baseball Encyclopedia: The Complete and Official Record of Major League Baseball. New York: Macmillan Publishing Co., 1969.

Becker, George. *The Mad Genius Controversy*. Beverly Hills, CA: Sage, 1978.

Benson, L. "An Approach to the Scientific Study of Past Public Opinion." *Public Opinion Quarterly* 4 (Winter 1967–68): 522–566.

Berelson, B. *Content Analysis in Communication Research*. New York: Hafner, 1972.

Berryman, Jack W. "The Tenuous Attempts of Americans to Catch Up with 'John Bull': Specialty Magazines and Sporting Journalism, 1800–1835." *Canadian Journal of History of Sport and Physical Education* 10, No. 1 (May 1979): 33–61.

Betts, John Rickards. *America's Sporting Heritage: 1850–1950*. Reading, MA: Addison-Wesley, 1974.

Block, David. *Baseball Before We Knew It*. Lincoln: University of Nebraska Press, 2005.

Blumer, Herbert. "Outline of Collective Behavior." In *Readings in Collective Behavior*, pp. 65–88. Edited by Robert R. Evans. 2nd ed. Chicago: Rand McNally College, 1975.

Bode, Carl. *The Anatomy of Popular Culture, 1840–1861*. Berkeley: University of California Press, 1959.

Boulding, Kenneth E. *The Image*. Ann Arbor: University of Michigan Press, 1956.

Brasch, R. *How Did Sports Begin: A Look at the Origins of Man at Play*. New York: David McKay, 1970.

Brown, Richard H. *A Poetic for Sociology*. Cambridge: Cambridge University Press, 1977.

____, and Stanford M. Lyman, eds. *Structure, Consciousness, and History*. Cambridge: Cambridge University Press, 1978.

Brunson, James E., III. *Early Image of Black Baseball: Race and Representation in the Popular Press, 1871–1890*. Jefferson, NC: McFarland, 2009.

Cahnman, Werner, and Alvin Boskoff, eds. *Sociology and History: Theory and Research*. New York: Free Press, 1964.

Caillois, Roger. *Man, Play, and Games*. Translated by Meyer Barash. New York: Free Press of Glencoe, 1961.

Canetti, Elias. *Crowds and Power*. Translated by Carol Stewart. New York: Viking, 1966.

Cantor, Norman F., and Michael S. Werthman, eds. *The History of Popular Culture: Since 1815*. London: Macmillan, 1969.

Cawelti, John G. *Apostles of the Self-Made Man*. Chicago: University of Chicago Press, 1965.

Chafetz, Henry. *Play the Devil: A History of Gambling in the United States from 1492 to 1955*. New York: Bonanza, 1960.

Childs, H.L. *Public Opinion: Nature, Formation and Role*. Princeton, NJ: D. Von Nostrand, 1965.

Collett, Ritter. *The Cincinnati Reds*. Virginia Beach, VA: Jordan-Powers, 1976.

Corzine, Jay. "Media Diffusion of Subcultural Elements: Comment on Fine and Kleinman." *American Journal of Sociology* 87, No. 1 (July 1981): 170–173.

Culin, Stewart. *Games of North American Indians*. New York: Dover, 1975; original publication 1907.

Cunningham, Hugh. *Leisure in the Industrial Revolution*. New York: St. Martin's, 1980.

Davis, Thomas R. "Puritanism and Physical Education: The Shroud of Gloom Lifted." *Canadian Journal of History of Sport and Physical Education* 3, No. 2 (May 1972): 1–27.

Davison, W. Phillips, and Frederick T.C. Yu, eds. *Mass Communication Research: Major Issues and Future Directions*. New York: Praeger, 1976.

____, et al. *Mass Media Systems and Effects*. New York: Praeger, 1976.

Diem, Carl. "Yours Is the Earth." In *Sport and Society: A Symposium*, pp. 111–129. Edited by Alex Natan. London: Bowes & Bowes, 1958.

Dizikes, John. *Sportsmen and Gamesmen*. Boston: Houghton Mifflin, 1981.

Dulles, Foster Rhea. *A History of Recreation: America Learns to Play*. New York: Appleton-Century-Crofts, 1965.

Dunning, Eric, and Kenneth Sheard. *Barbarians, Gentlemen and Players: A Sociological Study of the Development of Rugby Football*. New York: New York University Press, 1979.

Ellul, Jacques. *The Technological Society*. Translated by J. Wilkinson. New York: Vintage, 1967.

Encyclopaedia Britannica. 1959 edition. Vols. 2, 19.

Festinger, Leon. "An Introduction to the Theory of Dissonance." In *Current Perspectives in Social Psychology*, pp. 347–357. Edited by Edwin P. Hollander and Raymond G. Hunt. New York: Oxford University Press, 1967.

Fine, Gary Alan, and Sherryl Kleinman. "Mass and Specialized Media: Reply to Corzine." *American Journal of Sociology* 87, No. 1 (July 1981): 173–177.

Freedman, Stephen. "The Baseball Fad in Chicago, 1865–1870: An Exploration of the Role of Sport in the Nineteenth-Century City." *Journal of Sport History* 5, No. 2 (Summer 1978): 42–64.

Goffman, Erving. *Encounters: Two Studies in the Sociology of Interaction*. Indianapolis: Bobbs-Merril, 1961.

Goode, William J. *The Celebration of Heroes.* Berkeley: University of California Press, 1978.

Grobani, Anton, ed. *Guide to Baseball Literature*. Detroit: Gale Research, 1975.

Gruneau, Richard. *Class, Sports, and Social Development*. Amherst: University of Massachusetts Press, 1983.

Gusfield, Joseph R. "Moral Passage: The Symbolic Process in Public Designation of Deviance." *Social Problems* 15, No. 2 (Fall 1967): 175–188.

Hardy, Stephen. *How Boston Played: Sports, Recreation and Community, 1865–1915.* Boston: Northeastern University Press, 1982.

Henderson, Robert W. *Ball, Bat, and Bishop: The Origin of Ball Games*. New York: Rockport, 1947.

_____. *Early American Sport: A Checklist of Books*. Cranbury, NJ: Associated University Presses, 1977.

Holliman, Jennie. *American Sports (1785–1835)*. Durham, NC: Seeman, 1931.

Hughes, Everett C. *The Sociological Eye: Selected Papers on Institutions and Race*. Chicago: Aldine-Atherton, 1971.

Huizinga, Johan. *Homo Ludens: A Study of the Play Elements in Culture*. Boston: Beacon Press, 1955.

Keenan, Francis W. "The Athletic Contest as a 'Tragic' Form of Art." In *The Philosophy of Sport*, pp. 306–309. Edited by Robert G. Osterhoudt, Ph.D. Springfield, IL: Charles C. Thomas, 1973.

Kelly, Robert H. "Toward a Theory of Competition and Cooperation in Sports as an Indicator of Change in American Life." *Journal of Popular Culture* 4, No. 3 (Winter 1971): 604–614.

Kett, Joseph F. *Rites of Passage: Adolescence in America, 1790 to the Present*. New York: Basic Books, 1977.

Klapp, Orrin E. *Heroes, Villains and Fools: Reflections of the American Character*. San Diego: Aegis, 1972.

_____. *Social Types: Process, Structure and Ethos*. San Diego: Aegis, 1971.

Lasch, Christopher. *The Culture of Narcissism*. New York: Warner, 1979.

Lasswell, Harold D. "The Structure and Function of Communication in Society." In *Mass Communications*, pp. 117–130. Edited by Wilbur Schramm. Urbana: University of Illinois Press, 1972.

Ledbetter, Bonnie S. "Sports and Games of the American Revolution." *Journal of Sport History* 6, No. 3 (Winter 1979): 36–37.

Lee, Alfred McClung. *The Daily Newspaper in America: The Evolution of a Social Instrument*. New York: Macmillan, 1937.

Lee, Robert. *Religion and Leisure in America*. New York: Abingdon, 1964.

Leitner, Irving A. *Baseball: Diamond in the Rough*. New York: Criterion, 1972.

Lowe, Benjamin. *The Beauty of Sport*. Englewood Cliffs, NJ: Prentice-Hall, 1977.

Loy, John W., Jr. "The Nature of Sport: A Definitional Effort." In *Sport, Culture, and Society*, pp. 56–71. Edited by John W. Loy, Jr. and Gerald S. Kenyon. New York: Macmillan, 1969.

Lucas, John S., and Ronald A. Smith. *Saga of American Sport*. Philadelphia: Lea & Febiger, 1978.

Lyman, Stanford M. *The Seven Deadly Sins*. New York: St. Martin's, 1978.

McIntosh, P.C. *Sport in Society*. London: C.A. Watts, 1963.

McLaughlin, William C. *The Meaning of Henry Ward Beecher: An Essay on the Shifting Values of Mid-Victorian America, 1830–1860*. New York: Alfred A. Knopf, 1970.

McPherson, Barry C. "Sport Consumption and Economics of Consumerism." In *Sport and Social Order: Contributions to the Sociology of Sport*, pp. 239–275. Edited by Donald W. Ball and John W. Loy. Reading, MA: Addison-Wesley, 1975.

Miller, Douglas T. *Jacksonian Aristocracy: Class and Democracy in New York 1830–1860.* New York: Oxford University Press, 1967.

Molotch, Harvey, and Marilyn Lester. "News as Purposive Behavior: On the Strategic Use of Routine Events, Accidents and Scandals." *American Sociological Review* 39, No. 1 (February 1974): 101–112.

Montgomery, David. *Beyond Equality: Labor and the Radical Republicans, 1862–1872.* New York: Alfred A. Knopf, 1967.

Moran, Malcolm. "Striving for 100%, 100% of the Time." *New York Times* (October 29, 1979).

Moss, George. "The Long Distance Runners of Ante-Bellum America." *Journal of Popular Culture* 8, No. 2 (Fall 1970): 371–382.

Mott, Morris. "The British Protestant Pioneers and the Establishment of Manly Sports in Manitoba, 1870–1886." *Journal of Sport History* 7, No. 3 (Winter 1980): 25–36.

Natan, Alex, ed. "The British Attitude to Sport." In *Sport and Society; A Symposium,* pp. 11–35. London: Bowes & Bowes, 1958.

Novak, Michael. *The Joy of Sports.* New York: Basic Books, 1976.

Nye, Russell. *The Unembarrassed Muse: The Popular Arts in America.* New York: Dial, 1971.

Orem, Preston D. *Baseball: 1845–1881.* Altadena, CA: Published by the author, 1961.

Park, Robert E. *The Crowd and the Public and Other Essays.* Chicago: University of Chicago Press, 1972.

Park, Roberta J. "The Attitudes of Leading New England Transcendentalists Toward Healthful Exercise, Active Recreation and Proper Care of the Body: 1830–1860." *Journal of Sport History* 4, No. 1 (Spring 1977): 34–50.

Parrington, Vernon L. *Main Currents in American Thought,* Vol. 2: *The Romantic Revolution in America: 1800–1860.* New York: Harcourt, Brace & World, 1927.

_____. *Main Currents in American Thought,* Vol. 3: *The Beginnings of Critical Realism in America: 1860–1920.* New York: Harcourt, Brace & World, 1930.

Parsons, Talcott. *The Social System.* Glencoe, NY: Free Press, 1951.

Pessen, Edward. *Riches, Class and Power Before the Civil War.* Lexington, MA: D.C. Heath, 1973.

Peterson, Harold. *The Man Who Invented Baseball.* New York: Charles Scribner's Sons, 1973.

Peterson, Robert. *Only the Ball Was White.* Englewood Cliffs, NJ: Prentice-Hall, 1970.

Riegel, Robert E. *Young America, 1830–1840.* Norman: University of Oklahoma Press, 1949.

Rodgers, Daniel T. *The Work Ethic in Industrial America, 1850–1920.* Chicago: University of Chicago Press, Phoenix Edition, 1979.

Sagarin, Edward. *Deviants & Deviance.* New York: Praeger, 1975.

Schlesinger, Arthur M., and Dixon Ryan Fox, eds. *A History of American Life.* New York: Macmillan, 1934. Vol. 7: *The Irrepressible Conflict, 1850–1865,* by Arthur Charles Cole.

Schur, Edwin M. *The Politics of Deviance.* Englewood Cliffs, NJ: Prentice-Hall, 1980.

Seban, Martha M. "A Theoretical Consideration of the Internal Dynamics of Sport." *Sport in the Socio-cultural Process,* pp. 220–243. Edited by Marie Hart. 2nd edition. Dubuque, IA: Wm. C. Brown, 1976.

Sennett, Richard. *The Fall of Public Man.* New York: Vintage, 1978.

Seymour, Harold, and Dorothy Seymour Mills. *Baseball: The Early Years.* New York: Oxford University Press, 1960.

Solomon, Barbara Miller. *Ancestors and Immigrants: A Changing New England Tradition.* Cambridge: Harvard University Press, 1956.

Somers, Dale A. *The Rise of Sport in New Orleans 1850–1900.* Baton Rouge: Louisiana State University Press, 1972.

Spears, Betty, and Richard A. Swanson. *History of Sport and Physical Activity in the United States.* Dubuque, IA: Wm. C. Brown, 1978.

Stone, Gregory P. "American Sports: Play and Display." In *Sport and Society,* pp. 65–85. Edited by John T. Talamini and Charles H. Page. Boston: Little, Brown, 1973.

Takaki, Ronald. "The Black Child-Savage in Antebellum America." In *The Great Fear: Race in the Mind of America,* pp. 27–44. Edited by G.B. Nash and R. Weiss. New York: Holt, Rinehart, Winston, 1970.

Tarde, Gabriel. *Communication and Social Influence: Selected Papers.* Edited by Terry N. Clark. Chicago: The University of Chicago Press, 1969.

Thorn, John. *Baseball in the Garden of Eden: The Secret History of the Early Game.* New York: Simon & Schuster, 2011.

Turner, Ralph H., and Lewis M. Killian. *Collective Behavior.* 2nd edition. Englewood Cliffs, NJ: Prentice-Hall, 1972.

Tygiel, Jules. *Baseball's Great Experiment: Jackie Robinson and His Legacy.* New York: Vintage, 1984.

Veblen, Thorstein. *The Theory of the Leisure Class.* New York: New American Library, 1953.

Voigt, David Quentin. *American Baseball: From the Gentleman's Sport to the Commissioner System.* University Park: Pennsylvania State University Press, 1983.

Weber, Max. *Economy and Society.* Edited by Guenther Roth and Claus Wittich. New York: Bedminster, 1968.

Weiss, Paul. *Sport: A Philosophical Inquiry.* Carbondale: Southern Illinois University Press, 1969.

Wiggins, David K. "Work, Leisure and Sport in America: The British Travelers Image, 1830–1860." *Canadian Journal of History of Sport* 13, No. 1 (May 1902): 28–60.

Woodhouse, Margaret K. "A History of Amateur Club Rowing in the New York Metropolitan Area, 1830–1870." *Canadian Journal of History of Sport and Physical Education* 11, No. 2 (December 1980): 73–96.

Wylie, M. *Clear Channels.* New York: Funk & Wagnalls, 1955.

Ziff, Larzer. *Literary Democracy: The Declaration of Cultural Independence in America.* New York: Penguin, 1981.

Dissertations and Theses

Adelman, Melvin L. "The Development of Modern Athletics: Sport in New York City, 1820–1870." Ph.D. dissertation, Department of History, University of Illinois at Urbana-Champaign, 1980.

Cosentino, Frank. "A History of the Concept of Professionalism in Canadian Sport." Ph.D. dissertation, University of Alberta, Canada, 1973.

Frohlich, P.E. "Sport and the Community: A Study in Social Change in Athens, Ohio." Ph.D. dissertation, University of Wisconsin, 1952.

Haven, Jeffrey L. "Baseball: The Origins and Development of the Game to 1903." Ph.D. dissertation, Department of Physical Education, Brigham Young University, 1979.

Messenger, Christian Karl. "Sport in American Literature (1830–1930)." Ph.D. dissertation, Department of Philosophy, Northwestern University, 1974.

Riess, Steven A. "Professional Baseball and American Culture in the Progressive Era: Myths and Realities, with Special Emphasis on Atlanta, Chicago, and New York." Ph.D. dissertation, Department of History, University of Chicago, 1974.

Voigt, David Quentin. "Cash and Glory: The Commercialization of Major League Baseball as a Sports Spectacular, 1865–1892." Ph.D. dissertation, Department of Sociology, Syracuse University, 1962.

Walmsley, Louise Jordan. "Sport Attitudes and Practices of Representative Americans Before 1870." Master's thesis, Graduate School of Education, George Peabody College for Teachers, 1938.

Index

Numbers in **_bold italics_** refer to pages with photographs.

accuracy factor, press reportage 5
Adams, Charles Francis 10
Adams, Ivers W. 131–132
Adelman, Melvin L. (writing on): baseball public 74, 77; championship system 106; class structure 127–129, 133, 158nn54–56; corruption accusations 105, 156n67; cricket connections 47, 48; gate receipts 158n18; Knickerbocker backgrounds 51–52; player hiring 134
admission charges: and amateur ideal argument 133; benefit matches 116, 118; with enclosed ball fields 119; first time 63; public willingness 158n13; see also gate receipts, sharing practice
African American players 111–113, 157n111, 157n120
Albany Pythian Club 112
alcohol prohibition, Gusfield's study 60, 132
all-star/championship games 62–65, 106–110, 156n78
Allison, Doug 130
Alton Locke (Kingsley) 15
amateur ideal: American emergence 28–30, 32–33, 148n33; class structure factor 26–27; in compensation arguments 125–127, 132–135, 143; English origins 25–27, 148n24; in Knickerbocker origins 48; rowing competitions 27–29, 148n27; and sportsmanship ideal 23–25
American Almanac ... for the Year 1834 19–20
American Farmer 18–19, 31
American Indians, baseball origins 42–43
American Rural Sports 19
American Turf Register 19
The American's Shooting Manual 31
amusements, defined 10
Anatomy of a Revolution (Brinton) 3
Angell, Roger 1–2
Arnold, Thomas 15
athletic clubs, English 25–26, 46–47
Athletics, Philadelphia: Atlantics game 154n81; benefit match 116–117; championship games 107; compensation accusations 124; competition orientation 55; fraud accusations 108; gate receipts 120–121, 160n138; Mutuals match 101; play inconsistency 101–102, 102–103; Red Stockings game 131
Atlantic Monthly 18
Atlantics, Brooklyn: all-star game 62; audience behavior 87–88, 89; benefit match 116–117; championship games 106–107; club rivalries 90; competition orientation 55; Excelsiors' games 65, 88; gate receipts 120–121, 158n18, 160n138; play inconsistency 100–103; professionalism decision 135, 138; Red Stockings game 130–131, 156n67
attendance statistics 63, 64, 130, 154n81
audience, baseball: defining 74–75, 77; rowdiness 80, 87–90, 101; see also public, baseball
Austen, Jane 37
Avery, Walter 53

Babcock, S. 40
Bachelor Club 112
Baltic Club, New York 54, 56
Baltimore, Excelsiors' tour 65
Barbarians, Gentlemen and Players (Dunning and Sheard) 24
Barth, Gunther 85
base distance, significance 45
base-on-balls rule 100–101
baseball (base ball): early clubs 53–56, 151n117; origins of 16–17, 21; see also Knickerbockers, New York; rules and regulations
baseball guides 21, 84
baseball player concept 4
batting rules 82–83
Baxter, William 12
Beadle's Dime Base-Ball Player 20–21, 84, 104, 112
Bedford Club 56
Beecher, Henry Ward 14
Bellows, H.W. 17–18

168   Index

benefit matches 115–119, 158n35
Benson, L. 75
Berelson, B. 81
Berryman, Jack W. 97
Betts, John Rickards 95
bias factor, press reportage analysis 5
Birdsall, Ralph 42
Block, David 34, 35–36
Bluestockings Club, St. Louis 112
Blumer, Herbert 75
boat clubs, American 29–30
Book of American Pastimes (Peverelly) 42
The Book of Sports (Carver) 40–41
Boskoff, Alvin 3
Boston club 71, 131–132
Boston Marathon 160n130
Boulding, Kenneth E. 2–3
Boxiana (Egan) 30
boxing contests 18, 20, 95–96
The Boy's Book of Sports (Babcock) 40
boys' games, in baseball's origins 34–43
The Boys Own Book 36, 39–40
Brainard, Asa 130
bribes *see* fixing games
Brinton, Crane 3
Brooklyn: in all-star games 62; as baseball center 5, 54; early baseball clubs 47–48, 54; *see also* Atlantics, Brooklyn
Brooklyn Association Board of Managers 16
Brooklyn Base Ball Club 53
Brooklyn Club 47–48
Brooklyn Daily Union 112–113
Brooklyn Eagle (article topics): all-star game 64–65; amateur definition 138; amateur vs. professional clubs 137, 139; benefit matches 116–117; benefits of baseball 61, 62; championship matches 109; club rivalries 90; compensation of players 125, 135, 160n136; cricket benefits 67; Excelsiors tour 65; gambling 100, 103, 125; performance levels 70; play inconsistency 102–103, 156n67; pre–Civil War sports 20; revolving practice 98; walking contestants 95
Brooklyn Putnam Club 54, 56, 62, 70
Brooklyn Union Club 112
Brooklyn Union Star Cricket Club 47–48
Brooklyn Uniques Club 112–113
Brunson, James E., III 157n120
Building the Young Man (Wayne) 52
bunting innovation 84
Bynders, A.P. 48–49

Cabinet of Natural History 19
Cahnman, Werner 3
Callois, Roger 86
Cammayer, William 88, 119, 158n18
Canada, leisure class structure 27
Capitoline Grounds 120
Carlisle, Joseph 55
Cartwright, Alexander 44, 53, 70
Carver, Robin 40–41

Castle Garden Amateur Boat Club Association 29, 30
catching innovations 84
Catlin, George 43
Cauldwell, William 21
Chadwick, Henry: characterized 20–21; Old Chalk's criticisms 155n42; in Spalding Baseball Collection 149n35
Chadwick, Henry (writing on): attendance statistics 154n81; audience behavior 90; championship games 109; compensation of players 124–125; cricket benefits 61; gambling 104; gate receipts 160n138; New York Club 47; origins of baseball 41–42; postgame activities 151n114; professional athletics 94, 143; prose style 71; training benefits 118–119
Champion, Aaron B. 129–130
championship/all-star games 62–65, 106–110, 156n78
Channing, William Ellery 13
character values 24–25, 52, 61; *see also* amateur ideal
Chicago Excelsiors 66, 102, 152n35
Chicago Republican 102
Chicago Times 102
Chicago Tribune 102
Chicago Uniques Club 112
Chicago White Stockings 131
children's games, in baseball's origins 34–43; *see also* rules and regulations
cholera epidemic 18
Christian athlete 15–17
Cincinnati Commercial 89, 130
Cincinnati, Nationals' tour 65
Cincinnati Red Stockings 89, 107, 129–131, 156n67
cities, health conditions 17–18
Civil War 4
Clarke, William 39
class structure: amateur player ideal 26–28; baseball audience 77–80, 81; Eckford Club 54–55; in Knickerbocker origins 48, 49–50, 51–52; and player compensation 126–129, 132–133, 158nn54–56; and player status 85–87; recreation activities 23–24
Cloney, Will 160n130
Cole, Arthur C. 153n32
Collings, Yarning Lansing 39
Columbus, Nationals' tour 65
commercialization process *see* compensation, player
compensation, player: benefit matches 115–119; gate receipts 119–121; ideological perspectives 123–126, 132, 139–140, 143; and image transformation 132–134, 139–140; and overview 115, 121–122, 139–140, 158n35; professionalism decision 134–136; Red Stocking case 129–132; rule against 122–123; salaries 115–116, 129; sinecures 121–122
competition philosophies 50–53

Condit (Olympics player) 70
consumption of baseball, forms 76–77
Continental Club 56
conventions, baseball 56–58, 98, 155n89
Cory and Daniels 40
costs, attendance 79–80
Coyle, Arthur 17
craftsmanship image 71–72
Creighton, Jim 65, 115–116, 117
cricket: benefit matches 116; Chadwick's reporting 21; clubs in America 46–47; English class structure 26–27; and fly rule 57; gambling 99; image in America 60, 61, 66–67, 152n38; popularity of 10, 146n2; reader letter about 67–68
crowd 74, 77; see also audience, baseball; public, baseball
Culin, Stewart 43
Curry, Duncan F. 45
Curtis, George W. 16

Davis, James Whyte 53, 133
Davison, Phillip W. 81
Decker, William H. 29
defense-offense balance 82–83
defensive play, innovations 45
Devyr, Thomas 105, 157n13
DeWitt's Base-Ball Guide 21, 72, 84
dime novels 20
disease, urban living 17–18
Doubleday myth 34, 41–42
Duffy, Edward 105, 157n13
Dunning, Eric 24, 25, 27, 86–87

Eagle Base Ball Club 53, 54, 56, 61, 69–70, 100
Eckford Club, Brooklyn: all-star game 62; benefit match 117; championship games 107; gate receipts 160n138; Mutuals games 105, 106, 157n13; player backgrounds 54–55; professional status 138
Eddy, Daniel 52
Edwards, Lyford 3
Egan, Pierce 30
Ellard, George B. 130
Ellul, Jacques 71
Elysian Fields 47, 55
Emerson, Ralph Waldo 13–14
Empire City Regatta Club 29
Empire Club, New York 54, 56, 62, 70, 90
enclosed baseball grounds 88–89, 119–120
entertainment, baseball as 74, 90–92; impact of playing innovations 84; impact of rule changes 82–84, 142, 154n47; see also skill levels, press reporting
ethnic backgrounds, New York players 129
Eton rowing competitions 148n27
Eurekas, Newark 101
event, defined 152n18
Everett, Edward 18
Ewing, George 39

Excelsior Club, Brooklyn: all-star game 62; amateur status 135, 139; audience behavior 87; championship games 106–107; club rivalries 90; competition orientation 1, 54; at convention 56; fly rule adoption 68–69; formation of 54; in healthy exercise description 61; national tour 65; performance reports 70–71; player hiring change 134
Excelsior Club, Chicago 66, 102, 152n35
Excelsior Club, Philadelphia 112

Fashion Race Course series 62–65, 106–107
fielding innovations 84
firemen, volunteer 52–53
fixing games: gate receipts implications 120–121; implications of inconsistent play 101–103, 106; Mutuals-Eckfords match 105, 157n13; professional player reputation 2, 97, 104–105; see also gambling
fly rule 56, 66, 68–69
folk football 24
Forest City Club 65–66, 102, 152n35
Franklin, Benjamin 17
fraud see fixing games

Gaine, Hugh 38
gambling: baseball 99–106, 107, 108; horse racing 94; pool selling strategy 156n59; professional athlete reputation 96–97, 113–114; Puritan attitude 12; rowdy behavior link 89; rowing competitions 28–29; walking contests 95
gate receipts, sharing practice: in Chadwick's list 160n136; game fixing accusations 120–121; Knickerbocker refusal 133; origins 119–120, 158n35; in professionalism debate 135, 139, 142; see also admission charges
Getting On in the World (Mathews) 52
Goal Ball 40
Godey's Lady's Book 16
Godwin, Samuel 54
Gold Ball Match 107
Gosham, Alfred 130
Gotham Club, New York: all-star game 62; at convention 56; Eagle games 69–70, 100; earliest press account 21; formation 54; in healthy exercise description 61; substitution practice 98
Gould, Charles 130
grandstands 88–89
Graves, Abnerf 41, 42
Greenleaf, Daniel 10
Gruneau 27
Gusfield, Joseph R. 60, 132
gymnasiums, Y.M.C.A. 16

Hardy, Stephen 31
harness racing 96
Harper's 16, 130

Harper's Monthly 18
Harper's Weekly 61, 95–96, 101, 108
Hatfield, John 71
Hawkins, Abe 94
health beliefs 13–17, 61
Heenan, John C. 95
Henderson, Robert W. 34, 35–36, 39, 42, 44–45
Henson Club 112
Higginson, Thomas Wentworth 15, 18
Hippodrome tactics 104, 108, 118, 121, 157n13
Holliman, Jennie 30–31
Holmes, Oliver Wendell 18
horse racing 2, 18, 20, 26, 94, 96
Hughes, Thomas 15
Humphreys (Marion player) 70
hunting sportsmanship 23–24
Hurley, Dick 130

The Illustrated Family Gymnasium (Tail) 16
image, defined 2–3
image of baseball, overview of sport press contribution 1–7, 139–144; *see also* compensation, player; *New York Clipper;* skill levels, press reporting
income levels, New York players 129
Independent Baseball Club 54
Independent Boat Club Association 29
Indianapolis, Nationals' tour 65
infielder skills 84
inning rule 45, 50, 57, 83–84
intellectual renaissance, impact on sport 12–15
Invincible 29

Jefferson, Thomas 17
Jockey Club 25–26
Jones, Frank 102
Jones, L.B. 58
Junior Base Ball Clubs 52, 58–59, 122, 133–134

Katz, E. 81
Killian, Lewis M. 75
Kingsley, Charles 15
Klapp, Orrin E. 111
Knickerbocker (boat) 29
Knickerbocker Base Ball Club, New York: all-star game 62; competition orientation 50–53; cricket connections 46–48; English influence 32; first press accounts 21; fly rule adoption 68; in formation of organizational body 56–57; Gothams match 98; healthy exercise description 61; Ladies Day 80; nationalism description 62; organizational structure 48–49; origins 43–44; player hiring change 134; press treatment 150n72; rules and regulations 44–46, 48–49; Washington Club matches 54

Ladies Day 80
language style, press 3, 71, 145n17

Laswell, Harold D. 76
Lawrence, John 30
Leggett, Joe 107
leisure, defined 10, 11; *see also* recreation activities
Leonard, Andy 130
Lepell, Mary 37
Lester, Andrew 55
Life in New York 19
Lilly, Wait, Colman, and Holden 40
literature review, baseball scholarship 5–6
Little Pretty Pocket-Book (Newberry) 37–39
Louisville, Nationals' tour 65
L'Overture Club, Philadelphia 112
Lucas, John S. 11, 12

Magnolia Base Ball Club, New York 53
Magnolia Lunch and Saloon 55
Manley (Star player) 70
manly game image 60, 61, 138, 151n4
marathon prize money 160n130
Marion Baseball Club 70
Marylebone Cricket Club 25–26, 46, 48
Mathews, William 52
Matthews, Bob 71
McKibbin, John 55
McLaughlin, William 14
McVey, Cal 89, 130
McVey, George 89
The Meaning of Henry Ward Beecher (McLaughlin) 14
methodology 3–5
Millar, Henry 130
Miller, Douglas T. 85–86
Mitchell, S. Weir 16
Monitor Club, Philadelphia 112–113
Morning Programme 155n42
Morrisania Mutuals 107
Morrisania Union Club 98, 101–102, 108
Morrisey, John 95
muffin matches 72–73, 152n58
Murray, H.J. 70
Murray, L.J. 70
Muscular Christianity 15–17
Mutuals, Morrisania 107
Mutuals, New York: Atlantics game 100–101; Boston game 71; championship games 107; compensation forms 121, 125, 155n42; competition orientation 55; Eckfords games 105, 106, 157n13; formation of 54; gate receipts 160n138; player backgrounds 53; professional status 138; Red Stockings game 130

NABBP *see* National Association of Base Ball Players (NABBP)
Nassau Club 56
National Advocate 53
National Association of Amateur Base Ball Players 135–136
National Association of Amateur Oarsmen 30

Index

National Association of Base Ball Players (NABBP): championship system development 107–108; colored persons rule 112; compensation rules 122–123, 126, 135; formation 57–58; social gatherings rule 151n114
National Association of Junior Base Ball Clubs 58–59
National Association of Professional Baseball Players (NAPBBP) 21, 135
National Base Ball Club, Washington 65–66, 102, 130, 152n35
nationalism, in baseball promotion 62, 68
Native Americans 42–43
Natural History of a Revolution (Edwards) 3
Negro players, in press reports 112–113
New Jersey 55, 59
New York Ball Club 53
New York Baltic Club 54, 56
New York City: in all-star games 62; as baseball center 5; club rivalries 90; early baseball clubs 53–54; health conditions 17–18; newspaper circulation 82; population statistics 82; rowing clubs 29–30
New York Clipper (article/editorial topics): amateur baseball's decline 136; audience behavior 88; benefit matches 117–118; Boston reorganization 131–132; boxing 95; championship matches 108; compensation of players 124, 126, 134; corruption 104–105, 120–121; gambling 100; gymnasiums 16; playing inconsistency 101–102; walking contest 95
New York Clipper, establishment of 20
New York Club 47–48
New York Empire Club 54, 56, 62, 70, 90
New York Gazette 29
New York Gotham Club 21, 54, 56, 69–70, 98, 100
New York Herald (article/editorial topics): baseball organization formation 56; cricket's health benefits 61; Elysian Fields game 55; Knickerbockers 47, 150n72; pre–Civil War sports 20; professional *vs.* amateur players 126, 138–139; skill levels for baseball 69
New York Herald, early sports reporting 20
New York Knickerbockers *see* Knickerbocker Base Ball Club, New York
New York Magnolia Base Ball Club 53
New York Mercury 38, 101
New York Mutuals *see* Mutuals, New York
New York Regatta Club 29
New York Sun 20, 95
New York Times (article/editorial topics): all-star games 63, 64; amateurs *vs.* professionals 135, 137–138; benefit matches 118; championship matches 109; compensation rule 122; fraud and dishonesty 94; gambling 103–104; revolving practice 98; working class 86
New York Times, early sports reporting 20

New York Transcript 20
New York Tribune 16, 61, 90
New York Union Base Ball Club 46–47, 56, 62, 70–71, 138
New York Weekly Mercury 20
Newark Baseball Club 55
Newark Eurekas 101
Newberry, John 37–39
newspapers, growth statistics 19
Niagara Club 70, 87
nine-inning rule 50, 57, 83–84
Novak, Michael 82

occupational backgrounds, players 127–129, 132–134
offense-defense balance 82–83
Old Chalk 155n42
Olympic athletes, endorsements 160n133
Olympic Ball Club, Philadelphia 53, 56, 70
organized baseball concept 4
outfielder skills 84

Park, Robert E. 75
Patchen, S. 70
Pearce, Dick 84
Pearce, Dicky 65, 107
pedestrianism 94–95
periodicals, generally 16–20
Pessen, Edward 46–47
Peterson, Harold 44, 53
Peverelly, C.A. 42, 44, 151n120
Philadelphia Athletics *see* Athletics, Philadelphia
Philadelphia, Excelsiors' tour 65
Philadelphia Monitor Club 112–113
Philadelphia Olympic Ball Club 53, 56, 70
Philosophical and Practical Treatise on Horses (Lawrence) 30
physical fitness 13–14, 18–19, 52, 61
Pidgeon, Francis 123
Pierce, Dick 116, 117
Pinckey (player) 98
pitching rules 82–83
pluck, defined 151n4
pool selling 156n59
poolrooms 97
Porter, William T. 19
Pratt, John 95
press reporting, overview of contribution to baseball's image 1–7, 139–144; *see also* compensation, player; *New York Clipper*; skill levels, press reporting
prize fighting 18, 20, 95–96
professional players: England 26–28; Old Chalk's commentary 155n42; reputation 93–97; *see also* compensation, player
professional *vs.* amateur players, ambiguities: historical problem 160n134; hybrid forms 139, 159n126; marathon prize money 160n130; Olympic athlete endorsements 160n133; in press descriptions 136–139

prose style, press 3, 71, 145n17
public, baseball: composition of 77–80; defining 74–77; press' role 80–82, 153n32
Puritan ideals 11–14, 97
Putnam Club, Brooklyn 54, 56, 62, 70
Pythian Club, Albany 112

Queen, Frank 16, 20, 107

Reach, Al 116
Reach Baseball Guide 21
reader letters, topics: amateur definition 138; audience behavior 87; compensation of players 123; cricket *vs.* baseball 67–68; substitution practice 98
recreation activities: English history 23–24; health/physical fitness beliefs 13–19, 52, 61; impact of intellectual renaissance 12–15; nineteenth century variety 10–12; overview 9, 21–22; religious attitudes 11–16, 97; role of print media 17–20
recreation, defined 10, 11
Red Stockings, Cincinnati 89, 107, 129–131, 156n67
religion, attitudes toward recreation 11–16, 97
revolving practice 98–99
Riess, Steven A. 127, 129
riots, spectator 88
rivalries, club 89–90, 100, 107
Robinson, Jackie 157n111
Rockville, Illinois 65–66
Rockwell (Olympics player) 70
Rodgers, Daniel T. 16, 85
rounders game 35–36, 39
rowdiness, audience 80, 87–90, 101
rowing competitions 27–30, 148n27
Rugby School 15, 24–25
rules and regulations: colored persons 112; compensation for player 122–123; conventions for 56–58; in early baseball guides 21; fly balls 56, 66, 68–69; importance for baseball's transformation 45; inning structure 45, 50, 57, 83–84; at Knickerbocker Club founding 44–45, 50–51; local variations 56; post-game social gatherings 151n114; role of sport press 60; spectator benefits 82–84, 142, 154n47
Rushmore (Olympics player) 70

St. George Cricket Club 47
St. Louis Bluestockings Club 112
St. Louis, Nationals' tour 65
St. Louis Post-Dispatch 78
salaries 115–116, 129, 130
saloons 97
Sawyers, Tom 95
Sennett, Richard 89
Seven Lectures to Young Men (Beecher) 14
Seymour, Harold (writing on): all-star games 63; audience 74, 77, 80; baseball origins 35; class structure 126–127, 132–133;
infielder skills 84; Knickerbockers 48; Negro players 112; player hiring change 134; rule changes 82; sport reportage importance 20
Sheard, Kenneth 24, 25, 27
shortstops 44, 45
Silver Ball Match 64–65, 107
sinecures 121–122, 125
skill levels, press reporting: all-star games 64–65; ambivalence about 72–73; cricket reputation 66–67; fly rule adoption 68–69; and gambling accusations 100, 101–103, 105–106, 142; for image transformation 60, 140–142; increase in 69–72
Skinner, John Stuart 18–19
Slate, Alonzo 53
Smith, Ronald A. 11, 12
soaking runners 45
soccer, consumption theory 86–87
sociological approaches, for historical analysis 3–4, 146n36
Soda Bill 95
Solomon, Barbara 31
Somers, Dale A. 159n126
Spalding, Albert G. (pitching skills) 102
Spalding, Albert G. (writing on): audience behavior 88; baseball origins 34, 41–42; commercialization resistance 97; compensation of players 122; conventions 155n89; Excelsiors' tour 65; gambling 101; junior clubs 58–59; Knickerbocker organization 46; rule variations 56
Spalding Baseball Collection 149n35
Spalding's Official Baseball Guide 21
spectacle *see* entertainment, baseball as
Spirit of the Times (article/editorial topics): amateur *vs.* professional players 139; audience behavior 87–88; benefit matches 116; benefits of baseball 61, 62; boxing 95; compensation of players 118, 123, 125–126, 158n35; cricket *vs.* baseball 61, 66, 67–68; fly rule adoption 68–69; gambling 101, 103; game length 154n47; gate receipts corruption 121; horse racing 94; junior clubs 58; muffin matches 152n58; player inconsistency 106; revolving practice 99; substitution practice 98; walking contestants 95
Spirit of the Times: English influence 31; establishment of 19; reader letters 67–68, 87, 98, 123
sport magazines, early 18–19
sport, overview 10–15, 30–33
sport press, overview of contribution to baseball's image 1–7, 139–144; *see also* compensation, player; *New York Clipper*; skill levels, press reporting
Sporting Magazine 19
Sporting Times 136
sportsmanship ideal: English history 23–26; in Knickerbocker origins 44, 46, 48; *see also* amateur ideal

Spotswood, W. 38–39
Star Club 59, 70
Start, Joe 84, 89
status of players, changing 85–87, 111
stealing bases 84
Stetson, John 95
Stone, Gregory 83
stoolball 36
Story of Cooperstown (Birdsall) 42
substitution practice 50, 51, 57, 58, 97–98
success ethic 12, 50, 71–72, 85–87
Sunday Mercury 21, 54
Sweasy, Cal 130
symbolic meanings, baseball's challenge 60

Tail, R.T. 16
Tarde, Gabriel 76
theater norms 89
Thomas, Isaiah 39
Thorn, John 34, 55
Tom Brown's School Days (Hughes) 15
tours, baseball 65–66, 130–131
Town Ball 40
Tracey (Star player) 70
transcendental movement 13–14
Turner, Ralph H. 75
Tweed, William Marcy 121

umpires 45–46, 100–101
uniforms, Knickerbocker 49
Union Ball Grounds 119, 158n18
Union Base Ball Club, New York 46–47, 56, 62, 70–71, 138
Union Club, Brooklyn 112
Union Club of Morrisania 98, 101–102, 108
Union Cricket Club, Ohio 129–130
Union Star Cricket Club, Brooklyn 47–48
Uniques Club, Brooklyn 112–113
Uniques Club, Chicago 112
Unitarianism 13
Unknown Club, Weekville 112
urban areas, health conditions 17–18

Van Cott, Thomas 56
Vizetelly, Branston, and Co. 39
Voigt, David (writing on): baseball public 74; Chadwick's reporting 21, 90; class structure 126–127, 132–133; commercialization process 86; English influences 48; player status 83; rule changes 82; sportswriters' impact 153n32
volunteer associations, benefits 150n61
volunteer fire companies 52–53

Wadsworth, Lewis 45
Wadsworth, William Fenn 50
walking contests 94–95
Wansley, William 105, 157n13
Ward, James Montgomery 42
Washington Club 54
Washington Nationals 65–66, 102, 130, 152n35
Waterman, Fred 130
Wayne, Kenneth H. 52
Wear and Tear or Hints for the Overworked (Mitchell) 16
Weekville Unknown Club 112
Wenman, James 48
Western Monthly 79
Whip 55
White Stockings, Chicago 131
Wilkes, George 19
Williams, George 15
Wilson, Thomas 37
Wood, Thomas 95
Woodhill, William A. 53
work ethic and recreation 12
Wright, George 47, 64, 71, 84, 130
Wright, Harry: on admission charges 158n17; cricket background 47; departure to Boston 131; fielding innovations 84; Mutuals game 71; on Mutuals scandal 105; salary 130; in Spalding Baseball Collection 149n35
Wright, Henry C. 15
Wright and Ditson's Baseball Guide 21
Wyant (Marion player) 70

Y.M.C.A. 15–17
The Young Man's Friend (Eddy) 52
Young Men's Christian Association 15–17

Ziff, Larzer 31–32

www.ingramcontent.com/pod-product-compliance
Ingram Content Group UK Ltd.
Pitfield, Milton Keynes, MK11 3LW, UK
UKHW042015140426
5217IPUK00015B/1195